Aliens from Space

by Donald E. Keyhoe

ALIENS FROM SPACE

FLYING SAUCERS

THE FLYING SAUCER CONSPIRACY

FLYING SAUCERS FROM OUTER SPACE

Aliens from Space

THE REAL STORY OF UNIDENTIFIED FLYING OBJECTS

Major Donald E. Keyhoe

DOUBLEDAY & COMPANY, INC.
GARDEN CITY, NEW YORK

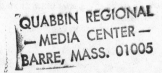

ISBN: 0-385-06751-8
LIBRARY OF CONGRESS CATALOG CARD NUMBER 73–83597

$7.95

001.9
1.6.81

In memory of my father, and to Helen, who loved him too

Acknowledgments

During my long UFO investigations I have had the assistance of many hundreds of Americans and also foreign officials, citizens to whom I should like to express my gratitude.

In addition, I should like to thank Vice-Admiral R. H. Hillenkoetter, Rear Admiral Delmer S. Fahrney, Colonels Joseph Bryan and Robert B. Emerson, and former Air Force Intelligence Major Dewey Fournet for their important evidence of UFO reality and for publicly confirming the official censorship. I am also grateful to the other members of the armed forces and government agencies who gave me leads—without violating national security—to hidden UFO reports and behind the scenes developments.

I am indebted to Senator Barry Goldwater, former Speaker of the House John W. McCormack, and other members of Congress for their valuable aid. I also wish to thank all the broadcasters and members of the press who have treated the subject seriously, among them Dave Garroway, Mike Douglas, Deena Clark, Lou Corbin, and Ken W. Purdy, the first national magazine editor to depict the facts and reveal the secrecy. During my thirteen years as director of NICAP I had the benefit of evaluations by our special advisers and by other scientists and engineers working with our thirty-one subcommittees—men like Clark McClelland, Robert Stevens, and other aerospace specialists at the Cape Kennedy subcommittee. Among the subcommittee heads were two capable

women to whom I extend my special thanks: Mrs. Idabel
Epperson, chairman of the Los Angeles subcommittee, who
secured the services of scientists and technical experts such
as Major Paul Duich, former Strategic Air Command navigator. Besides technical investigation, Chairman Epperson
organized the SKYNET reporting system, coordinated by
members Ann Druffel, Marilyn Epperson and a communications specialist.

The second woman chairman was Mrs. Jane Larson, head
of the Seattle NICAP, who also built up a competent investigating force, nailing down sightings by responsible witnesses
and revealing erroneous reports and hoaxes to strengthen
NICAP's prestige.

I also wish to thank Julian Hennessey, chairman of the
London subcommittee, who provided a special service by
organizing EURONET, a UFO reporting system including
hundreds of European airline pilots.

Besides appreciation for the subcommittees, I am grateful
for the hard work and achievements of Sherman Larsen, president of the Chicago Affiliate and David Branch, president of
the Southern California Affiliate. Over the years, both men
secured press support and public respect for NICAP by
presenting verified evidence and proof of secrecy.

A special tribute is due to Mr. and Mrs. Morris Frost, the
late Dr. Earl Douglass and the other members whose gen-
erous contributions enables NICAP to carry on investigations and the struggle against the cover-up.

And finally, I want to express my deep gratitude to editor
Howard Cady for his valued advice and encouragement during the recent years.

Foreword

Since the middle of 1972 new worldwide sightings of UFOs
—Unidentified Flying Objects—have put the U. S. Air Force
in a serious predicament.

Many AF members privately oppose UFO secrecy. Some
fear that increasing encounters by military and airline pilots,
here and abroad, may lead to a sudden development for
which millions of citizens would be completely unprepared.

In addition, many responsible scientists are now rejecting
AF denials of UFO reality. The American Institute of Astronautics and Aeronautics—the world's largest organization of
aerospace scientists and engineers—is now strongly urging a
new, full-scale, unbiased investigation, with no censorship.

Despite all this, AF Headquarters, following a high-level
policy, still publicly denies that UFOs exist, convinced this is
best for the country. But for years the Air Force has had full
proof of UFO reality.

During my long investigation of these strange objects I have
seen many reports verified by AF Intelligence, detailed accounts by AF pilots, radar operators and other trained observers proving the UFOs are high-speed craft superior to
anything built on Earth. Before the censorship tightened I
also was given the secret conclusions by AF scientists and Air
Technical Intelligence officers.

In many cases I was given valuable leads by Naval Academy
classmates, by contacts made when I was a Marine Corps
pilot and later when I was information chief at Civil Aero-

nautics (now the Federal Aviation Administration). During this period I was fortunate in making other valuable contacts when I was aide to Colonel (now General) Charles A. Lindbergh, and in World War II, when I went back on active duty.

After the war I returned to professional writing on aviation, espionage and other subjects. In 1957, after an independent investigation of UFOs, I was made director of NICAP—the National Investigations Committee on Aerial Phenomena. Utilizing the services of high-ranking retired and reserve officers, scientists and engineers, NICAP became the world's largest UFO research organization, with over thirty subcommittees in the United States and abroad.

The Board of Governors included military men fully informed on national security and UFO secrecy, among them Vice-Adm. R. H. Hillenkoetter, Rear Adm. D. S. Fahrney and Rear Adm. H. B. Knowles, Col. R. B. Emerson, U. S. Army Reserve, and Col. Joseph Bryan, USAF, retired. In a unanimous statement the Board publicly put its position on the line:

"The Air Force has withheld and is still withholding information on UFOs. NICAP intends to secure all possible verified factual evidence and make it available to Congress and the public. It will also attempt to end unwarranted secrecy."

By the mid-sixties we had analyzed nearly 11,000 UFO reports, over 2,500 of them from veteran pilots, scientists, tower operators, radar experts and other well-qualified observers. By concentrating on facts and exposing known frauds we had won the respect of many legislators and members of the press.

But there was still one big obstacle. Most scientists, misled by official denials, refused even to examine the massive evidence. Gradually some were convinced the problem was serious and they agreed to serve as scientific or technical advisers to NICAP, though at first they were openly skeptical.

Scientists' initial resistance was illustrated by the late Dr. James E. McDonald during the 1968 congressional UFO hearings. Under a special grant by the University of Arizona, Dr. McDonald had investigated hundreds of UFO reports, many with NICAP aid. I am quoting this scientist's statement regarding NICAP and myself because it shows his complete change from a skeptic, once he had checked the evidence.

The NICAP investigation, McDonald stated, was factual and serious—"a far better job than that of the Air Force." Before his own research, he said, he had strongly doubted that the cases I reported were factual records. But now, he told the House Science and Astronautics Committee, his opinion had been reversed.

"I must stress that much checking on my part has convinced me that Keyhoe's reportorial accuracy was uniformly high . . . his reliability must be recognized as impressive. . . . Within the past month I have had an opportunity to examine in detail a large amount of formerly classified official file material which substantiates to an almost alarming degree the authenticity and hence the scientific import of the case material upon which Keyhoe drew . . . for discussions of the UFO history" (p. 35 of the hearings record).

Since then the scientists' situation has had a significant change, with many belatedly examining the hard-core UFO evidence. This has been largely due to the failure of the AF-financed study at Colorado University, which was expected to bury the UFO subject. The CU Project's acceptance of AF denials has been sharply attacked and rejected by many scientists and technical experts in the aerospace and other fields.

The controversy now building up could finally lead to a showdown.

To help prepare the public, to reduce the impact of a forced admission or other sudden development is the purpose of this book. To aid those who are fighting the secrecy—inside or outside the Air Force—I have given the whole picture as I know it, with special attempts to offset unfounded "doomsday" warnings. I earnestly hope that this will help to arouse public and congressional support for an end to the secrecy—without recriminations—and for a new, practical program to learn the answers to the UFO problem.

We all have a stake in this. From all indications, this is one of the greatest problems our world will ever have to face—even if no danger is ever involved.

Contents

1

Strange
Surveillance

Behind a new curtain of secrecy, the U. S. Air Force is engaged in a dangerous gamble involving attacks on UFOs. Despite AF denials, unidentified flying objects are still operating in our skies.

During 1972, UFO encounters suddenly increased. The Aerospace Defense Command quickly stepped up interceptor pursuits. By strict ADC orders, pilots were silenced to hide the hazardous chases—and their true purpose.

In fear of public alarm, the AF has always denied firing on UFOs. Now this has been disproved by a special report at the Air Force Academy. As the director of NICAP—the National Investigations Committee on Aerial Phenomena—I was privately informed of this in October of '69.[1] After disclosing an attack by Soviet gunners, the Academy report describes a hidden AF chase:

We too have fired on UFOs. About ten o'clock one morning a radar site near a fighter base picked up a UFO doing 700 mph. The UFO then slowed to 100 mph and two F-80's were scrambled to intercept. Eventually one F-80 closed on the UFO at about 3,000 feet altitude. The UFO began to accelerate away but the pilot still managed to get within 500 yards of the object for a short period of time. It was definitely

[1] Photocopy of the AF Academy report in author's files.

saucer-shaped. As the pilot pushed the F-80 at top speed the UFO began to pull away. When the range reached 1,000 yards the pilot armed his guns and fired in an attempt to down the saucer. He failed, and the UFO pulled away rapidly, vanishing in the distance. [Pp. 462–63]

In this chase the pilot was not endangered, but some UFO pursuits have taken a grim toll. Several AF pilots have lost their lives while chasing these strange objects. In one case an AF plane and its two-man crew vanished without a trace. During another pursuit a UFO forced a pilot and his radar operator to bail out of their interceptor. The jet crashed in a city, killing a man and his wife and their two children. These and other accidents detailed later may have been meant as warnings against further AF attacks, not as outright hostility. But this does not lessen the dangers.

In December of '69, to avoid revealing the truth, the AF announced all UFO reports had been explained. In a surprising break with the AF, its chief UFO consultant, Dr. J. Allen Hynek, publicly exposed this claim. The Air Force, he stated, still had over 3,000 unsolved reports, many by scientists, veteran pilots and other top-rated observers. But the AF insisted all reported sightings were delusions, mistakes or hoaxes.

Hit by this official ridicule were thousands of competent observers including Astronaut James McDivitt, AF Wing Commander D. J. Blakeslee, jet manufacturer William Lear, astronomer Clyde Tombaugh, former ambassador Clare Booth Luce, Navy Capt. R. B. McLaughlin, Henry Ford II, Superior Court Judge Charles E. Bennett, Nathan Wagner, Missile Safety Chief at White Sands, pilots of all the armed forces and all major airlines, men and women in government and business, and other responsible citizens in all the fifty states.

In this same nationwide announcement the AF declared its investigation of UFOs was ended.

At that very time, AF interceptor pilots were trying to bring down these unknown flying objects by secret orders of the Aerospace Defense Command.

Since then, UFO pursuits have continued without a break, concealed from Congress and the public. This is not an indictment of the censors. Many strongly dislike the cover-up and harsh ridicule of witnesses. But high officials, caught in a serious dilemma, are convinced it is best to delay admitting that UFOs are real.

Though censorship has recently been tightened, a few AF pursuits have leaked out. In the early hours of September 14, 1972, an unknown machine, unlike any aircraft, was sighted at West Palm Beach International Airport. Two air traffic controllers of the Federal Aviation Administration, C. J. Fox and A. W. Brown, tracked the UFO as it maneuvered a few miles away.

"It was like nothing I've ever seen," Brown said later.

In the control tower, FAA supervisor George Morales scanned the gleaming craft through binoculars. Its elliptical, cigarlike shape was clearly outlined in the predawn darkness.

In quick succession, the UFO was reported by Eastern Airlines Captain B. F. Ferguson, city and state police and numerous citizens. By this time it was also being tracked by FAA operators at Miami International Airport and radarmen at Homestead Air Force Base.

At 6 A.M. two F-106 interceptors were scrambled at Homestead by orders from NORAD, the North American Air Defense Command. One jet pilot, Maj. Gerald Smith, climbed above the clouds and spotted the glowing UFO, but it disappeared before he could try to close in.

When newsmen called Homestead AFB, after learning of the jet scramble, an AF spokesman found himself on the spot. Ordinarily, press queries drew a standard answer: "We've proved UFOs aren't real, so we don't investigate any more." But a denial now would be useless—the press had the FAA controllers' reports. Seeing no other way out, the spokesman admitted the NORAD-ordered scramble.

During this censorship breakdown Major Smith told newsmen there was "something definite in the sky" over West Palm Beach. Two military radar stations, he said, had confirmed it.

"If it had proved hostile," another spokesman added, "we would have destroyed it."

To offset these admissions, when the censors regained control, the AF tried to discredit the evidence. The glowing UFO, it explained, was only the planet Venus. The FAA controllers' records spiked this claim. Their radar had tracked a hard, solid "target" less than sixteen miles away, and the visual reports confirmed it.

Luckily for the AF the story got only local coverage. Since the UFO had evaded the jets there was no scare angle to play up. But in other cases, unknown to most of the public, pilots have been frightened, even terrified, by close UFO encounters.

One such case, classified Secret, was buried for years in AF Project Report Number 10. The action occurred on a wintry night as an F-94 interceptor, with two AF pilots aboard, was cruising above the atomic energy station at Hanford, Washington. The jet was at 26,000 feet when the gunsight radar suddenly picked up an unknown object approaching at high speed. Then a red glow appeared ahead, outlining a disc-shaped machine larger than any known aircraft.

As the UFO raced toward the jet the pilot at the controls hastily banked to avoid a collision. The flying disc swiftly reversed direction, heading back toward the F-94. Believing it was an attack, the pilot hurriedly prepared to fire. But at the last moment the UFO whipped to one side.

Again and again, the disc flashed back toward the interceptor. Each time, the senior pilot started to fire, but the UFO dived or shot away at fantastic speed. For fifteen minutes, the flying disc kept up this grim cat-and-mouse game.

Then it came to an abrupt stop, flashed a red light twice, and streaked off into the night.

Many important cases, some as disturbing as the F-94 encounter, were hidden in AF Project Reports 1 to 12,[2] kept secret by this official admonition:

WARNING. This document contains information affecting the national defense of the United States within the meaning of the Espionage Law, Title 18 USC, Sections 793 and 794. Its transmission, or the revelation of its contents in any manner to an unauthorized person, is prohibited by law.

The penalties for violations range from five years in prison to a fine of $10,000.

Included in this censored evidence were impressive reports by Army, Navy, Air Force and airline pilots and other competent observers, among them a Royal Air Force wing commander.

Three AF Project 4 reports, stamped "SECRET," described B-29 bomber encounters in Korea. In one case the UFO was seen to be a cylindrical device with a rapidly pulsating exhaust trail. Turning in toward the bomber, the object closed "at high velocity" for a few tense seconds. Then it headed down, speeding under the B-29, and soon disappeared.

"The sources of these reports," AF project analysts stated, "are all World War II veterans and veterans of previous combat missions in Korea."

Listed in the Project 1 report were thirty-six confidential cases. Examples: McChord AFB, a round UFO tracked at great speed by a theodolite crew; four F-94s scrambled, unable to intercept. Terre Haute, Indiana, Chief Aircraft Communicator of CAA (now FAA) sighted high-speed UFO over airport. Larson AFB, Washington, radar tracked UFO at 948 mph; aircraft scrambled, could not intercept. Battle Creek, Michigan, flying disc 30–40 feet in diameter, with pol-

2 Photocopies of AF Project Reports 1 to 12 in author's files.

ished metal surface, came head-on at Navion private plane; pilot narrowly avoided a collision.

Several of these hidden cases were linked with a vital question:

Are there beings aboard some UFOs, or are they all under remote control?

One case which indicates the answer was concealed in the Project 9 report, stamped "CONFIDENTIAL." The source listed was a field-grade officer assigned to the White Sands Proving Ground, in New Mexico. The incident occurred at night while the officer was driving in open country. He was headed toward White Sands when strange lights appeared ahead, to the right of the road.

"I thought the Department of Army had a new type of pyrotechnics," the officer reported. A few minutes later he observed a series of lights approaching at an altitude of about 400 feet. He first thought this might be a C-119 or C-123 transport being used for an airborne drop of troops. But when the object made a right turn above the road he saw it was unlike any aircraft he knew.

"There were two rows of what appeared to be windows, brilliantly lighted. . . . I would estimate that they were five to six feet in height, and six to eight windows in each of the two rows."

Before he could get any closer the unknown machine went up at a ninety-degree angle and vanished in the darkness.

In another secret AF project case a UFO with lighted windows was sighted at Craig, Montana. When first seen it was only fifteen feet from the ground, moving so slowly that the windows were unmistakable. Since then other UFOs with windows have been reported by pilots and other trained observers. It seems obvious that these craft were designed to carry crews, though some may have been remote-controlled when sighted near Earth.

In 1967, after fifteen years of secrecy, the congressional "Freedom of Information" Committee forced AF Headquarters to release the long-hidden reports, for copying at the Pentagon. Though the photocopies secured by NICAP were marked "Declassified," all the Project Reports still bore the original SECRET or CONFIDENTIAL stamps, plus the warning which invoked the Espionage Law.

For those who have never doubted the AF denials this proof of UFO secrecy may be disturbing. And this is only a small part of the cover-up.

One of the most incredible censorship actions involved a high-ranking AF officer, Lt. Gen. Nathan F. Twining. In 1947, after a brilliant record in World War II, General Twining was serving as head of the Air Material Command. When the unknown flying objects made their first mass appearance he realized the serious possibilities and ordered a full AMC investigation. After three months of intensive checking and technical studies, the AMC opinion was requested by the commanding general of the Army Air Forces (shortly afterward changed to the U. S. Air Force.) On September 23, 1947, General Twining replied to the commanding general in a classified letter:

1. As requested by AC/AS-2, there is presented below the considered opinion of this Command concerning the so-called "Flying Discs." . . . This opinion was arrived at in a conference between personnel of the Air Institute of Technology, Intelligence T-2, Office, Chief of Engineering Division, and the Aircraft, Power Plant and Propeller Laboratories of Engineering Division T-3.

2. It is the opinion that:

a. The phenomenon reported is something real and not visionary or fictitious.

b. There are objects probably approximating the shape of a disc, of such appreciable size as to appear to be as large as manmade aircraft.

c. There is a possibility that some of the incidents may be caused by natural phenomena, such as meteors.

d. The reported operating characteristics such as extreme rates of climb, maneuverability (particularly in roll), and action which must be considered evasive when sighted or contacted by friendly aircraft and radar, lend belief to the possibility that some of the objects are controlled either manually, automatically or remotely.

e. The apparent common description of the objects is as follows:

(1) Metallic or light reflecting surface.

(2) Absence of trail, except in a few instances when the object apparently was operating under high performance conditions.

(3) Circular or elliptical in shape, flat on bottom and domed on top.

(4) Several reports of well kept formation flights varying from three to nine objects.

(5) Normally no associated sound, except in three instances a substantial rumbling roar was heard.

(6) Level flight speeds normally above 300 knots are estimated. . . .

3. It is recommended that: a. Headquarters, Army Air Force issue a directive assigning a priority, security classification and Code Name for a detailed study of this matter. . . .

4. Awaiting a specific directive AMC will continue the investigation within its current resources. . . .

> N. F. *Twining,*
> Lieutenant General, U.S.A.
> Commanding.

As a result of Twining's recommendation the secret UFO Project Sign was created. But for almost ten years there was not a hint of the vital "flying disc" conclusions by General Twining and the AMC technical analysts. In the late sixties former UFO Project coordinator Edward Ruppelt disclosed the AMC interplanetary conclusion, without naming General Twining or revealing any other evaluation details. The Ruppelt claim was immediately labeled false, with repeated denials year after year, such as this typical statement by Lt. Col. L. J. Tacker, AF Headquarters spokesman:

"There never has been an official AF conclusion that the flying saucers are real."

Meantime, top AF officials kept insisting there was no secrecy. In 1958, this flat denial was made by Assistant AF Secretary Richard E. Horner during a nationwide telecast:

"The Air Force is *not* hiding any UFO information. And I do not qualify this in any way."

Though Horner was only carrying out orders, as assistant secretary he was fully aware of the secrecy directives. One of the strictest orders was contained in JANAP-146, promulgated by the Joint Chiefs of Staff, titled Communication Instructions for Reporting Vital Intelligence Sightings from Aircraft (CIRVIS). This directive applied not only to military airmen but to airliner pilots and crews.

In Instruction 102, JANAP-146 stresses that CIRVIS reports are to be used only for information of *vital importance* to the security of the United States. In 201, it lists Unidentified Flying Object reports as requiring immediate transmission, preceded by the international "Urgency Signal," military precedence or emergency. In 206, it directs that all CIRVIS messages be transmitted to the Air (now Aerospace) Defense Command, the Secretary of Defense, and the nearest U. S. Military Command. After strong emphasis on securing immediate delivery, JANAP-146 warns that unauthorized transmission or revealing CIRVIS reports is prohibited under the Espionage Laws, with the penalties already listed.

Under the provisions of JANAP-146, hundreds of pilots reporting UFOs have been strictly muzzled and are still officially silenced. If they were allowed to reveal their encounters and sightings this would be a highly important addition to the verified UFO evidence.

Since 1947, UFOs have maneuvered over space bases, atomic energy centers, airports, cities, farms, obviously observing every aspect of our civilization for some highly important purpose. During the long surveillance the AF has made two full-scale evaluations of the verified evidence. In both analyses, detailed and documented later, AF scientists and Intelligence officers reached this secret conclusion:

The UFOs are spacecraft from a more advanced world, engaged in an extensive survey of our world.

One important phase of the UFO surveillance includes observations of our strategic defenses. Since early in 1967 a close watch has been kept on our huge Minuteman missiles, the intercontinental rockets so vital to our defense.

On the night of March 5, 1967, an unknown flying object was tracked by an AF radar station near Minot, North Dakota. It was heading for one of the Minuteman grids, where the missiles are kept in deep pits, pointed skyward for launching.

In seconds, alarms were flashed to Minot Air Force Base and to the missile defenders—AF "strike teams" equipped with fast armed trucks. A minute later the UFO came into sight, a circular metallic craft over 100 feet in diameter.

The missile guards, ready for action, tensely watched the descending machine. Lights flashing around the rim shone on a dome at the center, supposedly the control compartment. Whether the UFO was piloted or robot-controlled the men could not tell. Reflections from the rim lights kept them from seeing inside.

As the disc turned toward the nearest missile site three strike teams raced after it. Abruptly the UFO stopped, hovering at 500 feet. The guards trained their guns on the dome but held their fire, under orders to capture the machine undamaged if it should land.

Meantime, at Minot AFB, Intelligence had rushed a message to NORAD, the North American Air Defense Command. Fighter pilots were aboard their F-106 jets, ready for takeoff if NORAD ordered an attack. Five minutes passed with no answer. Then a missile officer anxiously called the base. The flying disc was now circling the launch control facility, the heart of the grid system. Operations was about to scramble the jets without waiting for NORAD when the UFO swerved upward and raced out of sight.

Disquieting approaches like this, with no hint of the aliens' purpose, are still going on near missile sites in North Dakota, Montana and Wyoming.

This Minot report is just one of thousands I have secured in twenty-two years, thirteen as director of NICAP, the world's largest UFO research organization. Besides NICAP reports I have convincing evidence obtained through sources established when I was a Marine Corps pilot and later the information chief at Civil Aeronautics—now the Federal Aviation Administration. Many of these reports confirm or duplicate proof of UFO reality the AF has tried to withhold.

During all this time AF members were silenced by a special order, AFR 200-2, later renumbered 80-17. AF personnel were forbidden to discuss UFOs with unauthorized persons "unless so directed, and then only on a need-to-know basis" (Section B-10). But with all the thousands of encounters and sightings some important cases inevitably became known, especially before the tightened censorship.

One leak which jolted headquarters involved an encounter on March 14, 1969. The witnesses were the pilots and crew of a KC-135 AF tanker based in Thailand and Col. Robert M. Tirman, an AF flight surgeon.

Colonel Tirman was in the tail section when he heard the pilots' startled voices over the intercom. When he reached the flight deck he was amazed to see a cylindrical machine, larger than the tanker, holding a position at their altitude. The crew knew that cylindrical UFOs existed—one had been sighted over Danang. But actually seeing the fantastic craft astonished all of them.

Though it seemed to be merely observing the tanker, the plane commander radioed a USAF base and asked for interceptors. In a few minutes the base called back—Intelligence was anxious for more details on this rare type of UFO.

The commander cautiously banked toward the weird-looking machine. There was no sign of the power source or controls. He was looking for ports or windows, or other indications of occupants, when the UFO veered away, disappearing in seconds.

In accordance with AFR 200-2, reports were rushed by radio code to the Secretary of the AF, the Directorate of Intelligence and the Foreign Technology Division at Wright-Patterson AFB. The details were secretly analyzed by technical experts and Intelligence. But in December of '69 this report was publicly discredited with all the rest.

Warnings of the secrecy hazards have been put on record, in spite of official pressures, by former military men who know the truth:

Col. Joseph Bryan, USAF, Retired, who was Special Assistant to the Secretary of the Air Force during nationwide UFO operations: "The UFOs are interplanetary devices systematically observing the Earth, either manned or remote-controlled, or both. Information on UFOs has been officially withheld. This policy is dangerous."

Vice-Admiral R. H. Hillenkoetter, Pacific Commander of Intelligence in World War II and later Director of the Central Intelligence Agency: "The Air Force has constantly misled the American public about UFOs. . . . I urge Congressional action to reduce the danger from secrecy."

Other military veterans urging that the public be given the facts include Lieut. Gen. P. A. del Valle, USMC, Ret., Rear Admirals D. S. Fahrney and H. B. Knowles, Col. R. B. Emerson, U. S. Army Reserve, and Col. Jim McAshan, U. S. Air Force Reserve.

In 1968, the House Space Committee was told that the cover-up was increasing the chance of panic when the public finally learned the truth. One warning came from a former

AF research psychologist, Dr. Robert Hall, head of the Department of Sociology, University of Illinois.

"The greatest risk of panic," Dr. Hall said, "would come from a dramatic confrontation between the assumed 'visitors' and a collection of humans who were unprepared and who had been told their leaders did not believe such visitors existed."

Even with no sign of occupants, the UFO machines have frightened many people. Dr. George Walton, a physicist, was driving in New Mexico with his wife when two flying discs came down near their car. The scientist jammed the throttle to the floor. For three nerve-racking minutes he drove at eighty-five miles an hour, frantically trying to escape. Then the lights of a small town appeared ahead and the discs climbed away, leaving the Waltons in a state of shock.

One harrowing experience, which the AF tried to keep hidden, was reported to me by a Department of Justice agency officer on field duty. His signed statement, given to me with the approval of his sector chief, duplicates his report to the AF. Later he told me of the powerful impact from this sudden encounter.

Just after midnight, January 12, 1965, Inspector Robert E. Kerringer, driving a Department of Justice agency car with two-way radio and armed with a .357 Magnum revolver, was on patrol duty north of Lynden, Washington.

The night was dark, with lowering clouds at 2,000 feet. Listening to radio chatter between other officers and sector headquarters, at Blaine, Washington, the inspector headed west along a tree-lined road.

Before joining the DJ agency, Kerringer had served six years in the Air National Guard, attending several AF schools. Now twenty-eight, a graduate of the agency's training academy, he was rated as an efficient officer, fully dependable in an emergency.

Driving at forty, Kerringer was a few miles from Lynden when a bright glow suddenly lit up the ground.

"It was so powerful," he told me, "I could see farm buildings in the distance. I was about to stop and get out when this huge shining thing swooped down, right over the car.

"It scared me half to death—I was almost paralyzed. The thing was round, about thirty feet in diameter, but the glare was so blinding I couldn't see any details. When it stopped, just above the road, it was less than fifty feet from me. I'd already hit the brakes, but I thought sure I'd ram it."

Kerringer was braced for the crash when the UFO shot up out of the way.

"I jumped out and saw it hovering above me. I was so rattled I pulled out my revolver, but something kept me from firing."

The strange machine remained above the DJ car for about three minutes. In the center of the disc was a round dark area; the rest was still glowing brilliantly.

"It hung there, motionless," Kerringer reported. "I had a strong feeling I was being watched. It could have been scanning me by remote control, or it could have been piloted. There was no way to tell."

He was reaching in for his radio mike, to call headquarters, when the flying disc began to move. Climbing faster than any jet, it vanished into the clouds.

"This may sound odd," the inspector told me, "but the worst scare hit me after it was gone. I was actually nauseated."

Two other DJ officers also sighted the UFO, and Blaine AFB told agency officials they had tracked it by radar, exactly where Kerringer saw it.

Although the AF had no authority over the inspector, a Blaine officer warned him to keep quiet. But afterward, remembering what he'd been through, Kerringer balked. When he learned I was trying to end unwarranted secrecy, through NICAP and other channels, he convinced his superiors that I should have his report, with his name and the agency's kept confidential.[3]

---

[3] Copies of the inspector's signed report in the author's files and at NICAP.

"The AF is making a bad mistake trying to hide this," he told me. "It could blow up right in their faces. People should be warned that such things can happen. I didn't believe UFOs were real. I had to be shown, and believe me, it was a rough way to learn."

Frequently, after startling experiences like this, witnesses have asked if I know what the AF is hiding. Has it learned why the UFOs are here? Does it think we're in danger? Does it know what kind of beings control the UFOs? What will happen if they land here?

The answers are of paramount importance. If humans and aliens should meet, the impact would be tremendous. Regardless of your age, sex, religion or race, many phases of your life would be affected. Even without meetings, communication with an advanced race would have powerful results. It might bring us knowledge that would change our world—aids to progress in many fields, from a civilization long past our stage of development. Contact with an advanced race might also bring trouble, even without actual hostility.

I intend to tell you all I have learned about the buried evidence, the important discoveries, the hidden gamble and other crucial aspects of this complicated problem. But first you should know about certain early developments.

When UFOs first made headlines, in June of '47, most people laughed at the flying saucer stories. I was one of the skeptics. It was hard to believe that we were being watched by a race superior to us—technologically at least.

Many AF officers would not even look at UFO reports. But others, like General Twining, were convinced the reports were true. There was no indication of the aliens' motives, and fear that they might be hostile increased after the first fatal chase.

On January 7, 1948, a large round machine descended over Kentucky, seen by the commanding officer and others at Godman AFB, by state police and thousands of citizens. As it hovered above Godman an interception was attempted by Capt. Thomas Mantell, a World War II ace, and two other fighter pilots. The wingmen lost contact in the broken clouds, but Mantell climbed out on top.

"I've sighted the thing," he radioed the Godman tower. "It looks metallic and it's tremendous in size. . . . Now it's starting to climb. . . . I'm going on up to twenty thousand feet. If I'm no closer I'll abandon chase."

This was the last message. Later Mantell's body was found near his wrecked plane, ninety miles from Godman. A newswire story said he had been chasing a flying saucer, but most people still disbelieved the reports and assumed there was an ordinary answer.

Soon after this, Project Sign began its investigation at Wright-Patterson AFB. It was staffed by top scientists and engineers, aided by Air Technical Intelligence officers.

For six months, project members analyzed the evidence, questioning pilots, radar trackers, scientists and other witnesses with special training. Most UFOs were found to be disc-shaped, usually domed, with a diameter about ten times their thickness at the center. They frequently maneuvered in formation, tracked visually and by radar. Second was the elliptical or "cigar-shaped" craft, some of them double-decked, with two rows of windows. Both types were capable of swift accelerations, great speeds and quick reversals in flight. It was clear they had a revolutionary power system far superior to anything known on Earth.

In unanimous agreement, the project scientists and Intelligence officers drew up this TOP SECRET conclusion:

The UFOs are spacecraft from another world, observing the Earth for an unknown motive.

In the Mantell case the pilot's death was not considered proof of hostility. His pursuit could have been viewed as an intended attack, causing defensive action.

On August 5, 1948, a TOP SECRET Estimate of the Situation was delivered to AF Headquarters. The spacecraft conclusion cleared the Directorate of Intelligence without a single dissent, before it reached the Chief of Staff, Gen. Hoyt Vandenberg.

By then, some project members and top-ranking HQ officers were convinced the aliens would make a full-scale survey of our planet before taking any action. This might take a long time—even an advanced race could find our world hard to understand. Fear of Earth diseases might cause a delay—there could even be a physical or mental bar to contact with humans. On that basis, this first group believed the secrecy should be continued until the AF had more information.

But other HQ and project members opposed a continued cover-up, and they urged Vandenberg to release the secret conclusion and start preparing the public. This would be far better, they told the general, than waiting until some sudden development forced a hasty admission. But Vandenberg flatly refused. Later I learned his reasons from project officers, one of them Capt. Edward J. Ruppelt.

"The general said it would cause a stampede," Ruppelt told me. "How could we convince the public the aliens weren't hostile when we didn't know it ourselves? Also he said we didn't have physical proof, like a captured spaceship, and a lot of scared people would grab at this to claim the conclusion was wrong, in spite of all the expert evidence. To hide the spaceship answer, the general ordered the secret analysis burned. But one copy was held out—Maj. Dewey Fournet and I saw it in 1952." (Major Fournet was the headquarters monitor of the UFO project.)

The existence of the TOP SECRET evaluation has been confirmed in a signed statement by Major Fournet, and by Lt. Col. George Freeman, former UFO spokesman attached to the office of the Secretary of the Air Force. Freeman's letter verifying the secret conclusion and Vandenberg's reactions was relayed to NICAP through the chairman of our subcommittee in London, Mr. Julian J. A. Hennessey.

After Vandenberg's decision Project Sign was renamed "Grudge" and the AF stepped up the debunking of UFO reports. In 1949 it announced all the reports had been disproved and the AF investigation was ended.

This statement was identical with the one made public in 1969. Afterward the AF shifted to secret operations—exactly as it did in '69. But in 1951, under a deluge of published reports, it was forced to admit its investigation had never stopped.

In spite of this admission, AF ridicule of witnesses continued. Some of the attacks were almost incredible, as in this public statement by Col. Harold E. Watson, Chief of Intelligence at Wright-Patterson AFB:

"At the end of nearly every report tracked down stands a crackpot, a religious fanatic, a publicity hound or a malicious practical joker."

During the fifties, the AF made strenuous efforts to bury all UFO reports. But some dramatic cases were impossible to hide.

One headlined scare which put the AF on the spot was reported by Capt. G. W. Schemel of Trans World Airlines. When it occurred, TWA Flight 21 had just passed over Amarillo, Texas, westbound. The time was 10:15 P.M., altitude 18,000 feet, visibility fifteen miles.

Captain Schemel had the controls, and his first officer was making an instrument check, when lights on an unknown machine abruptly materialized less than a mile away. The UFO's sudden appearance was almost unbelievable.

At a fantastic speed the strange craft came straight toward the plane. Just in time, Schemel dived, and the UFO flashed overhead in a blur of light. Through the cockpit door, the captain could hear passengers screaming. He pulled out of the dive, told the first officer to take over, and hurried back into the cabin.

It was a shambles. When the airliner dived, passengers with unfastened seat belts were thrown against the ceiling. As Schemel pulled out they fell back, landing on other passengers or in the aisles. One elderly woman, bleeding from a severe head cut, lay in a litter of hats and parcels. Seven other passengers and the two stewardesses also were injured, and some of the others were almost in hysterics.

Captain Schemel ran to the cockpit and radioed Amarillo Airport. Declaring an emergency landing, he asked for ambulances and doctors. By morning, the story had been broadcast around the country. The Air Force tried to explain away the "mystery object" as only an ordinary aircraft which Schemel and the first officer failed to recognize. But the terrific speed made this answer impossible. Civil Aeronautics investigators afterward proved there had been no conventional aircraft within fifty miles. But the AF would never admit that a UFO was involved.

Public foreign reports also add to AF debunkers' troubles. Since 1947 there have been thousands of global sightings, in sixty countries. Among the impressive witnesses on record are Gen. Paul Stehlin of the French Air Force, Australian Air Marshal Sir George Jones, Commandant-General A. B. Melville of the South Africa Union, and army and air force members in most of the civilized nations.

In some countries the evidence for alien spacecraft has been openly discussed by defense department officials. But in the United States the secrecy has been steadily increased.

In 1966, a new outbreak of UFO operations caused members of Congress, the press and many of the public to demand the truth. Besides sighting reports, wild space being stories were circulated.

In California, a tabloid newspaper said weird space beings had raped a nineteen-year-old girl. The paper stated she was alone on a beach when a spaceship landed nearby. Six humanoid creatures with bluish skin and webbed feet were said to have emerged and seized her. Nine months later, the tabloid claimed, she had a baby with webbed feet and blue skin. Fantastic abduction tales, stories of hairy space monsters and a claim of strange murders by aliens added to the general pressure.

To avoid a detailed congressional probe, the AF paid $523,-
000 for a supposedly unbiased investigation at Colorado University, headed by Dr. E. U. Condon. In the contract, Condon
and other CU officials pledged that "the work will be conducted under conditions of strictest objectivity." But a far
different approach was indicated privately by Robert J. Low,
shortly before he became the project administrator. In written suggestions to CU Vice President Thurston Marshall and
other university heads, Low made this interesting statement:

"Our study would be conducted almost exclusively by non-
believers. . . . The trick would be, I think, to describe the
project so that, to the public, it would appear a totally objective study. . . ."[4]

For over a year, as NICAP director, I saw the inside work-
ings of the Colorado Project. As you too will see later, it was
a strange and sometimes shocking operation. Most of the
scientists tried to make a serious, impartial examination of
the evidence. But out of almost 15,000 available UFO reports
—thousands by the most reliable, competent observers—
Condon and Low selected barely a hundred to check. Some
were such dubious reports that we had warned both men
against them. Very few responsible witnesses were interviewed.

On this flimsy basis, Condon issued a conclusion almost
parroting Air Force claims: No secrecy; no danger from UFOs;
no evidence that such objects even exist.

The Colorado Project and Condon's conclusions were
quickly denounced by former AF consultant Hynek, Congressman J. Edward Roush, chairman of the 1968 hearings,
NICAP technical advisers and other informed scientists and
engineers. The project and Condon's claims also were sharply
attacked by the American Institute of Aeronautics and Astronautics, which numbers most leading aerospace scientists
among its 35,000 members.

Furious at his critics, Condon let go a blast which amazed

4 Photocopy of the Low memorandum in author's files.

fellow scientists and others who had the image of a calm, objective investigator. Part of his outburst was aimed at publishers of UFO material and teachers who allow students to read such "pseudo science" in their study time.

"If found guilty," Condon declared, "they should be publicly horsewhipped and banned forever from their professions."[5]

In the battle now building up the Colorado Project is certain to be exposed as worthless, speeding the end of the secrecy. The official admission that UFOs are alien spacecraft will startle millions and probably frighten many at first. But once citizens know all the facts—and the lack of proven hostility—the hysteria should diminish.

For years we have realized we could be annihilated almost without warning by intercontinental and submarine-launched missiles. But we have learned to live with the danger because it is known. Once the country knows the truth about UFOs we probably will learn to live with this problem—which may be far less dangerous than the threat of World War III. At least, we shall be better prepared for whatever may develop.

Behind the scenes, highly placed secrecy opponents are working for a completely new, unbiased and open investigation of all the evaded and hidden evidence. It will probably lead to a full-scale crash program like the Manhattan Project, which produced the A-bomb, with thousands of scientists and engineers searching for clues to the UFOs' advanced technology.

But far more urgent is the need to communicate with the unknown aliens. Repeatedly, the officials in control have rejected all such plans—partly in fear of jeopardizing the hidden gamble.

If we had established communication when this was first suggested to top officials, by now we might not have to worry about certain aspects of the surveillance.

[5] Statement to educators and scientists in author's files.

One important and still unanswered question concerns injuries reportedly caused by UFOs.

In the AF Academy analysis report, there are sobering indications that UFOs have inflicted burns and other injuries on humans, and also that they have caused peculiar mental and physical effects.

The number of cases is relatively small—less than 1 per cent of the reported encounters. Some injuries may have been caused by control errors or by automatic devices used to keep humans from close approaches. But in a few serious cases there are no such easy answers, and the AF has suppressed or ridiculed this evidence to prevent hysteria.

It is imperative that we learn whether any injuries were deliberately inflicted. Even if none was intentional, the possibility of later hostile actions should not be ignored. As soon as possible we must discover the forces involved and try to create defenses—even though they may never be needed.

2

Unknown Forces

One of the most dramatic UFO injury cases on record occurred at Fort Itaipu, Brazil.[1] The Brazilian military leaders were so disturbed that they asked for U.S. aid in a confidential investigation. Although this happened in 1957, the case has never been closed.

The Fort Itaipu action came at a time of worldwide excitement. Shortly before this the Russians had launched *Sputnik I*, the first man-made satellite to orbit the Earth. It was quickly followed by *Sputnik II*. As evidence of aliens' interest in our first step into space, sightings of UFOs immediately increased.

At the White Sands rocket test area a disc-shaped craft descended for a brief landing. It was seen by Army military police, but it took off before they could reach it. Soon afterward, other MPs at White Sands saw a second UFO hovering fifty feet from the ground. It was described in an official Army statement as a controlled craft more than 200 feet long.

In the excitement the censorship started to break. Numerous sightings were reported by military and airline pilots, airport tower operators, a rocket engineer and other well-qualified observers. Adding to the tension, foreign officials released similar reports in South America, Canada, Australia, Europe and South Africa. But no injuries were reported—until the eerie incident at the Brazilian fort, on November 4, 1957.

It was about 2 A.M. when two sentries at Fort Itaipu saw a

[1] Confirmed and detailed in the AF Academy report, p. 459.

brilliant light above them. At first they thought it must be a star flaring up from some unknown cause. Then they realized it was an object coming down at tremendous speed, straight toward the fort. About a thousand feet above them the UFO abruptly reduced speed. Then it slowly descended, without a sound.

By this time the frightened sentries could see the object's shape through the orange glow around it. It was circular, at least 100 feet in diameter, and it was obviously under precise control.

Still silent, the strange machine stopped about 150 feet above the fort. Spotlighted by the orange glow, the sentries froze in their tracks. Each man was armed with a submachine gun, but neither one thought of firing at the UFO or sounding an alarm.

By then a steady hum, like the sound of a generator, could be heard from inside the hovering disc. Suddenly a blistering heat struck the two soldiers. It was instantly at full force, with no flame, no visible beam.

To the terrified sentries it seemed they were actually on fire. One, overcome by the intense heat, fell to his knees and collapsed. The other soldier, screaming from pain and fear, threw himself under a cannon for shelter. His cries woke up the garrison troops, but before any of them could get outside all the lights went out. Only a moderate heat penetrated the interior of the fort, but this, coupled with the total darkness, was enough to start a panic.

After a minute the heat ended, and moments later the lights came back on. Some of the Brazilian soldiers, running to their battle stations, saw the glowing UFO as it streaked skyward.

The burned sentries were taken inside and given medical treatment. Then the fort commander rushed a message to Brazilian Army Headquarters. Soon after this, Brazilian Air Force pilots were put on special patrols. The Fort Itaipu affair was kept secret.

Since the United States had far more knowledge of UFOs, high Brazilian officials asked the American Embassy for help in their investigation. As soon as possible, U. S. Army and Air Force officers were flown to the fort, accompanied by Brazilian Air Force investigators.

The burned sentries were still in a serious condition, but they were able to talk for brief periods. After recording details of the UFO's approach and the strange heat, the investigators took up the most important question:

Why were the sentries attacked?

In the search for a motive one U. S. Air Force officer recalled the Project Sign report. Some project members believed the Earth had been observed periodically by an advanced race, and their opinions were on record:

"Such a civilization might observe that on Earth we now have atomic bombs and are fast developing [space] rockets. In view of the past history of mankind [frequent wars indicating a belligerent human race] they should be alarmed. We should therefore expect at this time above all to behold such visitations."

According to this, the aliens' main purpose was to keep watch on our space developments, in fear that we would become a threat to other worlds. If this theory were correct, it might be stretched to link the launching of the Sputniks with the Fort Itaipu attack.

But this seemed preposterous, as all the investigators agreed. It would mean that the aliens were worried by our first feeble steps into space, by tiny spacecraft as primitive as a dugout canoe compared with an ocean liner. It would also mean that the burnings were intended as a demonstration of superior weapons they could use against aggressive explorers from Earth. But we were years from manned space travel, even to the moon. By human logic, we could not possibly menace an advanced space race now—if ever.

Even if the aliens believed in warnings far in advance, why

choose Fort Itaipu for a demonstration? Why not the Soviet base for launching Sputniks, or our rocket test areas?

One investigator suggested that only a harmless demonstration was intended. If so, the sentries could have been burned by an accidental increase in the heat-force. But this hopeful thinking still would not explain choosing a remote fort in a country unconnected with space travel experiments.

No reasonable answer could be found—the whole operation seemed senseless.

When a secret report on this case reached Washington, AF Headquarters had stopped the flood of publicity on UFOs, mainly by calling witnesses incompetent—or utter fools.

In the first White Sands incident, the object the MPs had seen landing was explained as the planet Venus. In the second White Sands case, the UFO which hovered at fifty feet was explained as the moon. To kill the report by an AF rocket expert, the AF publicly called him a "hoaxer"—then privately gave him a two-grade promotion after he ceased to discuss his sighting.[2]

But behind all the debunking the Directorate of AF Intelligence was seriously checking hundreds of sightings. When the baffling Fort Itaipu report was received, previous heat-force cases were quickly re-examined for possible clues to the riddle.

The most outstanding case involved an AF interceptor crew. Just before noon, on July 1, 1954, an unknown flying object was tracked over New York State by Griffiss AFB radar. An F-94 Starfire jet was scrambled and the pilot climbed steeply toward the target, guided by his radar observer. When a gleaming disc-shaped machine became visible he started to close in.

---

[2] Details of the MPs' reports and the AF explanations in the author's files and at NICAP. Promotion of the rocket expert after the AF labeled the report a hoax was admitted to the author in an official letter from the AF Missile Development Center.

Abruptly a furnacelike heat filled both cockpits. Gasping
for breath, the pilot jettisoned the canopy. Through a blur
of heat waves he saw the radar observer bail out. Stunned,
without even thinking, he ejected himself from the plane.

The cool air and the jerk of his opening parachute aroused
him. He was horrified to see the jet diving toward the heart
of a town.

The F-94, screaming down into Walesville, N.Y., smashed
through a building and burst into flames. Plunging on, the
fiery wreckage careened into a car. Four died in the holocaust
—a man and his wife and their two infant children. Five other
Walesville residents were injured, two of them seriously.

Soon after the pilot came down, at the edge of town, a reporter appeared on the scene. Still half dazed, the pilot told
him about the strange heat. Before he could tell the whole
story an AF car arrived. The pilot and the radar observer
were hurried back to Griffiss AFB. Interviews were prohibited,
and when the Walesville reporter's story of the sudden heat
was published the AF quickly denied it. There was no mystery, headquarters told the press, merely engine trouble.

Many in Walesville were bitter about the crew's bailing
out, especially the injured citizens and relatives of the dead
family. Other AF pilots had stayed with crippled planes—a
few at the cost of their lives—to keep from crashing in cities.
But after the AF statement many Walesville residents believed the airmen had jumped at the first hint of fire, without a thought of anyone below.

Although I investigated this case in 1954 there was one
angle I did not learn until early in '68. While the AF was
rechecking the Walesville disaster, also another heat injury
case, a headquarters officer I knew gave me the information:

"That F-94 pilot said there was a separate effect besides
the heat. Something made his mind black out—he couldn't
ever remember bailing out. He did recall the sudden heat
and he saw the radar observer eject himself. But everything
was a blank from then on until his parachute opened. That

partly snapped him out of it, but he still had a peculiar dazed feeling.

"The medicos told him it was the intense heat that caused the blackout. And they said the dazed feeling probably came from seeing the jet crash in Walesville. But he didn't believe them. He was sure there was something else besides the heat."

"What about the radar observer?" I asked.

"He was stunned, too, but he didn't black out. Of course he got out sooner than the pilot."

"It must have been terrible, seeing the jet dive into that town."

"It was, and those two men went through hell afterward. The pilot begged the AF to let him talk privately with the relatives of that family, and the people who got hurt, so they'd know what really happened. But they wouldn't let him. Both of those men were really muzzled."

Even today, the AF report on the Walesville crash remains buried, classified SECRET.

Several investigators believe this case indicates the aliens are not hostile. No attempt was made to injure the pilots after they bailed out. Apparently the heat-force was used only to keep them from closing in to attack. There are several other cases which appear to reinforce this opinion.

One encounter, over Uruguay, was reported by Carlos Alejo Rodriguez, a pilot and parachute instructor. He was flying near the Curbelo Naval Air Base when a domed UFO about seventy feet in diameter came toward him. When it stopped and hovered, Rodriguez decided to risk a closer look. Halfway to the flying disc he was almost suffocated by a wave of heat. As he hastily banked to escape, the UFO sped away and the temperature returned to normal.

In 1954, a French test pilot for the Fouga Aircraft Company saw a circular machine over the city of Pau. As he climbed toward it a heat blast hit him. On the verge of passing out he dived into cooler air. The UFO made no attempt to follow him down.

But regardless of the purpose, this strange heat-force can be dangerous, as the Brazilian case proved. If the temperature were increased it could be a deadly weapon. This is one more reason for the growing, tough criticism of the cover-up—some of it from unexpected sources.

One surprising attack has come from the RAND Corporation, often called the Air Force "think tank." RAND (for Research and Development) generally is known as a top consulting organization of military experts, scientists and engineers. Actually, it is at least semi-official in some operations, through its strong Pentagon connections.

For years, RAND has been the main AF policy maker. After an early evaluation for the AF, it rejected the UFO evidence. The new RAND analysis, almost a full reversal, worried the AF. Though RAND warned against publicity, the facts eventually leaked—I was privately given the report in 1970.[3]

Bearing the label "RAND DOCUMENT," this analysis confirms evidence of UFO reality, injuries to humans, interference with electrical power and other important aspects of the surveillance. Portraying the AF investigation as practically worthless, it urges an uncensored central reporting agency and serious, accurate information from the press.

This RAND analysis was drawn up not long after a new injury case was reported to the House Science and Astronautics Committee, during its UFO hearings in 1968 (p. 79 of the hearings record). The evidence was checked by the late Dr. James E. McDonald, who co-operated with NICAP in several hundred investigations.

This unique encounter occurred near Beallsville, Ohio, on the evening of March 14, 1968. The sighting was verified by reputable witnesses at different locations, but the main action centered around a nine-year-old boy named Gregory Wells.

[3] Photocopy also on file at NICAP.

Young Wells and his parents lived in a trailer which was about forty-five yards from a house owned by the boy's grandmother. On this particular evening, Gregory had been visiting his grandmother. It was near dusk when he left to return to the trailer.

Suddenly his grandmother heard him screaming. His mother, in the trailer, also heard his screams. When the two women ran out they found him rolling on the ground, his jacket on fire.

Between them, the women put out the flames. The boy was suffering from upper-arm burns and shock, and he was hurried to a hospital. While he was being treated, deputy sheriffs arrived, alerted by neighbors of the Wells. The UFO had already been reported by several witnesses. Separate reports described a cylindrical device moving at a very low altitude toward the Wells' property.

As soon as Gregory was able, he explained what had happened. He was halfway to the trailer when he saw a strange, lighted object hovering above trees across the road. As he stopped to watch it a tubelike appendage emerged from the bottom of the machine. Rotating to point toward him, it emitted a flash of bright light or flame. Instantly his jacket had ignited.

When the boy's mother and grandmother ran out, all their attention was focused on the boy and his burning jacket. In their excitement, putting out the flames, they did not look around until later. By then the UFO had gone.

No ordinary explanation for the sudden fire could be found. Gregory had nothing with him which could explain the swift-spreading flame.

The lack of a motive was even more puzzling. A test of human reactions to fire was unlikely—this had already been shown at Fort Itaipu. It could hardly be retaliation for recent AF attempts to down UFOs. Why strike at a nine-year-old boy in no way connected with the interceptor chases?

As in the Brazilian case there was no explanation—unless

aliens sometimes attacked humans for sadistic satisfaction. And the thousands of harmless encounters argued strongly against this.

Though the AF was quickly informed of the Beallsville affair, it avoided an investigation. Special UFO investigators were available at nearby AF bases, under a standing order by Maj. Gen. Richard O'Keefe, the Acting Inspector General.[4] The order was contained in a private briefing of AF base commanders.

"What is required," stated General O'Keefe, "is that every UFO sighting be investigated and reported to the Air Technical Intelligence Center at Wright-Patterson AFB."

Admitting that UFOs were a serious problem, General O'Keefe warned that sightings would increase, causing public apprehension. He directed base commanders to appoint UFO officers who knew investigative techniques, if possible men with scientific or technical backgrounds. He instructed that each UFO officer be equipped with a Geiger counter, a camera, binoculars, a magnifying glass and containers for samples. (This referred to directions for handling "actual or suspected UFO material," cited in AFR 200-2.)

Even though the AF feared publicity in injury cases, a UFO officer from an AF base in Ohio could probably have arranged a confidential interrogation of the witnesses. It might have yielded some slight lead to the unsolved heat-force riddle. But the AF decided not to take the chance. It still remembered how an injury case had backfired, just three years before.

The witness in this unusual UFO encounter was James W. Flynn, a rancher and dog trainer living at Fort Myers, Florida. Though the facts were reported to NICAP members at the time, the full story of the AF action is known to very few.

On the night of March 14, 1965, Flynn was camped in the Everglades after training some hunting dogs. It was after mid-

[4] Photocopy in author's files and at NICAP.

night when he saw a brightly lighted object descending about a mile away. Thinking it was a plane in trouble, he cranked up his swamp buggy and drove toward the light, which was visible through the trees. A fourth of a mile away he got out and proceeded on foot.

As he came nearer, Flynn saw that the object was not a plane but a large cone-shaped machine silently hovering a few feet from the ground. It was at least seventy-five feet in diameter at the base and twenty-five to thirty feet high. Four rows of ports or windows were visible, with a yellow light shining through them.

When he got closer Flynn heard a whirring sound, but he could see no equipment or occupants—there seemed to be a panel or wall just behind the windows.

After several minutes Flynn started to approach the UFO. As he stepped into the circle of light he raised his hand, intending this as a friendly gesture in case he was being watched. Instantly a narrow beam of light flashed out from under a lower window. It struck him on the forehead, knocking him unconscious.

When he came to, hours later, he was partially blinded. There was a painful bruise where the light beam had struck. The UFO was gone, but there was a charred circular area where it had hovered. The tops of the nearest trees also had been burned.

Flynn managed to drive back to Fort Myers, where he spent five days in a hospital. Besides the bruise on his forehead and the effect on his vision, he was found to have an impairment of deep muscle and tendon reflexes.

Press reports of Flynn's encounter came in the midst of a UFO "flap"—a big increase in published sightings. To avert any public alarm, AF Headquarters attempted to kill the story by discrediting Flynn. Reporters at the Pentagon were privately told the story was a hoax and that details would come later.

When Flynn was in the hospital Intelligence officers had

phoned him from Homestead AFB, Florida. Following the order by General O'Keefe, they obtained the basic report, then told Flynn they would interview him again when he left the hospital.

As soon as headquarters learned this the interview was canceled. But the plan to discredit Flynn was temporarily halted by news from Fort Myers. Dozens of leading citizens had joined in vouching for Flynn's veracity, among them Fort Myers *News-Press* editors, businessmen, police officers and Flynn's doctor. A day or so later, headquarters decided the impact was only local, and plans for a hoax statement were continued.

But unknown to the AF the case had been carefully investigated by a competent group including a NICAP representative, Capt. Charles H. Foresman, USN, Retired. The charred circular area was found just as Flynn had reported. So were the scorched treetops, which were between thirty and thirty-five feet from the ground. Scuffed places also were discovered on several tree trunks, indicating that a heavy object had scraped against the trees in descending.

For the story to have been a fake, Flynn would have had to climb the trees and scorch the tops and also scrape the trunks. There were no footprints around the trees. He would have had to create the charred circular area, again without leaving footprints. Topping it off, he would have had to hit himself on the forehead, hard enough to cause a bruise and affect his vision. Besides all this, Flynn's doctor stated that the impairment of his deep muscle and tendon reflexes could not have been faked.

When word of this report reached the Pentagon, AF Headquarters immediately dropped the plan for a public hoax claim. Newsmen who asked about the promised statement were told that the Flynn report had been checked by Homestead AFB but the conclusions had not been forwarded. Reporters who phoned the Florida base were told that Homestead knew nothing of the matter.

To nail this down, NICAP wrote to the base. In reply, Capt. Jon H. Adams, Chief of Information, sent the following brush-off:

"We here at Homestead have researched our files and find nothing concerning this particular incident where Mr. Flynn saw a brightly lit UFO and experienced a 'sledge hammer' blow as you described."

After the heat-force and Flynn cases, the mental effects cited in the AF Academy and RAND analyses may seem unimportant. Of course, some mental-reaction reports have been fakes. But others detailed by responsible citizens appear to be true. Most of the effects have not been serious, though there are potential dangers—even definite hazards.

One of the typically mild effects was reported by Russell Carter, a resident of Pierre, South Dakota. Carter was driving with his wife one night in '67, when a round, luminous device angled down toward their car. Leveling out at forty feet, it paced the Carters for four or five minutes.

"It was so bright you could drive without headlights," Carter reported. "The thing stayed at the same height, lighting up the area, and all this time a funny feeling went through my body. My wife said her face seemed to go numb."

But more disturbing reactions have been reported by a number of witnesses. The described effects have included dizziness, nausea, sharp headaches, sudden exhaustion and in a few cases memory blackouts during close pacing by UFOs.

Until the late sixties these reactions were blamed on excitement and fear of the unknown machines. Then it was discovered that most of the strange effects could have been caused by inaudible sound waves.

During studies aimed at noise abatement, scientists and engineers had already learned that audible sound, when sustained above high decibels, can cause heart attacks and other serious conditions. After checking various types of machinery and industrial equipment, they found that infrasonic sound waves (below our hearing level) and ultrasonic sounds (above our hearing range) also can create disturbing and sometimes dangerous effects. Among the reactions were fatigue, loss of balance, tension, nausea, headaches and sometimes fainting spells.

While this does not prove that inaudible sound waves cause the strange UFO effects, it has led to re-evaluation of certain reports, including the supposed blackouts.

In some close-approach incidents, witnesses were so numbed by fright that they could not recall all the details. Whether they blacked out part of the time is not certain. But a few other witnesses are positive that the UFOs caused complete blackouts. One Washington man who gave me a confidential report said he still had a blank spot in his memory, though the UFO encounter had occurred a year before.

"It was around two in the morning," he told me. "I was on Route Sixty-six, heading back to Washington, when this bright light showed up in the mirror. It was coming up fast behind me. At first I thought it was a spotlight on a car—maybe the police—and I slowed down. When it caught up I could see it was fifty or sixty feet in the air. Then it decelerated to my speed and I saw it had a round shape.

"It gave me a hell of a shock when I realized it was a UFO. I remember stepping on the gas. Then it came down closer and all of a sudden my lights got dim and the engine began to cut out.

"That's when it happened—this blacking out or whatever it was. The next thing I knew I was driving along five or six miles from where I'd been. There wasn't any sign of the UFO, and the engine and lights were back to normal. I kept trying to remember what happened after I blacked out, but it was all blank. The whole thing shook me up so much I didn't sleep for over twenty-four hours."

In a similar report, sent to NICAP from Australia, the witness had partial lapses of memory but not a complete blackout. The details were relayed by Constable Lenard Johnson of the Boyup Brook Police Station, who interrogated the witness, a local contractor.

At the contractor's request, his name has been kept confidential, although it was given in the report. From Constable Johnson's account it was evident that he was impressed by the witness.

When the encounter took place it was 9:35 P.M., October 30, 1967. The contractor was on the Kojonup-Mayanup Road, driving toward Boyup Brook, when his car came to a stop. The engine died, the headlights went out, and the car became stationary—all without any action by the witness. He had no sensation of deceleration or feeling the brakes go on.

After the car stopped, the contractor saw a beam or "tube of light" aimed down at his windshield. It was about two feet wide. Looking up along the beam he was startled to see an oval-shaped object about thirty feet in length. It was surrounded by a bluish glow which was steadily pulsating.

For several minutes the frightened witness remained in his stalled car, staring up at the weird-looking craft. Then the UFO moved away and the light beam disappeared.

"When it had gone," Constable Johnson quoted the contractor, "the witness found his motor running and his lights on." Strangest of all, the car was traveling at sixty to sixty-five miles an hour, as it had been before the UFO stopped it. The contractor had no recollection of starting the engine or speeding away from the scene.

Even though it is not certain that inaudible sound waves caused the reported effects, it could be a bad mistake to ignore the possibility. From studies of noise problems, some scientists and engineers believe that sustained, high-pitched audible sounds can lead to hallucinations—even suicidal and murderous impulses. If inaudible sound waves were generated by some powerful source they might possibly create similar reactions.

It is extremely important that we learn the answers to *all* the unknown UFO forces, not only so we can try to build defenses but also to help prepare the public. Until we know these vital answers, no preparation program can succeed.

In 1952, when hundreds of UFOs were operating over the United States, a group of ranking AF officers urged a radical change in policy:

Stop the interceptor pursuits and try to communicate with the UFO aliens.

Remembering how headquarters had rejected plans for a secret crash program, I felt sure this new plan also would be killed. A week later, there was a Pentagon rumor that the program had started. Although I didn't believe it, I went to see the press official in charge of UFO information—a civilian named Albert M. Chop. As I expected, he denied the rumor.

"Are you sure the Air Force has never tried to communicate with a UFO?" I asked.

"Positive," said Chop. "Oh, some pilot may have blinked his lights or tried a radio contact—but there's no official plan for communication. We can't set up any public scheme like that. People would take it as an official admission that the 'saucers' are interplanetary."

The AF fears of public hysteria were not without a foundation. Many headquarters officers remembered the panic caused by an Orson Welles broadcast in 1938, which reported a landing by monsters from Mars. The action was described in realistic news bulletins from New York and then, supposedly, from the scene of the landings.

Though the program had been announced as fiction, many people tuned in later and took the broadcasts as fact. Tens of thousands fled their homes, setting off a frantic exodus in several eastern states. Many were hurt in traffic accidents, and others collapsed from heart attacks. The panic lasted two or three hours, until emergency newscasts explained the Mars invasion story as fiction.

If the AF had waited until the '52 flap was over, it might have tried the communication plan after careful explanations to the public, emphasizing there was no proof of hostility.

Long before now we might have had answers to the most important questions—the purpose of the surveillance, the kind of beings involved, whether the UFO-caused injuries were accidents or not, and whether meetings with aliens are possible—and intended. By now we might have made actual contact. But the plan to communicate has always been suppressed.

Such a program would be hard to keep secret, and the AF is still afraid of alarming the public. But there is a far more powerful reason—a motive deeply involving the aliens' technical advances.

Several times, the enormous value of the UFO technology —for Earth nations—has been admitted by experts who know the great possibilities.

Rear Adm. D. S. Fahrney, former Navy missile chief, citing the UFOs' incredible maneuvers and high speed: "Such maneuvers would have to be the result of a tremendous technology of which we have no present knowledge. . . . If sightings continue, I believe there will be a contact which will give us important answers."

William Lear, aerospace genius and manufacturer of the Lear jet, after a close sighting from his executive plane: "The beings who operate the UFOs must have learned how to neutralize and control gravity. Once we can do this we won't have to depend on aerodynamics for lift."

Morton Gerla, past president of the New York section of the American Rocket Society: "UFOs are capable of performances beyond our technological ability." In a statement to NICAP, he emphasized the importance of learning the secrets of the alien machines.

(See Appendix B for scientists and engineers statements on the superior performance of disc-shaped craft.)

Almost from the start, certain high-level AF research planners were determined to learn the UFOs' technology if humanly possible. By the end of 1953 hundreds of UFO chases were on record—and three pilots had lost their lives. In 1957,

Representative (now Senator) Lee Metcalf asked the AF if its pilots were still pursuing UFOs. In the reply from headquarters, Maj. Gen. Joe W. Kelly admitted the continued chases.

"Air Force interceptors still pursue unidentified flying objects as a matter of security to this country and to determine technical aspects involved."

In the 1962 revision of AFR 200-2, the AF-UFO directive, headquarters made another significant statement:

"The Air Force will continue to collect and analyze reports of UFOs until all are scientifically or technically explained, or until the full potential of the sightings has been exploited" (Section A-2-b).

Probably few citizens realize the grave situation behind the UFO pursuits. Dr. Bruce A. Rogers, member of the NICAP Board of Governors, is one of the UFO authorities fully aware of this hazard. In 1970, he wrote me about the danger that some other Earth nation might learn the aliens' technical secrets. It could be fatal to the United States, he said, if an unfriendly country acquired this knowledge first:

"It could make a nation master of the world. . . . Possession of this knowledge could greatly influence the future of the United States and perhaps determine our survival."

To determine our survival. This is the key to the dangerous AF pursuits—the determination that we shall be the first nation to learn the aliens' technical secrets and to use them for our protection.

These are the high stakes in the hidden gamble.

It is a gamble against heavy odds. If it should fail, it might lead to a disaster which could involve us all. But if it succeeds it might indeed influence our future and determine whether we shall survive as a free nation.

3

The
Hidden Gamble

Just before dawn, on September 24, 1959, a large flying disc descended near Redmond, Oregon, setting off one of the most desperate pursuits the Air Force ever attempted and almost wrecking the censorship.

About 5 A.M., the hovering UFO was sighted near Redmond Airport. The witnesses, attached to the air traffic communications station, were members of the FAA—the Federal Aviation Administration.

At 5:10, the FAA rushed a report to the Air Force.

At 5:18, six F-102 jet fighters roared up from their base at Portland, heading for Redmond. As they took off, the tower radioed the pilots of a B-47 bomber and an F-89 fighter, on routine flights nearby, and ordered them to join the F-102s in a secret mission.

The purpose: to capture the UFO—and its crew, if one was aboard.

All the pilots were grimly aware of the fatal chases and narrow escapes in other capture attempts. But they also knew the mission's tremendous importance. If the UFO was still hovering at a low altitude they might be able to force it down without serious damage. Even then, the mission might not succeed. The spacecraft might be destroyed on the ground— by its crew or by remote control if no one was aboard.

But if the machine remained intact, the AF would have its

long-sought opportunity to learn the UFOs' technical secrets. The AF would move it to a safe hiding place. Then top scientists and engineers—with or without aid by a crew—would analyze the power system, the controls and any advanced weapons. Once they had the answers, the Defense Department would rush a program to duplicate the alien machines, also to build superior missiles using UFO-type propulsion. If the United States were the first to build an armed UFO force, no other Earth nation would risk an attack. And if no other country learned the secrets it could mean an indefinite freedom from war.

This was the goal—the powerful driving purpose behind the Redmond mission.

The first known witness at Redmond was a city policeman, Officer Robert Dickerson, who was cruising at the edge of town. When the glowing disc plunged out of the sky he thought it was a burning plane about to crash. He was astonished when it stopped at 200 feet and he saw the disc shape.

For a few minutes the strange machine remained motionless. Then it climbed up past Redmond Airport and stopped again, hovering northeast of the field. Dickerson drove quickly to the airport and reported the UFO to Flight Specialist Laverne Wertz.

Through binoculars, Wertz and other FAA men scanned the disc for several minutes. The glow had dimmed and they could clearly see odd tongues of flame—red, yellow and green —extending and retracting from the rim.

At five-ten, Wertz teletyped the Air Route Traffic Control Center at Seattle. His report was immediately relayed to the Military Flight Service at Hamilton AFB, California. Within minutes, the AF told Seattle that the Portland jets were being scrambled, also that AF radar was tracking the UFO at Klamath Falls, Oregon.

At Redmond, the FAA observers were still watching the UFO when they heard the roar of jets. As the planes dived toward the spacecraft the tongues of flame vanished. Then a fiery exhaust blasted from the bottom of the disc. Accelerating at terrific speed, it shot straight upward, almost in the jets' path.

The nearest pilot frantically banked to avoid a collision. As the UFO shot up past him another jet, caught in the churning air from the machine's exhaust, almost went out of control. Three other pilots pulled out of their dives and climbed after the fleeing disc. But even with extra speed from their afterburners they were quickly left behind.

As the UFO disappeared in clouds at 14,000 feet, one AF pilot, guided by his gunsight radar, climbed after the unseen craft. His approach apparently was registered aboard the disc, for it instantly changed course, tracked by height-finder radar at Klamath Falls. Even after the AF pilots gave up the hopeless chase, the radar operators were still tracking the UFO in high-speed maneuvers between 6,000 and 54,000 feet.

When the pilots landed, still tense from their frightening experience, they were hurried into an Intelligence debriefing session. After describing the UFO encounter they were ordered not to discuss the pursuit, even among themselves.

But hundreds of Redmond citizens had heard the diving jets. Several had seen the interceptors, and a few reported seeing an odd glow in the sky. The AF, fearing the capture attempt might be exposed, hurriedly explained the flight as a routine checkup, caused by a false radar return. The glow was brushed off as something imagined by excited witnesses.

Within hours, a new development upset the AF. When HQ learned of the disc's exhaust blast, it was feared that the UFO might be using nuclear power. Through the FAA at Seattle, Flight Specialist Wertz was ordered to make a flying check for abnormal radioactivity. Using a Geiger counter, Wertz and the pilot of a Tri-Pacer circled at various altitudes in the area where the UFO had hovered. The results, teletyped to the AF, were never released. But a newsman somehow learned of the test and broke the story.

The leak alarmed headquarters—the FAA would not be checking for radiation unless some unknown aerial object actually had been seen. If this proof of UFO reality were allowed to stand, after all the AF denials, it could cause an uproar in Congress and possibly set off a panic.

To block this the reported mystery object *had* to be debunked. After a futile search for some plausible explanation, HQ took a chance on this incredible official answer:

The object seen ascending near Redmond was probably a weather balloon.

To anyone who knew the evidence this was preposterous. Balloons drift with the wind; they have no engines, except for the long outmoded, slow dirigibles. It was impossible for any balloon to outdistance jets flying at 600 miles an hour. Reporters knew the answer was false, but the power of AF Headquarters kept them from open ridicule.

For the men back of the secrecy this had been a severe ordeal. They were already under sharp criticism by some ranking officers for recklessly endangering the lives of AF pilots. The Redmond disclosures brought new demands for an end to the UFO pursuits.

But to the high-level censor group there was no alternative. At least five other major nations were engaged in this unseen battle for the UFOs' technological secrets. For the security of the country, the AF had to get this information first, by any means possible. If they succeeded, it would justify all the hazardous chases, even the fatal pursuits.

As the Redmond excitement died down the HQ censors thankfully relaxed. Now, they thought, the Redmond case was safely buried, though it had been a close call.

But unknown to the AF, NICAP had obtained certified copies of the FAA logs. In earlier years, the FAA sometimes had been pressured into silence—as it has been since. But at that time there was no rigid order binding the agency, and many FAA members were worried about the cover-up.

The logs given to NICAP described the UFO, its maneuvers, the strange tongues of flame, the fiery exhaust and the disc's vertical takeoff to elude the interceptors. They also included the AF confirmations of radar tracking, scrambling of the Portland jets, and the Klamath Falls report on the UFO's evasive operations after the AF attack failed.

The official logs were signed by L. E. Davis, Chief, Redmond Air Traffic Communications Station, and by William F. Zauche, Jr., Chief, Air Route Traffic Control Center, Seattle. They were also confirmed in a letter from Eugene S. Kropf, Assistant to the Regional Manager, FAA Region 4, Los Angeles. A separate report from Flight Specialist Wertz verified the entire operation.

When the AF found that NICAP had the FAA logs, there was consternation at headquarters. The FAA was a highly competent agency, its airport and airways stations staffed by carefully trained men. Which would Congress and the public believe—the certified reports by expert FAA observers, or the AF's weak debunking claims?

Threatened with an end to secrecy, HQ risked the only step that might save them. The FAA was denounced for putting out false information and all of its evidence was denied. For a time the AF stuck to the balloon answer. But after a fight by several legislators and NICAP it gave in and admitted this was an error. Then HQ announced it had found the true explanation:

The FAA observers and Redmond witnesses had been misled by the planet Venus, which they took to be an unknown object maneuvering near the Earth.

This was as ridiculous as the balloon story, if not more so. If the FAA observers had been that stupid the agency would have fired them for incompetence. Top FAA officials insisted the logged evidence was correct, but the AF refused further discussion. The Venus answer is still listed as the proved explanation—one of the biggest deceptions in the long cover-up.

When the AF realized that UFOs were spacecraft, in the early years, the Air Defense Command was determined to capture one of these superior machines. This was confirmed to me in a personal conference with Gen. Sory Smith, Deputy Director of Information, and Maj. Jeremiah Boggs, a HQ Intelligence officer. In contrast with the later denials, Boggs frankly admitted that the AF had put out a special order for its pilots to capture UFOs.

"We were naturally anxious to get hold of one of the things. We told pilots to do practically anything in reason, even if they had to grab one by the tail."

Afterward I talked with an interceptor pilot I knew, who had been in on two chases. When I quoted Boggs' words about grabbing a UFO by the tail he looked at me grimly.

"That's a lot nearer the truth than you might think, even if he did make it sound like a joke. In our squadron at least we were told to ram one and bail out, if we could do it without getting hurt. I don't know anybody that tried it—I certainly didn't. After what happened to Mantell a man would be a fool to try a trick like that."

In the first year or two of mass sightings most aviation scientists and engineers scoffed at reports of UFOs' terrific speeds. It seemed impossible for any machine to fly that swiftly in our atmosphere—heat from air friction would burn it up. When the AF verified radar trackers' reports of high speeds some of its technical advisers decided the UFOs must be made of a super-metal which could withstand the heat and also brace the machines during violent maneuvers.

On one thing the AF and its technical analysts were fully agreed—no living creature could take the intense heat and the high-speed turns.

Then HQ discovered a startling report which had been suppressed at MacDill AFB in Florida. The chief witness was Capt. Jack E. Puckett, a combat veteran of World War II and since then the Assistant Chief of Flying Safety, Tactical Air Command, at Langley Field.

On August 1, 1946, Captain Puckett was flying a C-47 transport from Langley to MacDill, with Lt. Henry F. Glass, the co-pilot, and an unnamed flight engineer. Thirty miles from Tampa they saw a large UFO speeding toward them on a collision course.

"At about 1,000 yards," reported Captain Puckett, "it veered to cross our path. We observed it to be a long, cylindrical shape approximately twice the size of a B-29 bomber."

Apparently the machine was propelled by rocket power, for it trailed a stream of fire half its length. It disappeared at an estimated speed of 1,500 to 2,000 miles an hour.

But the startling part, to AF analysts, was this discovery: The unknown craft had a row of portholes. This was the first report of UFO windows.

Incredible as it seemed, the portholes indicated there were living creatures aboard—or at least that the UFO was equipped to transport some kind of beings in spite of the heat and swift turns.

Some analysts believed the portholes were an illusion caused by the high speed. But other UFOs with ports or windows were sighted later by competent observers. Besides the cases cited in Chapter 1, several others were listed in the secret Project Grudge Report:

Case 144. On the night of July 24, 1948, a projectile-like craft was encountered by Eastern Airlines Capt. C. S. Chiles and First Officer John B. Whitted. Both pilots described it as almost 100 feet long and double-decked, with two rows of windows.

Case 168, briefed from a report to the AF by the Netherlands Government: Arnheim, The Hague, July 20, 1948: an object with two decks, wingless, seen four times. . . . Very high speed comparable to a V-2 (the German rocket used against London in World War II).

Besides the window cases, Project Grudge included the official report which killed the super-metal theory:

Case 122. On April 6, 1948, Navy missile trackers and a scientist sighted an oval-shaped UFO high above White Sands Proving Ground. Tracked by theodolites, it was found to be flying at 18,000 mph. Suddenly it went into a steep climb, also registered by the theodolites, gaining twenty-five miles' altitude in ten seconds. The computed downward pull of gravity during this high-speed climb was almost unbelievable.

As you know, all that we usually feel on Earth is one G, the downward force caused by the planet's gravitational field. A pilot flying level feels the same effect. But if he pulls up sharply he will feel several Gs, because of the tendency of his body to continue in a straight line (inertia). Astronauts feel similar effects during blast-offs, from the powerful upward thrust of their rockets.

With a conventional type of flying machine, a sudden climb at 18,000 miles an hour would create a downward pull of several hundred Gs. Actually, it could never reach such a high speed in our atmosphere—the terrific heat from friction would set it afire and burn it up.

The only possible explanation was neutralizing gravity. At that time, if anti-gravity had been publicly linked with UFOs it would have been derided as science fiction fantasy. But a number of noted scientists and engineers privately accepted this answer, after analyzing the UFO evidence. Among them were Dr. Hermann Oberth, co-designer of the V-2 and a space travel authority, and aircraft manufacturers Grover Loening, Lawrence Bell and Igor Sikorsky.

How gravity control works was explained to me by Dr. Oberth while he was in the United States, aiding the Army in anti-G research at Redstone Arsenal.

"In a UFO with artificial gravity the surrounding air is held against the machine and drawn along as the ship moves—just as the Earth's atmosphere is held around the planet, in spite of the high speed of rotation, by the Earth's G-field.

"Since this 'cushion' of air prevents friction, the vehicle does not heat up. Also it moves silently—there are no eddies, no turbulence and no sonic booms.

"With ordinary propulsion, the UFOs' violent accelerations and maneuvers would endanger the spaceships—besides their burning from excessive heat. Also, the forces would crush any creatures aboard against the rear or sides of the machines, along with their being burned."

As an illustration, Dr. Oberth cited the Redmond case.

"The ship was not damaged or strained because it obviously was operating with an artificial G-field. Even the driving power of that violent ascent would not harm any beings aboard since the gravity-field force would apply simultaneously to them as well as the spacecraft. Even in swift changes of speed and direction, the passengers would feel nothing."

When AF researchers fully realized the astounding possibilities, headquarters persuaded scientists, aerospace companies and technical laboratories to set up anti-gravity projects, many of them under secret contracts. Every year, the number of projects increased. In 1965, forty-six unclassified G-projects were confirmed to me by the Scientific Information Exchange of the Smithsonian Institution. Of the forty-six, thirty-three were AF-controlled. The Navy had three; Army, one; the Atomic Energy Commission, one; NASA, two, and the National Science Foundation, six. In addition, there were at least twenty-five secret contracts which could not be listed.

At the start, some researchers warned the AF not to expect an early breakthrough—getting the answers might take years. To reduce the odds, the AF increased its attempts to capture UFOs.

In 1952, there was a sudden jump in sightings and low approaches. Fearing an attack, the Air Defense Command ordered pilots to fire on the alien machines, under the four-phase policy of air defense:

Detection, identification, interception and destruction. The link with UFOs was emphasized in AFR 200-2, which was then restricted to AF commands.

But top HQ officers soon realized the firing order was a

mistake. It was quickly canceled and the capture attempts were resumed.

Usually the AF avoids such action at low altitudes, to prevent publicity. But several times it has taken a chance—as it did in the Redmond case.

On the night of August 1, 1953, a squadron of AF fighters circled above Sequoia-Kings National Park in California. For three nights, a large disc-shaped UFO had descended over the park, seen once at close range by Park Superintendent E. T. Scoyen and some of his staff. The aliens' interest in the park puzzled the AF but it ordered the special mission in case the UFO returned.

Just before midnight, the pilots saw the disc slanting down at reduced speed. When it was well below them they started down, matching the UFO's speed as they leveled out above it. To the pilots, it seemed impossible for the spacecraft to climb without hitting one or two jets and seriously damaging the ship. Rather than take this risk, it appeared likely that the aliens would give in and land at the first safe spot.

But suddenly, without even slowing down, the UFO stopped in midair. The jets instantly overshot. Before the pilots could even begin to turn back the disc soared steeply above them and was gone.

News reports said witnesses had seen jets diving toward a UFO, but there was no documented proof, as in the later Redmond case, and the public soon forgot the story.

Just after the Sequoia-Kings Park mission several AF pilots had alarming encounters with UFOs. Near Moscow, Idaho, on August 9, a 200-foot disc plunged down toward three F-86 fighters. Its head-on approach gave the pilots a bad scare before it whipped aside. During a chase over South Dakota, three nights later, an F-84 pilot was so frightened that he radioed his base and asked to break off the pursuit. Similar incidents added to the tension; some pilots believed these actions were warnings, that the aliens might retaliate for the capture attempt at the park.

But most of the top censors were convinced this was not a great danger. Even now, after careful evaluations of the long surveillance, most of the AF men in control believe such attacks are unlikely. Here are some of their reasons for continuing the hidden gamble:

First, the extensive surveillance without open hostility must mean that the aliens have some powerful purpose requiring peaceful contacts with humans and gradual adjustments without aggression.

Second, the number of UFOs observing our world is not large enough for full-scale attacks; probably most of them are unarmed observation types which can easily avoid our jets by their high-speed maneuvers.

Third, we are not entirely defenseless. We have numerous missiles capable of reaching spaceships, even at very high altitudes.

Fourth, the aliens have repeatedly tried to avoid harming humans, so the few actual injury cases must have been accidental. One example frequently cited is a Navy encounter in 1953. A carrier squadron of AD-3s was practicing combat maneuvers when a huge rocket-shaped machine came down toward them. Decelerating to the planes' speed, it leveled off a thousand feet above them.

The squadron commander radioed a hasty order, then led his pilots in a steep climb toward the spaceship. Instantly the UFO swung around so that its tail was pointed away from the zooming planes. Then a terrific propulsion exhaust flamed out from the rear and the machine raced away. But for the hasty turn the fiery blast would have killed some of the pilots, perhaps all of them.[1] There are hundreds of other encounters on record where the UFO aliens have avoided injuring humans.

Though some of these reasons seem sound, by human logic, there is no proof that we are safe from alien retaliation. But

[1] Confirmed to Rear Adm. D. S. Fahrney and the author by a Navy Department commander.

foreign nations' efforts to get the UFOs' technical secrets have caused the AF to take the risk and intensify capture attempts.

For years, AF Intelligence has known of foreign air force struggles to get a UFO on the ground. One of the most determined countries is Soviet Russia. After constant failures by interceptor pilots, Soviet anti-aircraft gunners were ordered to fire on UFOs. Apparently the Russian high command hoped that a spaceship might be crippled and forced down without wrecking its power and weapon systems. One such attack was confirmed in the AF Academy evaluation drawn up in 1968.

"On July 24, 1957," the Academy report states, "Russian anti-aircraft batteries on the Kouril Islands opened fire on UFOs. Although all Soviet anti-aircraft batteries on the Islands were in action, no hits were made. The UFOs were luminous and moved very fast."

As in the United States and Russia, military pilots have persistently tried to force down UFOs in England, France, Brazil, Canada, the Union of South Africa, Norway, the Netherlands and several other countries.

Some foreign pilots are directed to attempt radio contact and order the aliens to land. If a UFO fails to obey, it must be shot down if possible. A Royal Dutch Air Force pilot had an experience of this kind on January 29, 1962, when he encountered a strange flying object over eastern Holland.

Following orders, the pilot radioed a command to land, using several frequencies. When the UFO showed no response, he prepared to attack. His F-86 Sabre jet was equipped with four 20-millimeter cannon and a Sidewinder rocket. Arming his guns and the rocket, the pilot closed in at full power. But before he was near enough for accurate aim the UFO streaked up out of range.

Though jet pursuits are the usual method for capture attempts, at least one country has tried a different plan. In 1954, AF Intelligence learned that Canada had set up a top secret project, after Royal Canadian Air Force pilots had failed to bring down a UFO. Hoping to lure aliens into landing, the Defence Research Board established a restricted landing field near its experimental station at Suffield, Alberta. All RCAF and commercial pilots were banned from the area.

At first, some Defence Research officials expected to use radio and searchlight signals to attract the aliens. But high military officers warned that this would expose the capture purpose and alarm the public, so the plan was abandoned.

Frequently, UFOs were sighted over Alberta by the RCAF. But there was nothing to indicate that the restricted field was reserved for the alien machines and none came near the area. Even if the aliens had known, they might not have risked landing, after the hundreds of earlier chases by the RCAF. In spite of the failure, the top secret project was continued for several years. Finally, Defence Minister Paul Hellyer revealed its existence, in 1967.

In the late fifties, as the number of futile U. S. Air Force chases mounted, some pilots were convinced that the UFOs were immune to gunfire and rockets. Several Intelligence analysts believed the aliens might be using some negative force linked with gravity control to repel or deflect bullets and missiles. But the top control group disagreed. In a special evaluation of U.S. and foreign reports they found evidence that UFOs were not invulnerable. Some had been temporarily crippled, apparently from power or control failures, and a few others had been completely destroyed by strange explosions. In one or two cases it appeared that missiles or jet rocket fire could have been the cause.

On November 13, 1957, an unidentified flying object exploded over the State Hospital at Crownsville, Maryland. A burned piece of metal fell on the hospital grounds, where it was quickly checked by Army Intelligence officers from Fort Meade and then relayed to the AF for technical analysis.

Similar explosions have been reported at several places in the United States. In one case a flying disc had exploded several miles from Richard Gebauer AFB. The witness was an aeronautical engineer and former Navy pilot. Other such disasters have been reported in various foreign countries, including New Zealand, France and England.

In 1953, an oval-shaped craft was sighted by Constable Florian Giabowski of the Ontario Provincial Police. As he watched from his patrol car the UFO disintegrated in a shower of brilliant particles. The blast also was witnessed by a pilot flying nearby. Immediately afterward, a peculiar blue rain began to fall. Samples tested by the Defence Research Board proved abnormally radioactive.

One puzzling U.S. report was given to me by Capt. William Call, a veteran Eastern Airlines pilot. The incident took place in 1954, on a night when three AF jets were scrambled to intercept a large UFO over Connecticut.

"We were circling over the airport at Hartford," Captain Call told me. "We were at eight thousand feet, on instruments in the overcast, waiting our turn to land. All of a sudden there was a tremendous flash—apparently from some terrific explosion. For a second I thought an A-bomb had gone off.

"The Hartford tower called and told us they had had a bad scare. An American airliner was 'holding' underneath us and the tower thought we'd collided.

"I can tell you this—none of us ever saw anything like it before. It lit up the sky for a hundred miles."

After checking the Hartford Airport report through the FAA, I called a private contact in the Pentagon, an AF officer who had helped me when he could do so without violating national security. But when I started to tell him about the mysterious flash over Connecticut he quickly stopped me.

"I'm tied up—I'll call you back."

He phoned me an hour later. "I'm calling from outside. Sorry I had to cut you off, but I've already stuck my neck out pretty far on this UFO deal."

"I should have waited and called you at home," I said. Then

I gave him the details of Captain Call's report. "I thought maybe you might give me some lead that wouldn't break security. There was a UFO chase over Connecticut that night. I got a private report on the scramble—it was about twelve minutes before that terrific flash."

"You think they're tied together?" said the Air Force man.

"I don't know. But it could be—a pilot might finally have hit a UFO and it blew up."

"If anything like that happened I'd probably never know it. I'm cleared for Top Secret—you know that. But anything that hot would be classified a lot higher. I honestly don't know. It could have happened. A pilot might have made a direct hit with a rocket—or a missile might have been fired from the ground. But I hope to heaven it was an accident on board—something that caused an explosion. The situation is bad enough now."

This was the first time I'd heard an AF source suggest a missile attack on a UFO. There had been several reports, but most of them seemed to be fakes. The only exception—a case still unproved—was a report relayed to me by the late Frank Edwards, well-known newscaster and public relations adviser to NICAP.

The source for the report was an officer on a Navy missile ship who personally gave Edwards an account of the action. One day in 1963, when the ship was stationed in the South Atlantic, a UFO approached the vessel and then stopped, hovering about four miles above it. According to the officer, an emergency report in a secret code was radioed to the Navy Department, which ordered an attack. A surface-to-air missile was launched, scoring a direct hit and completely destroying the UFO.

From a detailed discussion with Edwards, whom I had known for years, I knew he believed the report. But he told me the missile officer had insisted that his name be withheld. As director of NICAP I attempted to check the story, but I was unable to verify the report—even on a confidential basis.

Aside from this missile report, the number of UFO accident cases has convinced some HQ officers that eventually the AF will capture one of the alien spacecraft.

In the early sixties the failure of capture attempts was temporarily offset by optimistic reports from G-projects. Some researchers believed we would soon be able to duplicate UFOs. Several project heads had already gone on record, before the lid went down. Walter Dornberger, president of Bell Aerospace, had predicted airliner speeds of at least 10,000 miles an hour. G. S. Trimble, head of a huge Martin Aircraft G-project, put the figure at over 14,000 mph. Plane designer Alexander de Seversky predicted trips to the moon in three and a half hours, to Venus in thirty-six, to Mars in two days and to far-off Jupiter in six days.

By 1964, seven aerospace companies had Top Secret G-projects—Bell, Boeing, Convair, Douglas, Hughes, Lockheed and Martin. Other projects on basic theory and G-testing devices, listed by the Scientific Information Exchange, included AF Flight Dynamics, AF General Physics Research, RCA, the Massachusetts Institute of Technology, and outstanding researchers at twenty-one U.S. and foreign universities, among them Dr. Thomas Gold at Cornell, Dr. Bryce DeWitt at North Carolina, Dr. R. H. Dicke at Princeton and Dr. Herman Bondi at Kings's College, London.

By this time, an almost unbelievable picture had emerged from the researchers' discoveries and predictions and the verified UFO evidence:

Round-the-world airliner trips in less than two hours; space explorations at fantastic speeds, and a hair-raising military situation, with UFO bombers and missiles able to deliver surprise attacks 10,000 miles away in thirty minutes or less. Besides this, any alien hostility could probably be avoided—*if* they permitted us to build up a UFO force.

But in 1966 this optimistic picture faded. Though project

researchers were still working hard, they were nowhere near the control of gravity. When the leading scientists admitted they were baffled, the AF once again stepped up its attempts to capture UFOs.

Strangely enough, in spite of all the pursuits and attacks, UFOs had made brief landings in the U.S. and other countries. Probably the first ones were landing tests. In those that followed the aliens possibly were showing a readiness for peaceful meetings, hoping we would end our aggressive operations. Whatever the reasons, the landings and close approaches to airports are definitely on record.

In July 1962, a strange flying object descended toward the Camba Punta Airport in Argentina. Airport Director Luis Harvey immediately ordered the landing strip cleared. In a few moments, a UFO described as a "perfectly round flying object" approached at high speed. Then it stopped and hovered for three minutes. Though the Argentine Air Force had been alerted, no interception was attempted. But unfortunately some excited witnesses ran out for a closer inspection and the flying disc hurriedly took off.

That same year, on December 22, an actual landing occurred at the Ezeiza International Airport near Buenos Aires. In the pre-dawn darkness, a Panagra DC-8 jetliner was making its landing approach. As the airport lights came on the pilots were startled to see a disc-shaped object sitting at the end of the runway.

When the captain called the tower a traffic controller told him the machine had just landed. Since the UFO was blocking the runway, the captain pulled up into a holding pattern. For a minute longer the unknown craft remained on the ground, in the full glare of the landing lights. The DC-8 pilots expected to see airport cars speed down the field—or at least make a careful approach to the UFO. When no one appeared, the disc slowly lifted and climbed out of sight.

Since then, "touch landings" have been reported in several foreign countries. In one verified case a UFO remained on the ground almost half an hour—the longest known landing on record. The report on this unusual incident, which took place in Australia, was accepted as genuine by the regional director of Civil Aviation.

Shortly after midnight on May 24, 1965, a round, glowing object came down toward Eton Range, about forty-two miles from Mackay. It was sighted by three witnesses at an isolated resort hotel—J. W. Tilse, Eric Judin and John Burgess. Tilse was a veteran Australian airline pilot, with 11,500 flying hours.

The UFO, as Tilse later described it, was solid, metallic-looking, at least thirty feet in diameter. Below a circular platform was a bank of spotlights.

The frightened witnesses watched the machine approach over the treetops. Burgess, a World War II veteran, started to get a rifle and shoot at the descending craft, but Tilse warned him not to try it. When the disc landed the glow dimmed, but not enough to show whether there were ports or windows. Not knowing what might happen, the three men kept their distance.

For about thirty minutes the UFO remained on the ground. When it lifted, a tripod landing gear was briefly visible before it was retracted. The flying disc quickly accelerated and disappeared. Where it had landed was a ring three feet thick, the inner diameter twenty feet. Also, treetops were charred by the UFO's close passage.

"I always scoffed at these reports," Tilse admitted later. "But we all saw it. It was under intelligent control, and it was certainly no known aircraft."

The report and the evidence of the landing were checked and confirmed by NICAP investigator Paul Norman, an American engineer residing in Australia.

In the United States there have been several verified landings. One was in 1964, several miles from Socorro, New Mexico. Police Officer Lonnie Zamora was chasing a speeder when he saw an oval-shaped device in a gully off the highway. Abandoning the chase, he drove toward the UFO but when he stopped near it, a rocket-like exhaust flamed from underneath and the craft swiftly departed.

When the AF investigated, checking the evidence at the site, no one expected more than the usual debunking and ridicule. Instead, the AF admitted that Officer Zamora had seen an "unknown vehicle." The official statement, signed by a headquarters spokesman—Maj. Maston M. Jacks—astonished many people who knew the denial policy. Why it was ever released is still a mystery.

For some time, several NICAP advisers and other serious investigators have urged that the public should be prepared for eventual contacts with beings from unknown worlds. One strong supporter is a Stanford University professor, Dr. Magoroh Maruyama, who has had wide experience in anthropology, psychology and communications.

Up to now, the AF jet chases and UFO debunking have made a preparation program nearly impossible. But recent reappraisals of confirmed landings, by AF opponents of the capture attempts, have led to strong arguments for a new operation:

1) In all these years, the chases have failed. 2) Even if the UFO aliens do want peaceful meetings and adjustments, continued attacks could lead to open hostility. 3) Why not try a new operation—give the aliens a chance to land, unmolested? Stop all the chases, and order all pilots to keep clear of UFOs. Notify all military and naval bases, and all airports, so there will be no entrapment. It will probably take time, after all the attacks, but since the aliens have already made landings, they should be willing to try again. This could eventually lead to learning the UFO technology, without any more aggression.

So far, the top planners have withstood the pressure. Some of them fear the aliens would not land and make contact— or that it might take too long. Meanwhile, some other nation —perhaps a known enemy—might force down a UFO and learn the secrets of its superior performance.

But even if our Air Force did capture a UFO the results could be disastrous—especially if alien beings were aboard. To keep the capture hidden, the AF undoubtedly would try to cordon off the area, as it did when low-flying spacecraft were reported to have landed in Pennsylvania and New Mexico. Aside from this, there is no real plan for dealing with space beings.

Until we know what they are like, or at least have a fair idea, no realistic plan is possible. Without such knowledge, and careful preparations, understanding any such space creatures would be extremely difficult.

In a special study for NASA, the Brookings Institution has warned that a superior space race might be so highly advanced that we could not even communicate. But others who have carefully studied the UFO situation reject this bleak outlook.

Several communication experts—some in the AF and NICAP—now believe that the UFO beings have monitored and recorded a huge number of television and radio broadcasts during their long surveillance. If so, they would by now have acquired a colossal amount of information, in addition to their visual observations. But do they understand what they have seen and heard? Or are they uncertain—or dangerously misled?

Long ago, we should have tried to establish communication, to learn all we could, especially what the unknown space beings are like, physically and mentally. But until communication is finally attempted there is one important step that we can take.

We can try to see ourselves, our world, as the UFO aliens see us.

It is not easy. Most of us cannot even see ourselves as we really are. But in recent years serious work has been done on this problem by linguists, communications engineers, psychologists, biologists and others concerned with our present dilemma. In these private discussions, I have heard serious opinions based on our own space exploration plans, studies of possible extraterrestrial life, the UFO evidence, and the TV and radio broadcasts over the years which the aliens could have heard. The main purpose is to try to answer these questions: What do the UFO beings know about us—or what do they think, after observing us all this time? Some of the results are startling.

You may think it impossible to imagine yourself in the place of an unknown space being.

But if you try you can at least see the difficulties even an advanced race may have in attempting to understand the inhabitants of planet Earth. You may even get a glimpse, through space beings' eyes, of the human race—and our so-called civilization.

4

Through
Alien Eyes

In the huge number of broadcasts which UFO beings could have heard, there have been numerous unflattering comments on other-world creatures. Some could have been extremely disturbing, even alarming.

One such broadcast dealt with murdering spacemen. In 1963, after public reports of citizens shooting at UFOs, NICAP member Larry Bryant asked the Department of Justice if killing a space being would legally be murder. In the DJ answer, Assistant Attorney General Norbert A. Schlei stated:

Since criminal laws are usually construed strictly, it is doubtful that laws against homicide would apply to the killing of intelligent, man-like creatures alien to this planet, unless such creatures were members of the human species. Whether killing these creatures would violate other criminal laws—for instance the laws against cruelty to animals or disorderly conduct—would ordinarily depend on the laws of the particular state in which the killing occurred.

If any space beings heard and understood this broadcast statement, you can imagine the effect.

In 1960, Lt. Gen. Roscoe C. Wilson, AF Deputy Chief of Staff, announced Project Saint, a plan for a new space-defense operation. As quoted in a newscast, General Wilson said the intent was to create a device which would rendezvous with unknown objects orbiting the Earth. If they proved hostile they would be destroyed.

Two years later, Gen. Douglas MacArthur told the West Point graduating class that nations of the Earth would some day have to be united against attacks by people from other planets. "We speak," he said, "of ultimate conflict between the united human race and the sinister forces of some other planetary galaxy." Because of his rank and great military experience, this warning was broadcast by many stations.

Even before this, some scientists linked with our space program reported plans to establish large colonies on other planets—even if they were already inhabited. And this is only a small part of the irresponsible broadcasts about our space program which probably have poured into alien ears, along with a flood of often misleading information about our troubled world.

During a nationwide wave of sightings in 1965, a long, oval-shaped craft came down a few miles from Exeter, New Hampshire. Observed at close range by police officers, the machine hovered near the ground, with five brilliant red lights pulsating in sequence—1,2,3,4,5, then 5,4,3,2,1. The pulsations appeared to be signals. In several similar cases, police officers had flashed their spotlights in response, but this time no attempt was made and after a few minutes the UFO departed.

Under increasing pressure from reports of UFO signals, the AF Office of Scientific Research held a special discussion on communicating with beings from other worlds. The conference included Dr. William O. Davis, a former AF physicist who had helped analyze UFO evidence; Dr. John C. Lilly, a scientist noted for his Navy-sponsored experiments in communicating with dolphins; Dr. Paul Garvin, linguist for the Bunker-Ramo Corporation, and a government cryptologist, Lambros D. P. Callimahos.

During evaluations of UFO reports, Dr. Davis had made a

careful study of how alien explorers might communicate with humans. Contact with such higher-level beings, he said, would be seriously upsetting for Earth's inhabitants. In his opinion, the space visitors would realize this and delay communications while they tried to get us accustomed to seeing their spacecraft. During this period they would study our world and learn our languages (or those most frequently heard in broadcasts), so they would be ready for communication when we seemed at least partly prepared.

Some time before this, the RAND Corporation had worked out a similar plan for NASA, to guide our astronauts in future explorations of inhabited planets. These operations will include monitoring and recording any radio or television transmissions and probably computerized translation of languages, which is already under way. Members of an advanced race, such as the UFO operators, should be able to do all this and more, with superior equipment.

But would these explorers fully understand what they heard and saw? Can the UFO aliens tell the difference between truth and unfounded claims? Can they recognize humorous exaggerations and implied meanings behind the actual words?

Imagine for a few minutes that you are an observer from a world hundreds of years ahead of us, perhaps thousands. You are aboard a UFO surveillance spacecraft hovering high above our Atlantic coast, beyond the reach of interceptors. It is night, and you can see lighted cities below.

You are seated in a compartment containing a bank of electronic units which receive and record TV and radio transmissions. With the aid of automatic translators and other super-computers you understand English, French, Russian, Spanish and the languages of other major nations. When necessary you can get automatic translations of broadcasts from still more countries.

Switching back and forth, you tune in current news, a variety of programs, discussions of world problems and repeats of earlier TV shows and old movies.

You hear a newscast on the latest crimes in the United States: several murders, an airliner hijacking, a bomb explosion in a bank, the fatal beating of a merchant in a store holdup, the burning of a chain store to force "protection" payments. In a crime round-up, the newscaster lists our capital, Washington, as leading in murders, rapes, break-ins and stickups.

On other U.S. channels you hear surgeons discussing heart transplants . . . you see a Western with settlers and the cavalry fighting the Indians . . . the fantasy program "Bewitched," with Samantha's husband suddenly transformed into a dog . . . a report on the increase of drug addicts . . . a movie with a church wedding scene, followed by a shot from an old variety show, as a magician appears to be sawing a woman in half.

During a round-up on world conditions you hear a special report on the increasing misery in conquered Pakistan, and you recall the butchering of helpless men, women and children when India invaded the country.

You switch to previously recorded transmissions showing the almost constant wars—in Korea, Vietnam, Africa, South America and Asia. You remember other war-ravaged countries, such as Biafra, with its thousands of emaciated children dying of starvation. In a discussion of the "cold war," you hear a commentator's warning: The United States and the Soviet Union have ten times the number of hydrogen bombs and missiles needed to destroy all life on Earth.

It would seem such a warning would frighten everyone on the planet. Yet you have watched thousands of programs which showed not a sign of concern.

You turn off the receiving units and think back to some of these programs: "I Dream of Jeannie" . . . "The Ghost and Mrs. Muir" . . . "Laugh-In" . . . "Gunsmoke" . . . "Here's

Lucy" . . . "The Carol Burnett Show" . . . and older broadcasts such as "Mr. Ed, The Talking Horse."

Were humans really unconcerned with the threat of extinction? Or were these programs contrived to help them forget the danger, and also their other serious problems?

If you *were* an observer from an advanced civilization, could you fully understand what you have seen and heard? Could you tell fact from false claims? Could you recognize humor, harmless exaggerations and satire? Could you understand all the conflicting views of Earth nations? In short, could you end up with a fairly accurate picture of our world?

At one time I believed the UFO beings could do this after their years of surveillance. It even seemed likely they would understand the reasons behind the U. S. Air Force denials that UFOs exist. But now, after discussions with linguists, psychologists and others who have studied the problem, this seems more difficult.

The aliens' reactions to our broadcasts and their visual observations will depend on whether their mental processes, logic and emotions are similar to ours—or radically different.

Several well-known scientists believe there is a good chance that space visitors will resemble us in form. Among them are Dr. Melvin Calvin, Nobel prize winner and Director of the bio-organic group, Lawrence Radiation Laboratory, University of California; Dr. Clyde Tombaugh, the astronomer who discovered the planet Pluto; and Dr. C. F. Powell, another Nobel prize winner, Dean of the Faculty of Sciences, University of Bristol, England. These scientists agree that there are many inhabited planets in our galaxy with beings similar to those on Earth. Dr. Calvin estimates the number as a million or more.

By human logic, it would seem likely that beings like ourselves would seek out and contact their own kind. We have no proof that the UFO aliens are humanoid, but even if they are almost identical to us they could still be strangers with mental processes and emotions hard for us to understand—

at least in the first period of contact. However, the possibility of eventual understanding would be much greater.

Meantime, there may be some helpful clues to the UFO observers' opinions of us. Several years ago, I worked out six main phases of known UFO operations. Some of the surveillance appeared similar to our own space exploration plans.[1]

According to recorded sightings, UFOs were making sporadic observations of Earth more than two centuries ago. The AF Academy report states there were "many documented sightings throughout the Middle Ages, including an especially startling one of a UFO over London on 16 December 1742." Apparently these were just routine checks on a slowly progressing civilization.

Dr. Carl Sagan, astronomer and NASA adviser, believes the Earth has been under occasional observation back into prehistoric times. The AF Academy analysis goes even farther, discussing possible evidence of space visitors thousands of years ago. It is a fascinating suggestion, which we'll examine later. But the six-phase documented evidence is a more definite source for clues to the aliens' knowledge of humans.

Phase One. In the two hundred years before World War II, unknown flying objects—discs or rocket types—were occasionally sighted by astronomers, ship captains and other responsible witnesses. Europe was the most frequently observed area; UFOs were seen over Italy, England, Germany, France and sporadically at other parts of the globe.

During this first period the UFO aliens probably saw the conflicts in Europe, the first sailing ships, steamboats, trains, and the fragile airplanes of the early twentieth century. Few approaches to Earth inhabitants were reported, but with long-range observation devices they would not be needed. Almost certainly, some UFOs would be equipped with telescopes and cameras far ahead of anything we have achieved—and already

[1] In 1965, I briefed my evaluation in a report to NICAP members. Later I allowed Frank Edwards to quote from this report. By error, Edwards credited it to a Navy source. There was no Navy connection.

we can pick up two-foot objects on Earth from 500 miles in space.

In this first phase there were a few U.S. reports. One verified case occurred in 1904, when three glowing objects came down near the U.S.S. *Supply*. In a close triangle formation, they leveled off near the ship, seen by most of the crew. Then they quickly climbed out of sight. The incident was reported to the Navy Department by Lt. Frank Schofield (World War II Commander-in-Chief of the Pacific Fleet). The official report was published in the U. S. Weather Bureau *Review*.

By this time the aliens could have heard the early "wireless" signals, and possibly they listened to some of the newscasts and soap operas of the thirties. But no radio messages from UFOs were recorded, and there were no known landings. In general, the UFO beings showed little interest in our slow technical growth. It was not until World War II that they began to exhibit concern about our changing world.

Phase Two. During this war UFOs were often seen by both Allied and Axis pilots and crews. Singly and in formation, they paced fighters and bombers, maneuvered over ground forces, and circled above the half-wrecked cities. In the European theater they flew over V-2 bases as the rockets were launched against London, and they also paced the first German jets.

In the Pacific, UFOs frequently appeared above the embattled islands and along the bombing routes to Tokyo. One was described as descending near Japan just after the first A-bomb explosion, at Hiroshima. If the aliens needed to know humans' reactions to UFOs, they had many chances to learn. One encounter took place just after U.S. planes had bombed a Japanese oil depot, in Sumatra. Capt. Alvah Rieda, a B-29 bomber commander, had been ordered to stay behind and photograph the damage. As he circled over the sea of flame an oval-shaped device suddenly appeared off the right wing. Thinking it was some enemy weapon, Rieda frantically tried to shake it off, but the UFO instantly matched every turn.

If the machine was piloted, some space being may have seen the tense faces of Rieda and his crew in the glare from the burning oil depot. After eight frightening minutes the object shot straight upward and disappeared in the overcast. (Signed report sent to the author at NICAP.)

After watching this great war, with its burning cities, aerial battles, furious ground attacks and torpedoed ships, the aliens may have decided that in spite of our technical advances the inhabitants of Earth were barbarians at heart.

Phase Three. After the 1947 mass appearances, UFO operations steadily increased. In 1952 more than a thousand sightings were reported as spacecraft maneuvered over cities, airports, military bases and atomic energy centers.

In July of '52 UFOs flew over the White House, the Capitol, Washington Airport, and other parts of the city. Afterward the aliens could have heard their spacecraft explained as "mirages" by the Director of AF Intelligence, Maj. Gen. John M. Samford. They also could have heard Samford's admission of "several hundred interceptor chases" (with no hint of capture attempts), then the general's claim that in all these flights not one unknown craft had been seen.

During this phase the aliens could have heard stories describing them as twelve-foot giants with hypnotic eyes, hairy monsters with claws, and other frightening creatures. In contrast, they might have listened to cultists' reports of golden-haired, godlike beings who had come to save us by ending all the ills of our world. (Evidently it was a tougher job than they expected.)

At first, when no UFO communications were heard on Earth, some investigators thought such advanced beings might not use radio or television transmissions. Since then, UFOs with antennae have frequently been reported, and there is evidence that the aliens not only hear our radio but also understand at least some messages. In numerous cases, when AF flight commanders or tower operators radioed pilots to close on UFOs or try to box them in, the alien machines have instantly reversed course or performed other evasive maneuvers. After the 1952 action at Washington Airport, veteran Traffic Controller Jim Ritchey told me of identical UFO reactions. When he radioed a Capital Airlines pilot to make a quick turn toward the nearest unknown object it shot straight up, accelerating from 130 to 500 miles an hour in four seconds. The same thing happened twice when Senior Controller Harry Barnes radioed pilots to attempt interceptions. Barnes later told me he was certain that the unknown visitors were listening to his instructions. A similar incident was reported by a Marine Corps squadron leader, Maj. Charles Scarborough, after an encounter with sixteen flying discs over Texas. With all the U.S. and foreign reports on record the evidence appears conclusive.

After the advent of television the aliens may have matched actions and gestures with spoken words, to help their automatic translators. We can only guess at the effect of television. Adding pictures of life on Earth to voice broadcasts might make it easier to understand humans. But with all the conglomeration on TV there could be some weird results.

Phase Four. In 1957 the Sputniks launched us into the Space Age, as shown in Chapter 2. From the speed-up of our space plans, the aliens must have realized that manned spaceships would reach the nearer planets before the end of the century. Their surveillance was quickly increased, with closer observations of launching bases and sometimes even pacing of our missiles and rockets.

Phase Five. Since 1957, there have been hundreds of broadcasts about our space exploration program. Some could have alarmed any space beings who heard them. Here are a few examples:

1) Before A.D. 2000, we shall have planet colonies containing millions of Earth people, according to space experts such as Dr. Simon Ramo, head of Space Technology Laboratories, Dr. G. G. Quarles, chief scientist of the Army Ordnance Missile Command, and the late Andrew G. Haley, former

president of the American Rocket Society. Because of over-population, we shall have no alternative, in the opinion of Col. J. E. Ash, former head of the Armed Forces Institute of Pathology. The first colony will be on Mars; giant spaceships will make daily trips to the Red Planet, carrying thousands of construction workers and engineers to erect sealed cities or to build them underground.

2) A statement by Dr. Kraft Ehricke, then chief consultant at Convair Aircraft: "The solar system and as much of the universe as man can reach are man's rightful field of activity."

3) Suggestions by Prof. Harold Lasswell of Yale University for getting control of an inhabited planet by setting one group against another, and also bringing back live spacemen as specimens.

4) An endorsement of the Mars plan by Dr. James B. Edson, Director of Army Research and Development: "Once Mars has colonies independent of the Earth, then if Earth is destroyed man can carry on in this reserve world."

5) Suggestions by scientists for improving Earth's weather by changing other planets' orbits with H-bomb explosions, and also for propelling Saturn into an orbit nearer the sun to make it suitable for colonists from Earth. (Changing the orbits of planets could upset the balance of the solar system. Dr. George Gamow, author of *One, Two, Three—Infinity*, has stated that the Earth's ice ages were caused by some violent disturbance on Saturn. Even a smaller-scale tampering with a planet's climate might be disastrous for its inhabitants.)

Perhaps the UFO beings can recognize most of such statements as unfounded speculation. In 1962, the Space Science Board said our space explorations will be in accord with the "peaceful nature" of our country. And the NASA plan prepared by the RAND Corporation also states that our astronauts will proceed with caution in exploring an inhabited planet, treating the aliens with utmost consideration.

But will the UFO beings believe this, after hearing the

other broadcasts? Barely two months after the Space Science Board announcement, a new space-war warning was delivered by Brig. Gen. John A. McDavid, Director of Communications-Electronic for the Joint Chiefs of Staff. As quoted in newscasts, General McDavid said that meeting beings of higher intelligence was likely to lead to conflicts.

During Phase Five, UFOs sometimes came within fifty feet of cars and pedestrians. If the alien observers hoped we were becoming accustomed to their presence they must have been disappointed. Most humans were badly frightened by the encounters.

Even when the UFOs were not extremely close some witnesses were thrown into panic. On the night of October 6, 1961, a large spacecraft appeared over Santa Rita, Venezuela, its glow lighting up the town. As it moved slowly over Lake Maracaibo the brilliant light illuminated several fishing boats. Most of the fishermen leaped overboard and frantically swam ashore. But one man, Bartolme Romero, went down, apparently overcome by fear. As Phase Five ended, the aliens must have realized that few if any of Earth's inhabitants were prepared for meeting space beings.

Phase Six. Ever since 1963, TV and radio broadcasts have frequently given a grim picture—with good reason—of conditions on Earth. If the UFO beings have been tuned in they will have learned about our riots, terrorist attacks, steadily growing crime, the almost uncontrolled traffic in drugs, the partial breakdown in morals and other evidence of a world in trouble. They also will have heard more predictions about planet colonies and the use of armed spaceships if we meet resistance. They could have heard plans to send missionaries to planets, regardless of any religion the inhabitants already may have. Far worse, they may have heard official admissions that our spacecraft are not fully sterilized, and warnings that this could cause epidemics against which other-world beings had no protection. Steps to improve sterilization are being taken, but the aliens may not know this. The admitted risks might seem an ominous indication of what to expect if our astronauts and colonists land on inhabited planets.

Phase Seven, when and if it comes, would probably be the final operation—contact, landings and attempts to carry out the purpose behind the long observations of our world.

Since 1969, in trying to estimate the effect of Earth broadcasts and the aliens' visual observations, I have been privately assisted by a group including linguists, an anthropologist, educators, a psychologist and a communications expert. Only one believed the UFO observers could get a true picture of our world—which would be bad enough. The others decided the aliens might partly understand us but they could be badly misled about some aspects of life on Earth, and they probably would not realize that the majority of humans were against crime and that they hoped for a peaceful world.

"If we could only communicate," one linguist told me, "we might be able to straighten out the mistakes—or the worst ones."

But incredible as it may appear, some top space scientists now have a deep fear of communicating with any advanced beings—even those on distant worlds—and this fear has spread to some high official planners.

One scientist on record is Dr. Albert Hibbs of Caltech's Jet Propulsion Laboratory. When asked how we should reply to the first message from another world he tersely answered:

"Hang up! Look what happened to the Indians."

Dr. Carl Sagan says we should refrain from transmitting "because we do not know the intentions of a superior galactic society."

Dr. Thomas Gold of Cornell University warns that trying to communicate could be a grave mistake. "Anyone who sends out a signal is courting disaster."

But already space signals are on record, evidently beamed at the Earth—evidence that advanced civilizations are aware of our existence and our technical progress. Failing to answer is no guarantee against space visitors—some analysts believe the UFO surveillance is a follow-up of attempts to communicate.

The first definitely known transmission was in 1899, when electronic genius Nikola Tesla received strange signals at his Colorado laboratory. Tesla reported they were intelligent transmissions from space, and he was convinced that advanced beings were trying to signal us. In 1921, Guglielmo Marconi, inventor of the "wireless," picked up code signals from space. In 1924, when Mars was closest to Earth, a photographic record of radio signals was made by Dr. David Todd, professor of astronomy at Amherst College. Unexplained signals also were picked up in 1927, 1928 and in 1964, according to Dr. Ronald Bracewell of the Radio Astronomy Institute at Stanford University.

In 1959, NASA intercepted signals from an unknown satellite circling the Earth. It was in this same year that the National Science Foundation set up a program to listen for messages from space—a project which led to the reception of strange signals and the sudden fear among certain scientists.

The listening project was begun without publicity, at Green Bank, West Virginia, where a radio astronomy observatory was operated by the National Science Foundation. The director of the observatory was Dr. Otto Struve, one of the most distinguished astronomers in the world.

In 1960, Dr. Struve startled the scientific world and the public by announcing the program called Project Ozma. In a sober report to the press, he stated there must be at least one million inhabited planets in our galaxy. Many of the more advanced civilizations, he said, probably suspected or definitely knew of the Earth's existence. It was vitally important, he emphasized, that we try to establish communication, at first by listening for intelligent messages or signals. Most professional astronomers, at this time, avoided discussing other-world life for fear of ridicule. But Struve's impressive background and reputation carried weight, and since he had studied this problem for thirty years his disclosure of the official search was taken seriously and widely publicized.

The Project Ozma director was Dr. Frank Drake, and in 1960 he publicly stressed the great benefits we might receive from contacts with advanced worlds—guides to ending disease and prolonging life, to living without wars, speeding up space travel and learning the secrets of the universe. Once he said the project might intercept messages between alien spaceships, but both he and Struve avoided discussions of UFOs, which could have caused trouble—the AF was already uneasy about this listening project.

Early in 1961, Drake and his staff took their first major step—focusing on Tau Ceti, one of the nearest suns likely to have planets. Though they had discussed this for weeks, none of the scientists was prepared for what happened.

In less than two minutes strong signals were heard, unmistakably an intelligent code. To the startled listeners such an immediate success was amazing. But it was clear they had tuned in a civilization on a planet of Tau Ceti.

After a short time the signals faded out, leaving the scientists almost stunned. Describing the impact later, Dr. Drake admitted that the "spooky signals" had had an unexpected effect. "Everybody was throwing up his hands," he said.

To avoid possible hysteria the story was temporarily suppressed, but it was too dramatic to keep hidden. When it did break, a debunking explanation was quickly released—relayed from the Pentagon.

The supposed space signals, officials insisted, actually had come from a secret military station—so important that it could not be publicly identified.

If this had been true, Project Ozma could have continued with no excitement. It could not possibly explain the incredible actions which followed.

Abruptly, Dr. Struve declared Project Ozma closed. Astonishing the reporters who had heard him announce the search, he completely reversed his statements on the project's importance. It was folly, he said bluntly, to listen for other-world messages. Then, curiously, he added that even if such signals were received it might be unwise to answer. When the press asked when the project might be reopened, he brushed them off with, "Come back in a thousand years."

What could have caused this noted scientist to expose himself to ridicule with such a strange performance? Inevitably, there was conjecture that the Tau Ceti message had been deciphered—and that it had caused sudden, deep fear.

Though it was hard for me to believe, I tried to check through well-placed sources in Washington. So far as I know, this was only a rumor. But *something* powerful was involved in Struve's sudden reversal. The proof of this is the development which followed, perhaps the most unbelievable of all.

In November of '61, when the Project Ozma story was half forgotten, a secret meeting of scientists was held at Green Bank.

The purpose: to estimate the number of worlds capable of communicating with Earth.

Heading this secret meeting was the man who had ridiculed the subject—Dr. Otto Struve. Working with him were Dr. Melvin Calvin, Dr. John C. Lilly, Dr. Frank Drake, Dr. Carl Sagan and several others fully informed about the urgent problem.

After long, careful discussions and calculations, the entire group approved the secret estimate. Known as the Green Bank Formula, it may prove to be the most important conclusion in our history:

There are between 40,000,000 and 50,000,000 worlds which are either trying to signal us or are listening for messages from Earth.

Fantastic as this is, the very remoteness of these worlds dulls the impact on most people. When the Green Bank Formula became known, there was no public alarm.

Since then, Project Ozma has continued listening for space signals, at the larger station in Puerto Rico. Its operations are now under the AF Office of Scientific Research, and any dramatic messages will probably be kept secret.

The true story of the Tau Ceti incident may never be revealed. It seems almost certain that Dr. Struve was persuaded to conceal the facts in the best interests of the public, though it meant a humiliating ordeal.

Whatever happened, it was apparently the cause of the fear which still affects some space scientists. A few warn that it is dangerous even to listen to space messages. Arthur C. Clarke, the highly respected space-travel authority, believes that a malevolent super-race might transmit vicious, compelling information which could cause us to destroy ourselves.

Fear of contacting an advanced race has also extended to communicating with UFO beings. Some of the scientists know the evidence, the secret AF conclusions and the attempts to capture the UFO spacecraft. Even though there is no strong evidence of hostility, a few scientists have warned that we must not expect all space beings to be friendly—our visitors might enslave or destroy us. Dr. Thomas Gold, in a similar warning, added that such space beings might even consider us as food.

Aside from these "doomsday" warnings, we urgently need to learn all we can about the UFO beings. In the Brookings Institution report to NASA on the impact of the Space Age, a five-page discussion of possible visitors was included, though UFOs were not mentioned. Any discovery of intelligent space beings, the report stated, could have a severe effect on the public:

"Societies sure of their own place have disintegrated when confronted by a superior society. Others have survived even though changed. Clearly, the better we can come to understand the factors involved in responding to such crises the better prepared we may be."

In refusing to attempt communication with UFOs, some AF HQ officers have argued that it could not be concealed and it might frighten the public. But ever since 1961 there has been a special transmission system which could have been used secretly. Known as the "ultracom," it was developed by Westinghouse, to create a beam free from interception. Dr. Patrick Conley, a Westinghouse official, has explained ultracom as an ultraviolet beam almost impossible to intercept. Its short wavelength is absorbed by the atmosphere, preventing direct contact between space vehicles and the Earth. Besides radio, it can also carry TV signals.

"Manned space vehicles could use ultracom for intercommunication," Dr. Conley stated, "without being heard on Earth."

It is highly probable that the UFO aliens use this or a similar system, which would explain why we have not heard messages between the surveillance spacecraft.

Soon after the ultracom system was proved interference-free the AF was urged to install the equipment in several planes and try to make contact with the UFOs. But even though the plan was backed by some high-ranking HQ officers, the control group feared it would leak out and the tests were banned. Repeated efforts since then have also met with failure.

With all the pressure on the AF, it may seem a miracle that the resistance did not collapse years ago, along with the cover-up. It would have, if the AF had stood alone—it never has had the power to enforce such a large-scale censorship. But the Air Force has not stood alone.

The Central Intelligence Agency is the power behind the UFO secrecy. Though it is not widely known, the CIA has authority over the Intelligence departments of all the military services. It has strong influence with the heads of the Army, Navy, Air Force and Marine Corps. It can exert pressure—though it does not have full control—on the Federal Aviation Administration, the Coast Guard, the Federal Communications Commission and most other government agencies—except the FBI.

The CIA take-over of the Air Force investigation occurred

in 1953. (Vice-Admiral Hillenkoetter was not involved; his tour as CIA director had ended before this.) Since then, the Central Intelligence Agency has used its power to guide and support the Air Force deception of Congress, the press and the public. This is not an attempt to crucify the CIA, harsh as it may seem. Faced with a serious decision, it took the course it believed wisest for the nation. But regardless of motives, the CIA and the AF now have put the country in a dangerous predicament. It could hardly be worse if they had deliberately planned it.

5

The CIA
Takes Over

It was after a tough, two-pronged fight against UFO secrecy that the CIA took control of the Air Force investigation. Even now, not many people know the full story of that behind-the-scenes battle.

Oddly enough, it was a report from Secretary of the Navy Dan Kimball which led to the CIA's drastic action.

In April of 1952, Secretary Kimball was flying to Hawaii when two disc-shaped craft streaked in toward his Navy executive plane.

"Their speed was amazing," he told me later, in Washington. "My pilots estimated it between fifteen hundred and two thousand miles an hour. The objects circled us twice and then took off, heading east. There was another Navy plane behind us, with Admiral Arthur Radford on board. The distance was about fifty miles. I had my senior pilot radio a report on the sighting. In almost no time Radford's chief pilot called back, really excited. The UFOs were now circling their plane—they'd covered the fifty miles in less than two minutes. In a few seconds the pilot told us they'd left the plane and raced up out of sight."

After landing, Secretary Kimball had a report radioed to the AF, since it was officially in charge of the UFO investigation. When he returned to Washington he had an aide ask the AF what action had been taken. He was informed it was against orders to discuss case analyses, even with witnesses who made the reports.

It was a mistake the AF soon regretted, for Kimball was not a man who could be easily pushed around. The secretary knew that Navy and Marine Corps pilots had made numerous verified reports, also tower operators and other Navy personnel. On checking, he found that the AF had insisted on getting all copies of reports, without even a preliminary Navy investigation. As in his own case, the AF had refused to answer any questions about these sightings, except for a few that were already known to the press, which it had tried to debunk.

As soon as he learned this, Secretary Kimball had a conference with Rear Admiral Calvin Bolster, Chief of the Office of Naval Research.

"I want ONR to make a full investigation of all Navy and Marine reports from now on—also try to get duplicate reports from the witnesses in unexplained earlier cases. This is to be kept separate from the Air Force project."[1]

When the AF heard of this there was a hasty conference at headquarters. They were already in a tight spot. The big "flap" of 1952 had started, with UFO reports coming in from all over the country, and both Capitol Hill and the press were demanding explanations. If Kimball's bucking the AF got out it would be headlined news and the censors would be in trouble. But tangling with the Navy Secretary could make it a lot worse—he might make the Pacific encounter public, along with other Navy evidence. The HQ group was still trying to find an answer when a new development hit them.

From an inside source, they learned that a Naval Aviation photographer had photographed a UFO formation. By Kimball's orders, the movie film was being evaluated at the Navy Photo-Interpretation Laboratory, near Washington. From the first analysis, it seemed certain that genuine UFOs had been photographed. If so, this could be a worse threat than the Navy investigation.

[1] Confirmed to the author by Rear Admiral Bolster, in 1953.

Contacting the head of the photo laboratory, the AF quoted the UFO jurisdiction order and told him to deliver the film immediately for Air Force analysis. When the demand was relayed to Secretary Kimball he ordered the Navy experts to continue analyzing the original film, sending the AF only a copy.

By this time, all the sighting details had been carefully checked. On July 2, 1952, Warrant Officer Delbert C. Newhouse was driving to a newly assigned station with his wife. Near Tremonton, Utah, they saw a group of twelve to fourteen flying objects maneuvering at high speed. Newhouse, a veteran Naval Aviation photographer, described them later as unlike any aircraft he had ever seen, comparing them with pans inverted on other pans—typical discs.

Using a Bell & Howell camera with a three-inch telephoto lens, Newhouse shot about forty feet of film before the UFOs flew out of sight.

At the Navy laboratory, photo analysts spent three months—over 600 working hours—evaluating the color film. After thorough technical tests, they agreed it was impossible to duplicate the maneuvering UFOs under simulated conditions. In their final analysis, they also ruled out conventional objects:

Aircraft. "With the lens used, aircraft would have been identified clearly five miles away. The objects' speed at that distance would have been 653.3 miles an hour. . . . At that time, there was no group flying by aircraft capable of such speeds, and certainly not capable of such maneuvers at those speeds."

Balloons. "With the telephoto lens used, balloons could have been identified up to five miles. The speeds if they were only 2½ miles away would be 326.75 miles an hour, in excess of any wind-blown balloons."

Birds. "No bird is sufficiently reflective to cause the film to react as strongly as it has done." The analysts also made it plain that with such speeds it would be ridiculous to explain the UFOs as birds.

With all ordinary answers disproved, the Navy experts agreed on the only possible conclusion:

"Unknown objects under intelligent control."

In the fall of 1952 the Navy evaluation was delivered to the Air Force. Though the censors had expected the conclusion, they were dismayed by the Navy's technical backup. So far, their own analysts had been stumped in their efforts to debunk the Utah film. Now the Navy experts had made it impossible. There was not a single loophole—except for an obvious and dangerous lie.

Stalling for time, the AF asked the Navy not to take any action until their own analysis was completed. Secretary Kimball, certain they could not explain away the film, agreed to a short delay.

During all this time, the CIA had been keeping a close watch on the UFO problem and the AF operations. (As Admiral Hillenkoetter told me afterward, this had been going on since 1948, when he was the CIA director.)

But in '52, though neither the AF nor the Navy knew it, the CIA was solidly behind the cover-up. When it learned of the Navy investigation and the Utah film conclusion it decided that Kimball had to be stopped. It would be a risky job. Kimball might defy them and publicly release the film analysis along with the strongest Navy evidence. It might be better to avoid him and try to convince President Truman that Kimball should be silenced. But this too might backfire—no one could be sure of Truman's reaction.

The CIA decided to wait for the November election. General Eisenhower's victory gave them a break—Secretary Kimball would soon be replaced by a Republican, and now he probably would not push any fight with the Air Force.

The agency heads proved to be right. As Secretary Kimball knew, preparing a strong case against the censorship would take time. In the aftermath of the election it would be difficult to launch a drive against the AF, and as an outgoing cabinet officer he would not have much chance of success. But his efforts had not been wasted; if the new secretary decided to go ahead, Admiral Bolster would have all the evidence.

Even though the Kimball threat seemed ended, the CIA knew another Navy fight could erupt, and the AF had shown it was not tough enough to cope with such a danger. The only answer was to seize control of the AF investigation and insist on a hard-boiled, ruthless censorship, to kill off public belief in UFOs.

To carry this out, the CIA arranged a meeting of scientists and AF representatives at the Pentagon, for a confidential analysis of the UFO evidence. Supposedly, this was to be a careful, objective examination of the best verified reports. Actually, the CIA-selected scientists were known skeptics. Most of them had no real knowledge of UFOs and they considered the subject nonsense. Since the CIA agents would have full authority, they could limit and offset the evidence, steering the scientists toward a completely negative verdict. The agency heads had little doubt of the outcome.

Most of the AF group were opposed to the cover-up, at least privately. Deliberately or not, they were led to believe that the CIA was worried about the growing censorship hazards. Completely unaware of the true CIA stand, they expected to present irrefutable proof of UFO reality and then join the agents and the scientists in discussing plans to end the debunking.

The AF group to be summoned to this conference included a general from Wright-Patterson AFB; Cols. William A. Adams and Wesley S. Smith of the Directorate of Intelligence; Maj. Dewey Fournet, Headquarters Intelligence Monitor of the UFO Project; Capt. Edward J. Ruppelt and other project officers, and Albert M. Chop, HQ press official handling UFO information.

Unsuspected by the CIA, Major Fournet and several headquarters officers had secretly worked up a plan to give the public the facts. This was six weeks before the CIA conference was arranged. I had been working privately with some of this group and I had been told of the plan off-record, first by Chop, later by Fournet and Ruppelt. It was such a daring scheme that at first I couldn't believe they would get away with it.

During the '52 excitement, Fournet had been the key figure in evaluating the hundreds of reports. As headquarters monitor, he knew the full UFO story and he now was convinced the secrecy should end. Because of his special assignment, he frequently had contacts with high-ranking HQ officers. Some of them, he discovered, were strongly opposed to the cover-up, and after guarded discussions they aided him in developing a plan for action.

The key was a special press conference, called with no previous announcement which would alert the opposition. Reporters first would be shown the Utah film. The Navy analysts' conclusions would follow, with no hint of AF debunking. Then the strongest UFO reports by impressive witnesses would be released, some confirmed by radar tracking, with all ordinary explanations ruled out. Finally, a new Intelligence evaluation of UFOs would be presented, drawn up by Major Fournet and based on hundreds of reports he had analyzed, with the aid of project scientists and Technical Intelligence officers. The conclusion: Alien spacecraft observing our world. There would be no hint of the AF capture attempts.[2]

It was an incredible plan, but with the higher officers' private help it could succeed. To reduce the chance of public alarm, the secrecy would be frankly admitted and then explained as intended to keep from frightening the country while the AF tried to learn more about UFOs; since there was no proof of any hostile purpose, the AF now felt sure the public would take the disclosure without any serious hysteria. This also would help to take the censors off the hook—indicating their genuine concern for the citizens. And once the press had the documented story, the control-officers would probably be

[2] Confirmed by Lt. Col. Joseph Bloomer, AF Intelligence, Capt. Ruppelt and Albert M. Chop.

afraid to deny it. At least this is what the Fournet group was counting on in this daring operation.

Before the CIA meeting Fournet decided not to mention the plan until the main discussions were over. But he still expected the scientists to accept the AF evidence and agree on the need to prepare the country.

The CIA conference began on January 12, 1953. It was controlled by three representatives of the Central Intelligence Agency—Agents Philip G. Strong and Ralph L. Clark, and CIA scientist Dr. Marshall Chadwell. After the five-day ordeal ended, a grim-faced Intelligence colonel gave me the bad news, confirmed later by Fournet, Ruppelt and Chop.

"We were double-crossed. The CIA doesn't want to prepare the public—they're trying to bury the subject. Those agents ran the whole show and the scientists followed their lead. They threw out the Utah film—said the Navy analysts were incompetent. We had over a hundred of the strongest verified reports. The agents bypassed the best ones. The scientists saw just fifteen cases, and the CIA men tried to pick holes in them. Fournet had sightings by top military and airline pilots—even scientists. The agents made it seem as if the witnesses were dopes, so the scientists brushed off the whole Fournet report—said he didn't have the slightest evidence of interplanetary spaceships. Ed Ruppelt had a program for a special tracking system and they threw that out. I know those CIA agents were only following orders, but once or twice I almost blew up."

Luckily the Fournet group had not given any hint of their secret preparation plan. In February they made a determined effort to put over the special press conference. They seemed on the verge of winning—then the CIA moved in. That afternoon, at the Pentagon, Chop told me what had happened.

"They killed the whole program. We've been ordered to work up a national debunking campaign, planting articles in magazines and arranging broadcasts to make UFO reports sound like poppycock."

Within a few days Chop quit the Air Force, but I learned more about the CIA take-over from Captain Ruppelt.

"What Al Chop told you isn't the worst of it. We're ordered to hide sightings when possible, but if a strong report does get out we have to publish a fast explanation—make up something to kill the report in a hurry, and also ridicule the witness, especially if we can't figure a plausible answer. We even have to discredit our own pilots. It's a raw deal but we can't buck the CIA. The whole thing makes me sick—I'm thinking of putting in for inactive."

Major Fournet had already been put on inactive duty, with orders not to reveal his UFO conclusion. His secret report was bottled up at HQ as "an unfinished Air Force document."

Under the new CIA-dictated policy, even the highest-rated AF observers were ruthlessly slandered. One victim was Wing Commander D. J. Blakeslee, a famous ace in World War II. Blakeslee was flying a jet fighter over Japan one night when he heard the pilots of two other AF planes report a UFO to an Air Force base. Guided by ground radar, he sighted the object, a machine with rotating red, green and white lights. Cutting off his own lights, he tried to close in. Apparently his jet was not seen at first, but in a moment the UFO drew away and disappeared. When he saw it a second time he went to full power and switched on his lights. This time the unknown craft raced off at terrific speed, vanishing in five seconds.

In a debriefing report an Intelligence lieutenant colonel stated Blakeslee had held responsible command assignments and was stable and thoroughly reliable. The device sighted, he said, was definitely "an Unidentified Flying Object."

After the CIA took over it learned this report had been cleared for me. Under orders, the AF hurriedly explained the UFO as the planet Jupiter. The AF radar which tracked the UFO had a range of a few hundred miles. On that night Jupiter was 366 million miles from the Earth. But the CIA deliberately tried to make fools of Wing Commander Blakeslee, the other pilots and the AF radar experts.

In 1953, the true story of the Utah film was made public by Walter Karig, Special Assistant to the Secretary of the Navy. Evading the Navy analysis, the AF rushed out this answer: The UFOs were only sea gulls.

Not all AF officers gave in to the CIA without a fight. One report that set off a row came from Prof. Henry Carlock, Chief of the Physics Department, University of Mississippi—who was also an Air Force Reserve colonel.

One night in '57, Carlock observed a UFO over Jackson, using a 100-power telescope. In a public report he described a maneuvering device with three portholes. In Washington, a CIA agent told an AF public information officer to release a debunking explanation. As it happened, the PIO knew Carlock.

"The colonel's a good astronomer," he told the CIA agent. "It's a damned shame to ridicule him—I know he saw what he reported."

"We can't help it," the agent said. "You'll have to say it was a delusion."

After an argument, the PIO wrote out a press release. But somehow it never reached the reporters.

In smearing commercial pilots, some debunkers have made vicious attacks. In one case, a veteran American Airlines captain reported sighting three UFOs, which also had been seen by his co-pilot, passengers, and the crews of five other airliners. A HQ spokesman, protecting himself by anonymity, withheld mention of the other witnesses and publicly implied the captain was drunk. After the captain went on the air to end ridicule of his family and himself, his company was forced to silence him.

Some of the hasty debunking is not only harsh but unbelievably stupid. One pilot who was given "the treatment" was Ernest Stadvec, an AF bomber captain in World War II, now the owner of a flying service in Akron.

Stadvec was flying over Ohio one night, with two pilots as passengers, when a bright-glowing UFO dived at his plane. Just as a collision seemed certain the object stopped abruptly. Then it climbed away at rocket-like speed, leaving the three pilots stunned by the near-disaster.

When the story broke, an AF spokesman hurriedly called the press, without even questioning the witnesses. Implying that Stadvec was alone, he said the object which frightened him was only the star Capella.

Stadvec hit back with an angry public retort.

"This AF man never bothered to investigate. Two other pilots were with me and they'll both testify that the UFO almost crashed into the plane. I've been flying 19 years, thousands of hours at night, and I'm certainly not going to be scared out of my wits imagining some star is diving at me."

But the AF never retracted the senseless Capella explanation.

At least once, under this hard-boiled cover-up policy, the AF has publicly denounced a foreign government picture of a UFO. This photograph of a round-shaped flying device was taken in broad daylight from a Brazilian survey ship, as Brazilian Navy officers and crewmen watched the UFO's maneuvers. Following extensive laboratory tests under government supervision, the photograph was certified as authentic by the Brazilian Navy Secretary, Admiral Garson de Macedo Soares, and other high Navy officers. It was then released by the President of Brazil.

When the picture was televised in the United States the Air Technical Intelligence Center called it a fake. Lt. Col. L. J. Tacker, a HQ spokesman, stated that the U. S. Navy had determined it to be a hoax. The Navy denied the AF claims, but they were repeated for months to Congress and the press. This deliberate insult, which caused ill feelings in Brazil, should have been retracted long ago, with a full apology. But under the CIA-AF suppression policy the picture is still listed as a hoax.

Even members of Congress are not immune to the pressure. The late Senator Richard B. Russell once sighted UFOs while in Europe. Someone tipped off an aviation columnist, Tom Towers, and he wrote for details.

"I have discussed this with the affected agencies of the government," Senator Russell replied, "and they are of the opinion that it is unwise to publicize the matter at this time."

As Senator Russell was a congressional leader, Chairman of the Senate Armed Services Committee, this was hot news, and Towers printed the letter as proof of high-level censorship. The CIA hastily contacted the senator and from then on he kept silent.

For years, the CIA and the AF have shown an astonishing disregard for congressional authority. Absolute denials of any spaceship evidence have been sent to legislators, signed by directors of legislative liaison, whose specific job is to give straight answers to Congress. Included in this group there have been several generals, among them Maj. Gen. Joe W. Kelly and Maj. Gen. W. P. Fisher.

Not even lawmakers with high security clearance can get the true answers. When Congressman John McCormack was House Majority Leader he made strong efforts to learn the AF conclusions. In a personal discussion and a letter, he told me he could not get the facts, even in closed sessions with high AF officers. Senator Keating, an Army Reserve general, not only was denied the AF conclusions but given a false explanation for the 1952 Washington sightings.

Senator Barry Goldwater, a major general in the AF Reserve, told me he tried repeatedly to get the truth about UFOs. As a general he was cleared for Top Secret. But the crucial UFO information, he discovered later, is classified at a higher level.

Even after some lawmakers were tipped off about the 1948 Top Secret conclusion, AF Headquarters denied its existence. Scores of legislators have received the following statement, which was sent to Congressman Thomas N. Downing after a specific inquiry:

"There never has been an AF or Air Technical Intelligence Center top secret estimate of the situation which declared that UFOs were interplanetary." This was signed by Col. Gordon B. Knight, Chief of the Congressional Inquiry Division. At least five other CID colonels have sent the same denials to members of Congress.

One of the most disturbing aspects of the cover-up operation is the heavy pressure sometimes used against individuals. Capt. Edward Ruppelt is believed by many who know the inside story to have been a tragic victim of such action.

After going on inactive duty, Ruppelt wrote a book on UFOs which jarred the censors with its massive verified evidence and disclosures about the secrecy. In letters to me he firmly opposed the cover-up and he swore he would never follow the Air Force "line." He frequently gave me valuable leads, and when I became director of NICAP he steadily co-operated, praising the organization for its struggle against secrecy.

But in 1959 this suddenly ended. Ruppelt was then working with an aerospace company with Air Force contracts. Something happened which obviously put him under heavy pressure to stop criticizing AF UFO activities. One explanation—which is unproved—is that the AF implied his company contracts and his job might suffer if he did not co-operate. Perhaps there is another answer, something powerful enough to make him give in. The main target was his revealing book. Somehow, he was forced to repudiate it completely.

Adding three chapters at the end, Ruppelt reversed all he had disclosed, rejecting all his strong evidence and ridiculing expert witnesses—some of whom had become personal friends. Now, he said, he knew that the UFO sightings were only illusions, mistakes and hoaxes—the standard AF line.

I knew Ed Ruppelt well. He had courageously revealed what he believed the public should know, and this violent change was bound to hurt him deeply. He was also a sensitive man, and when the revised book appeared there were sharp attacks on his integrity, some even by former friends who should have guessed the truth. Like several others who knew Ruppelt well, I have always believed that the enforced retraction and bitter criticism were partly the cause of his premature death from a heart attack.

The drastic action taken against Ruppelt should have been a warning for NICAP. But there had been no serious CIA interference in our three years of operation, though we knew we were being watched. Several times, the CIA had tried to pressure witnesses who had reported sightings to NICAP. In 1957, two CIA agents had forced NICAP adviser Ralph Mayher to give them a UFO film. The agents promised Mayher the AF would return it with a technical analysis, but all he received was a section with the best frames cut out. It was mailed in a plain envelope, with no analysis or other AF link. And once a CIA agent had come to our Washington offices while I was away, apparently intending to discover what confidential material we were holding for congressional hearings. But the staff had been prepared against any such attempt, and the agent learned nothing of importance.

Though NICAP was a private organization, there were scores of high-ranking retired or former officers and hundreds of influential citizens on our Board of Governors, in the Panel of Special Advisers, and our nationwide associate membership. Believing we were fairly safe from any strong action, we had unconsciously let down our guard.

When the attack came it was a swift blow aimed at a high-level target. The effect was immediate and disastrous. To the few of us who knew what happened it seemed at first impossible—even for the powerful CIA.

6

Invisible
Control

It was early in '62 when the CIA struck at NICAP, to block a threatened showdown which would have ended the cover-up. Here for the first time are the full details of that incredible operation and its stunning climax.

The explosive situation which led to the CIA action built up on Capitol Hill in 1961. In the preceding session, NICAP had sent a confidential report to Congress with proof of UFO reality, the censorship, and increasing hazards from secrecy.

The confidential report was approved by the NICAP Board of Governors, including veteran military men with extensive knowledge of the UFO evidence: Vice-Adm. R. H. Hillenkoetter, former CIA director; Rear Adm. H. B. Knowles and Army Reserve Col. Robert B. Emerson, both of whom had made careful evaluations of the UFO reports; former AF Monitor Dewey Fournet, and J. B. Hartranft, Jr., an AF lieutenant colonel in World War II, since then president of the worldwide Aircraft Owners and Pilots Association.

In March 1961, House Majority Leader McCormack privately told me he had urged an investigation by the Science and Astronautics Committee, headed by Congressman Overton Brooks.

By this time, after studying the NICAP confidential report, scores of legislators had come out against UFO secrecy, among them Senators Dodd, Goldwater, Keating, Kefauver, Proxmire and Smathers, and Congressmen Addonizio, Baumhart, Downing, Hardy, Metcalf, Scherer, and L. T. Johnson.

Representative Hiestand urged the Secretary of the AF to reveal the facts. Representative Lindsay, later the mayor of New York, called UFO sightings a matter of vital importance. "The security of the U.S.," he said, "does not always demand total secrecy. . . . The American people are fully capable of understanding the nature of these problems."

Representative Leonard Wolf, a member of the Space Committee, told the House of Representatives: "I believe that publication of the NICAP Report (with one confidential section on foreign angles deleted) will help to reduce the dangers cited by Vice-Admiral Hillenkoetter and the other NICAP officials." Stressing that the NICAP Report was a careful evaluation in contrast to frauds and delusions about UFOs, Wolf strongly urged open hearings.

In May of '61 a UFO investigation was announced, to be carried out by three members of the House Space Committee. The subcommittee was to be headed by Congressman Joseph E. Karth of Minnesota. Karth had already publicly criticized the censorship, and he insisted that the hearings should be open.

An AF fight against hearings had been started by Maj. Gen. W. P. Fisher, Director of Legislative Liaison. In letters and conversations with lawmakers he hammered away with this argument: "Hearings would only benefit the sensation seekers and publishers of science fiction." Other ranking HQ officers followed up, trying to kill the investigation. But the drive for hearings was moving too rapidly.

In August, Chairman Brooks of the Space Committee gave the AF its hardest setback. Until then, he had not favored hearings, though he had reluctantly agreed on the UFO subcommittee, after strong urging by Majority Leader McCormack. But he still refused to sanction open meetings or even privately examine NICAP's documented evidence.

But in early August something caused a surprising change.

Without explaining what had happened, Chairman Brooks scheduled a private conference with Admiral Hillenkoetter and me. We were asked to bring a cross section of our strongest and best-documented evidence, also proof of official censorship and an explanation of the secrecy dangers. Later on I learned that Brooks had a deep respect for the admiral's achievement in organizing the CIA and directing it for three years, besides a high regard for his brilliant Navy record. In ignoring the NICAP confidential report, he had failed to realize that Hillenkoetter was a Board member almost from the beginning.

The conference was set for August 24, but our hopes were quickly ended. Congressman Brooks was taken seriously ill, and he died soon afterward. His successor was Congressman George P. Miller, who bluntly announced he would not order hearings.

The chances of ending the cover-up seemed almost zero. But in February of '62 a congressman who had strongly supported Karth asked me to come to his office.

"There's another way to break this," he said. "I've talked it over with some of my colleagues and I'm sure we can count on Karth, Downing, Moss, Kornegay—as many as we want on the House side. Maybe we can get McCormack, if it won't jeopardize his Majority Leader position. In the Senate, I'm certain we can get Keating, Goldwater, Proxmire, Dodd and two or three others already on the record against UFO secrecy.

"Now first, we want you to give us one of the hottest cases NICAP's got, fully documented. It's got to be powerful and exciting, with enough expert witnesses so it'll hit the front pages and the network newscasts."

"I know one big case that would do it," I said. "But without hearings, how—?"

"I'll explain in a minute. Tell me about this report."

"Admiral Del Fahrney gave me the lead to it—he's been a NICAP member since he retired as the Navy missile chief. I can get him to confirm it to you. The detailed report was obtained from the chief witness by Capt. James Taylor, and Fahrney arranged for him to verify the whole thing for me. You can double-check this with Taylor if you want to. He's retired now, and he told me I could use his name."

"Okay," said the congressman. "Give me a rundown."

On the night of the UFO encounter, a four-engine Navy transport was flying west over the Atlantic, its altitude 19,000 feet. At the controls was Cmdr. George Brent, a Navy pilot for ten years. (To protect the officer his name has been changed.) Brent had crossed the Atlantic more than two hundred times. On this trip he was bringing two flight crews home from special duty in Europe. Including his own crew there were over twenty-five pilots, navigators and flight engineers aboard the transport.

The plane was about fifty miles from Gander Airport, Newfoundland, when Brent saw a cluster of lighted objects ahead. Apparently they were on the surface of the ocean, or close to it.

As the commander circled for a better look all the lights suddenly dimmed. Then they swiftly spread out and disappeared—except for one which streaked up at the transport. Within seconds, the object reached the plane's altitude, now clearly visible as a huge flying disc with a glow around the rim. To the stunned men in the cockpit it seemed about to hit them head on. Then it tilted sharply and shot to one side.

Reducing speed, the flying disc swung around to pace the transport. To the dazed men in the cockpit and the cabin it was an incredible sight. The UFO was enormous, well over 300 feet in diameter and at least thirty feet thick at the center. From the glow around the rim the Navy men could see the reflecting surface, apparently smooth metal.

After about ten seconds the big disc tilted up steeply, accelerating to an estimated speed of over 2,000 knots before it disappeared.

When Brent radioed Gander a tower operator told him they

had tracked the UFO on radar. When the plane landed, the entire crew was interrogated by AF Intelligence officers. At their destination, Patuxent Naval Air Station in Maryland, Brent and the rest were questioned again by Naval Intelligence and required to sign full reports. Later, a government scientist (supposedly from the CIA) confidentially showed Brent secret UFO photos—one portraying a disc like the one over the Atlantic. In a final interview, the commander was interviewed by Air Technical Intelligence officers at Wright-Patterson AFB. But none of the Navy or Air Force men, or the government scientist, would answer any questions about the UFOs.

"That's a powerful case," the congressman said. "It's exactly what we need."

"Those witnesses are probably afraid of reprisals," I told him. "They may not agree to a public report."

"Tell them we'll guarantee immunity. If you have any trouble I'm sure Admiral Hillenkoetter can persuade them to appear."

"You mean he's in on this?"

"Not yet, but we expect him to be. Now, here's the strategy. We intend to call a press conference—there's nothing to stop members of Congress from getting together and talking with the press. We want Admiral Hillenkoetter to spearhead the show. With his terrific Navy record and being CIA director three years the press will play it up as a top-level deal.

"But first we'll have a private bipartisan meeting, not connected with any committee, and we'll keep it under wraps. We'll have Hillenkoetter and you and two or three NICAP Board members there, after we've lined up those Navy witnesses. We'll have that commander give us the report first, then the other witnesses, so we can be sure it's airtight. We should also go over two or three other hot cases you and the other NICAP Board members can certify, and any new documentary proof of censorship since your report to Congress."

"There's one thing that should have a big impact," I said.

"In the fall of '61 we managed to get a photocopy of an AF Intelligence sketch of a flying disc. It was taken from a restricted manual for AF Intelligence officers, entitled *AFM 200-3*. We can use it because somebody slipped up and forgot to reclassify it as Confidential when the Restricted classification was canceled."

"What does it show?" asked the congressman.

"There's an AF bomber in the lower foreground. Above it is a typical flying disc with a domed center, coming in toward the bomber. But here's the important part. This official sketch is linked with a key statement in the manual: 'The Air Technical Intelligence Center is responsible for the prevention of technological surprise.' So here is AF Intelligence, in this hidden manual, implying a possible 'technological surprise' by UFOs after flatly denying they exist. The payoff is this claim in AF Special Project Report 14, p. 93:

" 'It is still impossible to develop a picture of what a flying saucer is. . . . Out of 4,000 people who said they saw flying saucers, sufficiently detailed descriptions were given in only 12 cases. Having culled the cream of the crop, it is still impossible to develop a picture. . . . to derive a verified model . . .' "

"That's very good," the congressman said. "We'll make copies of that photostat and those AF statements, and give them to the press. As I see it, we'll have McCormack or Karth open the press conference, with Goldwater or some other senator confirming the purpose. They'll come right out and say this congressional group is seriously concerned about the UFO problem and the censorship. Then Admiral Hillenkoetter will take over. He'll repeat his statement that UFOs are real objects under intelligent control and that the AF is hiding the truth. Then he can produce the Navy witnesses in that Atlantic case. When they finish with their story we can follow up with a few other strong NICAP-verified cases, and Hillenkoetter can go into the proof of secrecy, and the dangers from covering up. To wind it up, the congressional

group will go on record as demanding an end to official secrecy. If it's handled right, with network TV along with the
wire services, it'll blow the lid off. Unless the Air Force gives
in, Congress will have to hold a full-scale investigation—an
open one."

"If you can do this without scaring the public, it should be
a big start toward preparing people."

"We'll use the same approach the Fournet group intended," the congressman assured me. "You said they were
going to play up the lack of any proven hostility. We'll do
the same—maybe Admiral Hillenkoetter should open on that
angle. Naturally some people will be a little frightened, but
if we handle it carefully I don't think they'll get hysterical.
I'm counting on Hillenkoetter for that. You think there's
any doubt he'll go along?"

"No, I'm almost certain he'll agree; he's hit the secrecy
pretty hard. I've known him since we were classmates at the
Naval Academy. If he does take it on he won't pull any
punches."

"That's why we want him. Will you sound him out?"

"Sure. His office is in New York—he's head of a shipping
line. I'll fly up if necessary; I'd rather not phone about it.
But he's expected down here in a few days—"

"That'll be okay," said the congressman. "Let me know
as soon as you can."

The more I thought over this breakthrough scheme the
better it looked. Most of this Congress group had openly
opposed the secrecy. From personal knowledge, I was sure
that McCormack, Karth and Goldwater would put up a real
fight. Karth, I knew, had counted heavily on NICAP evidence
and assistance in open hearings. After a misunderstanding
about protocol, which I quickly corrected, Congressman
Karth wrote me that he expected strong NICAP evidence
of the interplanetary answer. It was his belief, he said, that
we would produce proof of UFO reality in a hearing—proof

that UFOs "actually were craft (of sorts) from other planets." Otherwise, he told me, he would not have been interested in holding hearings. On receiving details of the available proof, he accepted NICAP's offer of full co-operation. Indicating his determination to resist any possible pressure, he sent me this underlined statement:

"*I am not a captive of the Air Force.*"

If Hillenkoetter acted as spearhead, it would of course add greatly to the national publicity. From the start, his Navy record had been outstanding. A star man at Annapolis, he was graduated Number 20 in a class of 457. He had served with distinction in submarines, on destroyers and battleships. In his early career, he carried out several diplomatic missions in Europe and South America. During his attaché service in Paris, Madrid, Lisbon and Rome he won high foreign decorations, including that of "Officer in the French Legion of Honor."

Hillenkoetter was executive officer of the U.S.S. *West Virginia* when World War II broke out, and he was wounded when the Japanese sank the battleship. After a tour as Chief of Intelligence in the Pacific, he went on to action in the Solomons and New Hebrides, followed by a special assignment as Director of War Planning and Control. He was present at the Japanese surrender on the U.S.S. *Missouri*, and afterward he was given command of the ship.

In 1947, President Truman promoted Hillenkoetter to vice-admiral and made him the first director of the new Central Intelligence Agency. After three years he returned to naval duty, serving as the Navy Inspector General. Then in 1957 he retired and became head of a New York shipping line.

In his five years on the NICAP Board he had played an important role in combating UFO secrecy. If he did accept the Congress group role, it probably would result in the biggest break in the cover-up.

Before contacting Hillenkoetter, I took steps to locate Commander "Brent." I knew his real name, but phoning

Naval Personnel for his present station could be a mistake. To avoid any link with the UFO subject I used a go-between, a friend who dealt with various government departments as a personnel specialist. Though he had a serious interest in the UFO riddle he kept it quiet. I knew he could be trusted —we had exchanged suppressed information several times, with no resultant leaks. As he is now in private industry I can safely disclose the part he played, but not his name. I'll call him Jack Morton.

I had a special reason for selecting Morton. In 1959 he had met a Navy pilot stationed in Washington. After they became close friends Morton mentioned his interest in UFOs. Later the pilot revealed he had a close sighting while on a Navy transport. When Morton gave me the details, in confidence, I suspected this was the Atlantic encounter case. But the pilot refused any contact with NICAP, fearing a possible leak to the Air Force.

When I saw Morton, at his home, I told him the situation and he agreed to find out "Brent's" station. I asked if he thought the Navy might have a "flag" on the commander's file—a notice to refuse information and report any queries.

"I don't think so," said Morton. "That was some time back. But to play safe I'll just say I know the commander and I heard he was being transferred here. Then I'll ask for his ad- dress so I can write him. It should be routine."

"Thanks," I said. "Say, about that Navy pilot you know who had a sighting. If he really was one of the witnesses in that Atlantic case, do you think he'd agree to join the com- mander at that press conference?"

"I doubt it. He took eight months to decide on telling me about that sighting."

"If he really was one of those witnesses he could be a big help. He might get in touch with some he knew personally and ask them to join in. The congressman who told me about this said they'd guarantee immunity."

"How could they be sure? Maybe if Admiral Hillenkoetter

promised to protect them they'd agree. I'll ask this pilot during the weekend, that is, if this was the same case. Meantime, I'll get the dope on the commander and phone you tomorrow."

But the next day passed with no word. Morton's secretary told me he had taken time off, but calls to his home went unanswered. The following night, after repeated calls, I drove out to his house. No one came to the door, but soon after I returned home Morton telephoned.

"I've got to make this quick," he said hurriedly. "That Navy call raised hell—they did have a flag on that commander. A clerk said she'd check on his station, but she didn't call back. In less than an hour two CIA agents showed up at my office. They had me get rid of my secretary—"

"Hold it a second, Jack," I broke in.

"Don't stop me—I'm taking a big chance calling you. Those two agents really gave me the third degree. They made me tell them who wanted the commander's address and why. I could tell that the Congress meeting deal worried them. They grilled me until I told them about the whole plan and Admiral Hillenkoetter. That's all there is—"

Morton stopped for a moment. I heard his voice indistinctly, then he came back on.

"My wife's scared to death. I could be in trouble calling you—they ordered me not to see you or tell you anything. But I saw you at the house tonight and I knew you'd keep on until you got to me. Look, I've got to go—for heaven's sake don't try to call or see me again."

After Morton hung up, I felt a sudden guilt at involving him in this operation. And yet we had no reason to expect trouble. Twice before this, Morton had acted as go-between and secured the addresses of military witnesses in fairly important cases. There had been no repercussions. Also, both the CIA and the AF knew I had the Atlantic encounter report but had made no attempt to contact the witnesses. The main reason was a suggestion by Admiral Fahrney, in 1959, that we plan to use this startling case and the Navy air crews' testimony when we got congressional hearings. We were both confident that the Navy Department would produce these witnesses without resisting a congressional committee summons.

But apparently the CIA and the AF fully realized the potential danger in this case and had continued their safeguard, even with no sign of trouble.

Whatever the answer, the damage was done now. With the CIA aware of the Congress group plan, it would go all out to block it. There was still one chance. If Admiral Hillenkoetter was determined to go ahead, regardless of opposition, the Congress group would probably back him in an open fight. I knew that he should be warned about the CIA agents' action—especially since he had not yet been told of the Capitol Hill plan. To avoid endangering Morton I decided to fly to New York for a private meeting.

Next morning I phoned my secretary, Mrs. Lelia Day, from Washington Airport.

"I'm flying to New York. If necessary you can call me at—"

"Wait," she said hastily, "there's an important letter here you should know about. No one else knows about it yet. I could read it to you, but—"

"Hold it. I'll be right in."

When I saw Mrs. Day's face I knew there was bad news. She silently handed me the letter, went out and closed the door.

As I had guessed, the letter was from Hillenkoetter.

Dear Don:

In my opinion, NICAP's investigation has gone as far as possible. I know the UFOs are not U.S. or Soviet devices. All we can do now is wait for some action by the UFOs.

The Air Force cannot do any more under the circumstances. It has been a difficult assignment for them, and I believe we should not continue to criticize their investigations.

I am resigning as a member of the NICAP Board of Governors.

As I reread this incredible letter some of Hillenkoetter's public statements flashed through my mind:

"The UFOs are unknown objects operating under intelligent control. . . . The Air Force is still censoring UFO sightings. Hundreds of authentic reports by veteran pilots and other technically trained observers have been ridiculed or explained away as mistakes, delusions or hoaxes. . . . It is imperative that we learn where the UFOs come from and what their purpose is. The public has a right to know. . . ."

The most important statement of all was the one Hillenkoetter had signed on August 22, 1961, which was sent to Congress after the death of Space Committee Chairman Overton Brooks:

Acting with the majority of the NICAP Board of Governors, I urge immediate Congressional action to reduce the dangers from secrecy about Unidentified Flying Objects. . . . Two dangers are steadily increasing:

1. The risk of accidental war, from mistaking UFO formations for a Soviet surprise attack.

2. The danger that the Soviet Government may, in a critical moment, *falsely* claim the UFOs as secret Russian weapons against which our defenses are helpless.

For the third time I went over the admiral's astonishing letter of resignation. There was no hint that he had been told about the Congress group's exposé plan. Yet it was the only believable explanation. But Hillenkoetter had been absolutely convinced that the cover-up *should* be exposed. How could he have been pressured into this complete reversal?

Threats would not have worked—I knew this tough fighter too well to believe that. The only answer was persuasion at a very high level that it was his duty to help block the Capitol Hill showdown—and to attempt a change in NICAP policy. But this would still require some powerful reason for continuing the secrecy. That it was some frightening situation, to be kept from the public at all costs, I refused to believe. With all the confidential sources I had established since '49 I would have had at least an inkling. In an effort to find some clue, I went back over all the main points of the UFO evidence. But the cause of the admiral's action was still a mystery.

Regardless of the CIA and AF sincere motives, their long suppression of the truth about UFOs is the greatest public deception in American history.

On October 29, 1962, withholding information from the public was admitted by Defense Department Assistant Secretary Arthur Sylvester. If the ends justified it, he said, it was not wrong to keep the public in the dark. In AF Regulation 11-30, withholding information "in the public interest" is admitted as official policy. In AF Regulation 11-7, it is stated that sometimes information requested by Congress may not be furnished "even in confidence."

In regard to UFOs, the CIA and the AF realize it is impossible to deceive all of Congress and the public. Their aim always has been to keep the *majority* convinced that none of the reports has been correct.

To carry out this program, they have been forced to resort to the "Big Lie" technique to insure success. But in doing this they have built up a foundation for dangerous alarm if an outbreak of mass UFO operations suddenly disproved the false claims.

After several publicized landings in 1964, the UFO censorship officials were warned that sudden proof of UFO reality might cause an uncontrollable wave of fear. Several AF Headquarters officers were considering, belatedly, what steps to take in such an emergency, when the first phase of a new crisis abruptly began.

Increasing from the first week in '65, UFO encounter reports grew into an avalanche. As the months went on, bizarre stories of new discoveries and alien beings became public. Before the end of the year, the censors faced the worst crisis since the UFO surveillance began. And the end was not in sight.

7

Seeds
of Panic

Just before dark, on January 3, 1965, an Electra airliner was approaching Washington when a strange flying object hurtled toward the plane. To the terrified crew they seemed only seconds from a fatal collision. Then the UFO suddenly veered away.[1]

This was the start of the great '65 flap which finally led to the worst crisis Air Force censors ever experienced.

By January 5, scores of new reports were pouring in to the Air Force. That afternoon, a huge flying disc flashed over the NASA station at Wallops Island, Virginia. The satellite-tracking chief, Dempsey Bruton, calculated its speed at over 100 miles a minute. On that same day the Navy disclosed that two UFOs had been tracked by radar at the Naval Air Test Center in Maryland. One had made a sharp turn at 4,800 miles an hour.

Caught off guard by the sudden deluge, the AF rushed out some unbelievable answers.

Dempsey Bruton, and other Space Administration observers at Wallops Island, were labeled incompetent. Without the slightest investigation, AF Headquarters said the Navy radar was found to be faulty, then for good measure it branded the radar operators as inexperienced.

[1] Captain's report given to NICAP.

Within forty-eight hours, dozens of other factual reports were hastily explained as mistakes or hoaxes.

During this first period, a few stories of weird space beings were broadcast as humorous sidelights. Since most of them were obvious frauds, few people took them seriously. The straight sighting cases were dramatic enough without any wild space creatures.

On January 25, two UFOs landed separately near Williamsburg, Virginia, stalling witnesses' cars. The reports were confirmed by state police. Two days later, an alien craft came down near Hampton, Virginia. Among the witnesses were two NASA research engineers—A. G. Crimmins and Maj. John Nayadley, a retired AF jet pilot.

"I watched it through binoculars," Crimmins stated. "It was zigzagging as if searching for a landing spot. I could see flashing lights on the edge or rim of a rapidly rotating disc."

The UFO made a touch landing, then climbed steeply out of sight. Without any checkup, AF Headquarters hurriedly explained it as a helicopter the NASA engineers failed to recognize in their excitement. Too late HQ learned that Langley AFB had ruled this out—no helicopters were flying in the area.

Under the strict CIA policy, the AF had to debunk sightings as quickly as possible. With all the pressure, as reports piled up, foul-ups were inevitable.

One harried spokesman denied the AF had any landing reports from Virginia. That very afternoon AF investigators were checking the Williamsburg cases, and the press quickly hit the denial. To offset the blunder, HQ rushed the UFO Project chief, Maj. Hector Quintanella, to Richmond for a debunking tour. Stressing delusions and hoaxes, Quintanella told reporters not a single UFO report was genuine. Since his witness ridicule included responsible Virginians, the tour turned into a flop.

An even worse blunder followed an unusual case in Vermont. The witnesses included the state pathologist, Dr. R. S.

Woodruff, and a high state police official. The two men were riding in a police car near Bethel when a red-lighted UFO flashed overhead. Two more followed at precise intervals, holding the same course and altitude. Motorists behind the police car also witnessed the operation. The UFOs' speed was calculated by the police official as about 2,000 mph.

To cope with the flood of reports, two or three HQ officers were trying to help the regular debunkers, and one of these emergency spokesmen drew the Vermont case.

"The UFOs were only meteors," he told Pentagon reporters.

Within twenty-four hours the roof fell in on this unfortunate spokesman. Meteors come down in haphazard fashion, much faster than 2,000 mph, as several newscasters pointed out, and they either burn up or hit the Earth. To descend together, slow down and level off in precise line formation would be utterly impossible. TV commentator Frank Edwards summed it up in an ironic jibe at the AF.

"You'd do a lot better, gentlemen, if you'd just draw your answers out of a hat."

But the AF ordeal had only begun. Stimulated by the publicity, witnesses started to reveal important encounters they had kept secret in fear of ridicule. One of the first was a startling report by a veteran pilot, withheld since 1959. A Navy pilot in World War II, he was now chief service engineer for a large industrial company. For business trips he used his private plane, a Cessna 170.

On August 13, 1959, he was flying over New Mexico when his electric and standard magnetic compasses began to spin instead of showing the course. Then he saw three round gray machines speeding toward him. Before he could dive away they flipped around in front of the Cessna, circling it at close range. The pilot tensely sat it out—to attempt an escape could mean a collision.

After circling the plane several times, the UFOs sped away, then the compasses returned to normal. The pilot called the nearest airport to report the encounter, but an FAA tower operator broke in and told him to keep radio silence.

"He said for me to fly at once to Kirtland AFB. When I landed there I was hustled to an office and interrogated by an AF major—the base UFO officer. Then he told me that being so close to those objects I might develop radiation sickness. He said if I developed any unusual illness to let the AF know and get to a government hospital right away. He warned me to keep this secret from everybody but my wife and to make sure she kept quiet, too."

In a signed report secured later by a NICAP subcommittee chairman, Paul Cerny, the pilot said the possibility of serious radiation effects had kept him and his wife in a state of fear for weeks.

In hundreds of cases, people in planes and cars have been fairly close to UFOs with no serious results. However, a few spacecraft are known to have been radioactive. In 1956, Captain Ruppelt revealed that an instrumented AF test area had recorded abnormal radiation when UFOs flew overhead.

During December 1964, a landing near Grottoes, Virginia, brought added proof. Horace Burns, owner of a gun shop, was driving in the country when a large metallic craft came down nearby, landing about a hundred yards from the road. Before it took off he noted a blue fluorescent band around the base.

The touchdown area was checked by a Harrisonburg college professor, Ernest Gehman of Madison College, and his Geiger counter showed high radiation. This was confirmed by two Dupont engineers from the company plant at Waynesboro, Virginia, who also made extensive Geiger counter checks.

"It was a 'hot' area—radioactive," engineer Lawrence Cook reported. "We spent forty-five minutes in the field. . . . This was definitely an accurate reading."

Even though the landing-spot radiation was abnormal, the engineers had no ill effects. The UFO's radiation was unknown. But even experienced investigators fully aware of the cover-up found it hard to believe this was a serious threat. Over the years, a few people had reported slight burns, effects like deep suntan, after being near UFOs. But no radiation link was ever proved in NICAP investigations. It was unbelievable that the CIA or the AF would expose citizens to the risk of deadly radiation to keep from admitting that UFOs are real.

Apparently most of the public had the same belief; when the Cessna pilot's story broke there was no alarm. But in a follow-up, two newscasters tied in the Dupont engineers' report, exaggerating it to indicate dangerous radiation. A sensational newspaper recalled a scare article titled "I Was Doomed By A Flying Saucer," in which an anonymous writer said he was dying from radiation burns caused by a beam from a UFO. Unhappily for the AF, this misleading build-up got an added spurt from the James Flynn injury case. Spotlighting the beam angle, a network newscast told how Flynn had been knocked unconscious by a UFO in the Everglades. (Detailed in Chapter 2.)

Though there was no sign of panic, the publicity worried the Air Force. Pushed into a corner, they had little choice. Rejecting all the reports, headquarters denied any knowledge of UFO radiation, and the publicity died down.

But new developments constantly kept the AF on edge. An airline co-pilot released a long-hidden report of a near-collision with two UFOs. Several passengers had been thrown out of their seats by the captain's violent evasion maneuvers. Dave Garroway spotlighted the cover-up on an ABC network program. A congressman exposed an AF attempt to conceal its UFO directive, which contained censorship orders. In contrast to Pentagon debunking, several foreign nations publicly confirmed UFO reports. One was New Zealand, where the Deputy Director of AF Operations told the press they were taking the sightings seriously.

On through June, pressure on the Air Force continued.

On June 4, Astronaut James McDivitt photographed an unknown device from his *Gemini IV* spacecraft. Shortly after this, Astronaut Frank Borman sighted another unidentified space object as his *Gemini VII* passed over Antigua. Both these reports quickly became public, through NASA.

The AF was just starting to explain away the Borman sighting when an Arthur Godfrey broadcast jarred the debunkers. During his regular nationwide program, Godfrey disclosed for the first time an alarming UFO encounter. It had happened at night, as he was flying in his private executive plane with co-pilot Frank Munciello. They were nearing Philadelphia when a brightly lighted object came in toward the right wing. Godfrey hastily banked to avoid a possible collision. In a quick reverse, the UFO took up a position close to the left wing. When Godfrey tried to pull away it matched every move.

"It stayed there on the left wing, no matter what I did," Godfrey said. After several tense minutes, the unknown machine veered away and disappeared. During the broadcast, Godfrey admitted that he and Munciello were scared by the UFO's close approaches to the plane.

Overnight, Godfrey's report became a headache for the censors. Not only was he a national figure, he had flown Navy, Air Force and commercial planes, including jets, and he was rated an expert pilot. And to top this he was a colonel in the Air Force Reserve.

Calls and letters came in from the public, even some members of Congress, demanding the AF reaction. Do you accept Godfrey's report? If not, what have you got to say? Are you going to claim he was drunk? As these and tougher questions piled up, some of the Pentagon newsmen kept pushing for answers, one or two with malicious humor.

"Going to give him the usual?" asked one reporter. "Incompetent observer—or a practical joker? Or was he having a delusion?"

Just the thought was enough to make even an AF general

shudder. Godfrey was known for a quick and fiery temper. Even the slightest hint of AF debunking would bring a blast —on the air—which they would not soon forget.

But in spite of Godfrey and the astronauts' reports, public excitement decreased as the wave of sightings diminished. Weary AF spokesmen had decided the flap was finally ending when a news flash from the Antarctic ended their hopes.

On July 3, 1965, an enormous flying disc was tracked and photographed at an Argentine scientific station on Deception Island. For twenty minutes, the huge spacecraft maneuvered at terrific speed over the Antarctic base, observed through binoculars by scientists and the station operating staff. Color photographs were taken, showing the UFO as it maneuvered and also while it hovered above the base. During this time the object also caused strong EM interference with radio and instruments for measuring the Earth's magnetic field. In addition, the UFO was witnessed by Chilean scientists at a separate Antarctic base. Detailed reports were confirmed by the Secretary of the Argentine Navy and the Chilean Minister of Defense.

Within hours, news of the Antarctic sightings was flashed around the world. Because of the scientists involved and the high official confirmation, most of the press and the public took the reports seriously. At this same time UFO operations suddenly increased around the globe and these too received serious press coverage, in the United States as well as abroad.

At Lisbon, Portuguese officials reported a huge UFO with the same EM effects as the Antarctic spacecraft. In New South Wales, an aviation expert described a UFO landing on a beach. A leading French space authority, Alexander Ananoff, observed a flying disc near Dreux and photographed it as proof. On July 14, a UFO descended near an Australian space station, interfering with its tracking of *Mariner IV*; it was also observed by control-tower operators at Canberra Airport. Two days later a similar alien craft was sighted near Buenos Aires. Frightened motorists reported UFO chases in a dozen countries. In Australia two people leaped from their car; in South America and the United States several drivers took to the ditch.

By mid-July, the U. S. Air Force was swamped with reports from all over the country, and the debunking system had almost broken down.

On July 15, the Charleston *Evening Post* took a sharp dig at the Air Force: "Confronted by a UFO report, the service immediately begins to crank out of the wild blue yonder the same pre-recorded announcement it has been playing for 20 years: 'Scratch, scratch, the Air Force has no evidence, scratch, scratch, the Air Force has no evidence . . .'"

Then on July 31 the harassed debunkers were caught cold, as sightings abruptly zoomed in the Midwest. In Oklahoma, Kansas, Nebraska, Texas and five other states, formations of UFOs were seen by astronomers, state police, newsmen and thousands of other reliable citizens. At the ordnance depot in Sidney, Nebraska, a guard captain and other witnesses reported a large UFO with four smaller ones behind it in diamond formation. The weather bureau at Wichita tracked dozens of alien craft on its radar.

As these reports clattered in on AF Headquarters teletype, a follow-up bulletin gave the censors a shock. In violation of AFR 200-2, two Air Force bases—Tinker in Oklahoma, and Carswell in Texas—had publicly confirmed radar tracking of UFO formations.

Whatever caused this astonishing break was never explained. The admissions were quickly retracted as errors, after angry calls from the Pentagon. To repair the damage, a fast explanation for the sightings was given to the press:

The glowing objects reported in the Midwest were only the planet Jupiter and the stars Betelgeuse, Rigel, Aldebaran and Capella.

This official AF answer was still being quoted in newscasts when veteran astronomers shot it full of holes.

Not one of the stars named was visible in the United States at the time of the sightings. They could be seen only from the other side of the world.

"This is as far from the truth as you can get," said Director Robert Risser of the Oklahoma Science Foundation Planetarium.

A few of the press had started criticizing the Air Force, but after this false answer was exposed press attacks became an avalanche.

Fort Worth *Star-Telegram*: "They can stop kidding us now about there being no such things as 'flying saucers.' Too many people of obviously sound mind saw and reported them independently."

Cascade, Idaho, *News*: "The official government policy is . . . denying the existence of anything it can't explain."

Meriden, Connecticut, *Journal*: "Many reports in AF files were made by qualified pilots who in flight have encountered UFOs with fantastic flight patterns. These officers are not quacks."

Richmond *News Leader*: "Attempts to dismiss the reported sightings . . . serve only to heighten the suspicion that there's something out there the Air Force doesn't want us to know about."

Similar editorials and demands for a full, open investigation came from newspapers in many states. In the midst of all this, it was discovered that the AF had told Vice-President Humphrey, Senator Birch Bayh and other legislators that *all* UFO reports had been explained. (AF letters to these lawmakers—originals or photocopies—forwarded to NICAP.) The disclosure brought more criticism from the press.

Dallas *Morning News*: "The AF says all sightings can be explained in terms of known phenomena." Then, quoting a UFO Project statement, the newspaper added the AF admission that 633 cases were unexplained.

Seattle *Times*: "Do you ever get the feeling that . . . the AF makes its denials six months in advance?"

Even a few foreign papers joined in the attack. In Canada,

the Shawville, Quebec, *Equity* stated: "There is a strong belief that the military chiefs know more about the UFOs than they are letting on, but are keeping it a well-guarded secret so as not to panic the public."

At the end of July, press and broadcast attacks were still mounting. The barrage stunned the Air Force. Before this, most of the press had accepted the denials of UFO reality. Without this powerful support the cover-up would have collapsed long ago.

Early in '65, less than 20 per cent of the public believed in UFOs, according to polls and private AF and NICAP estimates. The figure was now over 33 per cent and steadily increasing. In barely four weeks, millions of skeptics had been convinced that the UFOs were real and the AF was hiding the truth.

Ever since the tense summer of 1952, the censors had soberly realized the threat of mass belief. With each flap, majority belief had come a little closer. But never had it been such a danger as now.

For the censors, the first big fear was a flood of sightings observers had never reported. By AF estimates, not over 10 per cent of all U.S. sightings had been made public. (After a special analysis, NICAP agreed with this figure.) In mid-July, the AF had about 9,000 UFO reports. If the 10 per cent estimate was correct, then approximately 81,000 sightings were still unreleased.

If the anti-AF trend continued, more and more witnesses would report their withheld sightings, and this flow of evidence could become a tidal wave, swamping the Air Force. A great number of these reports of course would be incorrect. But from documented cases given to me confidentially over the years, by top-rated witnesses, I knew there would be massive, impressive proof from scientists, pilots, aerospace engineers and reliable observers in many professions and trades.

Such a mass of factual evidence, combined with new UFO

reports and blasts from the press, would soon convince the majority of citizens that the UFOs were surveillance space-craft from an advanced civilization. Under tremendous public pressure the Air Force would have to admit the truth—to a nation almost completely unprepared.

This was the grim possibility the AF faced as the black month of July came to an end.

It was soon plain there would be no letup in August. And besides all the public sightings several AF reports leaked out. In one incredible secrecy break, United Press International was given two striking AF radar cases, which it put on national press wires:

Personnel at the U.S. Radar Base in the Keeweenaw Peninsula today reported "solid radar contact" with up to ten unidentified flying objects moving in a "V" formation over Lake Superior. The objects were moving out of the southwest and were heading northeast at "about 9,000 miles per hour."

"Seven other objects were spotted over Duluth," the UPI said. "Jet interceptors gave chase, but they could not maintain the speed of the UFOs and were easily outdistanced."

Another wire story reported an oval-shaped device which was photographed by Robert Campbell, a Sherman, Texas, newscaster. The *Christian Science Monitor* analyzed the negatives and published this serious comment:

Many Texans definitely saw something that even experienced investigators now admit defies explanation. . . . [It] appeared as a bright light in the sky with lesser lights clustered around it. It was photographed. Careful study of the negatives now shows something was there. The camera was in sharp focus. . . . It makes the clearest case yet for a thorough look at the saucer mystery.

On through '65, fear of UFOs was shown in numerous cases which became public. One such encounter involved two Texas deputy sheriffs. On the night of September 3, Deputies B. E. McCoy and Robert Goode sighted a large UFO from their patrol car. In the moonlight they could see it was oval-shaped, about 200 feet long. As they were watching it through binoculars the UFO came down swiftly toward the police car, with the moonlight casting a huge, fast-moving shadow on the ground. As lawmen, they had proved their courage many times. But the sight of this strange machine looming up fifty yards away sent them racing off at 110 miles an hour.

By this time many of the press had planted fear of panic as the reason for AF secrecy. In a typical explanation, the Medford, Oregon, *Mail Tribune* said the AF could fear "that a sudden disclosure might have drastic emotional effects."

Even though sightings became fewer, suspicion that the AF might be hiding something ominous remained, as the year ended.

In February of '66 UFO operations appeared to have reached a low level. While important sightings still were being reported the crisis seemed ended, though to the AF it was a haunting memory.

Then without any warning Phase Two violently erupted.

The actual outbreak, at Dexter, Michigan, occurred on the night of March 20. But dozens of police officers had had an unpublicized preview six nights before.

On March 14, at 3:50 A.M., Deputy Sheriffs B. Bushroe and J. Foster saw several disc-shaped objects maneuvering above Dexter. Then four UFOs were sighted flying in a line formation. By this time three other police agencies had reported similar sightings, and radar tracking had been confirmed by Selfridge AFB.

In an official report Deputy Bushroe detailed the sightings, then added:

"This is the strangest thing that Deputy Foster and myself have ever witnessed. . . . These objects could move at fantastic speeds, and make very sharp turns, dive and climb, and hover, with great maneuverability."

For some reason the March 14 incidents had little publicity. Then on March 20 two or three lights were reported as moving around in a swamp area near Dexter. The next night similar lights were supposedly seen near Hillsdale, Michigan.

In hundreds of far more important cases there had been only local press stories, or none at all. Why the Dexter and Hillsdale reports exploded into nationwide publicity is still a mystery to many experienced investigators.

Overnight, the tension of 1965 revived. Newsmen descended on Dexter. On Capitol Hill, House Minority Leader Gerald Ford demanded a congressional investigation, and other lawmakers backed him up. To reduce the excitement the AF hurriedly sent Dr. Hynek to Michigan. His investigation was barely started when headquarters phoned a peremptory order:

"You will hold a press conference tomorrow morning and explain those reports!"

On the nights of the twentieth and twenty-first, there had been verified reports of flying discs, besides the conflicting stories of moving lights near the ground. Hynek had no explanation for the high-speed maneuvering UFOs. Put on the spot by the HQ order, he attempted to focus attention on the ground light stories.

Avoiding any direct claim, Dr. Hynek told assembled reporters the cause could have been marsh gas, created by decaying vegetable matter in the swampy areas.

Without waiting for Hynek to finish, newsmen ran for the phones, and the marsh gas story quickly broke all over the country.

Never had an AF UFO explanation gotten such a furious reception.

"AIR FORCE INSULTS PUBLIC WITH SWAMP GAS THEORY," the South Bend *Tribune* headlined its attack. The Richmond *News Leader* admonished the AF for suppressing evidence and trying to discredit witnesses. The Houston *Chronicle* sarcastically hit at the AF for attempting to prove UFOs were a product of witnesses' imagination. The Indianapolis *News* urged a congressional inquiry to quiet public alarm.

National ridicule of the marsh gas answer built up so rapidly it was almost as if the '65 barrage had never stopped. Adding to the AF troubles, marsh gas experts publicly exposed the explanation. On the Johnny Carson show, Dr. Albert Hibbs, a California Institute of Technology scientist, emphatically rejected the answer. Press and TV commentators quoted a leading authority, M. Minnaert, author of *The Nature of Light and Colour in the Open Air.*

The methane marsh gas, according to Minnaert, can produce lights known as "will-o'-the-wisp." They resemble tiny flames, from one half an inch to five inches high, not over two inches across. Sometimes they are on the ground, at other times about four inches above it. At times they are blown a few feet by the wind before dying out.

Though Hynek was blamed, incorrectly, for trying to debunk all UFOs as swamp gas, the AF was the main target. Syndicated columnist Roscoe Drummond hammered at the need for a new, full-scale inquiry. So did many news editors, also members of Congress—both Democrats and Republicans. Cartoonists and TV comedians had a field day, deriding the swamp gas answer. *Time, Life, Newsweek* and other magazines played up the story, and networks carried daily UFO reports from pilots, tower operators and other witnesses from coast to coast.

Complicating the problem, "scare" stories were printed or broadcast. On March 23, a man named John T. King reported shooting at a UFO closing in on his car. He was driving near Bangor, Maine, he told police, when he saw a domed flying disc on the ground near the highway. As it came toward him his lights dimmed and the radio stopped. Believing he was in danger, King seized his Magnum pistol. The UFO was only fifty feet away, he said, when he opened fire. At the third shot the disc took off "at tremendous speed."

During March several UFOs also were reported to have smashed into cars and trailers. Few people believed such stories, but even the hoaxes added to the AF burden.

By now the AF was in a serious predicament. To reduce the clamor for a full-scale congressional investigation, it reluctantly agreed to a brief hearing by the House Armed Services Committee.

On the day before the hearing, the AF gave the press a photograph of a disc-shaped craft, one of two experimental models the Canadian AVRO Corporation had contracted to build for the U.S. military services. In 1955, the AF had announced that the AVRO device was to be a revolutionary interceptor, designed to fly at 1,500 miles an hour and to maneuver at incredible speeds. The public was told it would undoubtedly be reported as a "flying saucer" until it became well known.

The obvious purpose of reviving the AVRO story was to make it appear that AVROs had been operating for years and had caused many UFO reports. If this had been stated as fact it would have been a deliberate fraud.

The AVRO was a complete failure. On June 24, 1960, the Army officially stated it would lift only a few feet and was difficult to control. Its top speed was thirty-five miles an hour. After spending $10,000,000, the Army, Navy and Air Force canceled the Canadian contract.

The picture of the rejected AVRO was printed in many papers. But there was no sign that the public was misled by this out-of-date photograph.

The brief hearing by the Armed Services Committee was little more than a farce. Chairman E. Mendel Rivers told AF officials that the UFOs could not be just written off, but they stuck to their debunking claims:

1) No information has been withheld. 2) The AF has never ridiculed witnesses. 3) There is no evidence that UFOs are from other worlds—or that they even exist. 4) There are

no unexplained photographs or radar reports. 5) There never was a Top Secret Estimate of the Situation which concluded UFOs were alien spaceships.

Some committee members made it plain they did not accept all the AF denials. But Chairman Rivers decided against a full probe and ended the hearing. After this victory headquarters expected an encouraging drop in mass belief. Then a new Gallup poll shook the censors.

Nearly *half* the public—46 per cent—now believed UFOs were real.

It was a hard blow—the AF knew it could be on the brink of disaster. In any new wave of sightings debunking would fail, press attacks would increase and an aroused public majority would force an end to the cover-up.

Even if there was no panic, high AF officers knew they would be denounced for the long deception, though it had seemed the wisest course and best for the public. Any sudden admission now would be inviting disaster, and a hasty preparation program was impossible. But the only hope for continuing the secrecy was a drastic change in their operations.

During the Armed Services Committee hearing there had been a discussion of possible evaluation help by university scientists, and HQ decided this might be a way out of their dilemma. First, they would arrange for a UFO study at a well-known, respected college. This would be announced as a new, independent UFO investigation, entirely free of AF control.

Without waiting for a detailed plan the AF quickly tried to secure a contract. But either university scientists were afraid of "flying saucer" ridicule, or they were dubious about the AF debunking. A month passed with no success, and new developments increased the debunkers' problems.

On April 25, Florida Governor Haydon Burns and a group of newsmen had a close sighting of an unknown flying object. They were aboard the governor's Convair, on a campaign tour, when the strange craft began to pace the plane. Governor Burns told his chief pilot to close in for a better look but the UFO immediately climbed away. The report received wide publicity.

About this same time a leading aviation expert alarmed the AF with a public disclosure of massive UFO evidence. The revelation was made by the Director-General of the International Air Transport Association, Knut Hammarskjold. Addressing an aviation-space writers' meeting, Hammarskjold said he was given a huge number of UFO reports when he became head of IATA—verified encounters by hundreds of pilots and crewmen on U.S. and foreign airlines which were members of the transport association. All this evidence from trained observers, Hammarskjold said, convinced him that the UFOs were probably observation machines from outer space.

When the press queried the AF it refused to comment. An attempt to discredit the IATA director might have caused him to release all this powerful evidence.

The AF was still vainly seeking a university contract when newscasts played up a report by an Apollo Space Project engineer, a pilot and former AF navigator. On June 23, 1966, Project Engineer Julian Sandoval and other witnesses sighted a UFO about 300 feet long, near Albuquerque, New Mexico. The spacecraft, Sandoval said, departed at incredible speed, swiftly reaching six Machs (six times the speed of sound) before it disappeared.

But the most upsetting to the AF was a public release by Dr. Hynek, sharply contradicting official denials in the Armed Services Committee hearing. The chief UFO consultant revealed that the AF did have unexplained radar reports and photographs of UFOs. He also disclosed that sightings had reached a new high since early in '65, and that many of the reports defied analysis. Calling for an end to witness ridicule, he said the truly puzzling reports came from reliable, stable, educated people—including scientists.

At the Pentagon the first angry reaction was to fire Dr. Hynek; then HQ realized it would set off another press barrage.

By this time, claims of UFO aliens' hostility had begun to spread, against the background of disclosures and factual sightings.

One story involved a New Hampshire couple, Betty and Barney Hill. Under hypnosis after a reported close UFO encounter, they supposedly recalled that space beings from a landed spacecraft had taken them from their car after they stopped on a lonely road to observe the strange machine. During the hypnotic state, induced by a prominent psychiatrist, they described embarrassing physical examinations by the aliens before they were returned to their car.

Separate investigations, including one by NICAP, indicated the supposed abduction probably was an intense psychological reaction—a purely imaginary experience caused by fear after an actual close UFO approach. The story was unlike the usual "contactee" claims, most of which have proved untrue, and the Hills' reputation as good citizens made a deliberate hoax seem unlikely. When part of the story was published in a Boston newspaper, some people who had scoffed at such tales had a more serious reaction. While the report was not widely accepted, a surprising number of readers began to consider if it could possibly be true.

This was quickly linked with one of the Gallup poll findings. Belief in other inhabited planets had greatly increased since early in '65. Now, 34 per cent of the public believed there were intelligent beings in many parts of the universe, making it easier to accept reports of alien visitors to Earth.

Unfortunately, the Hill story helped to set off more disturbing reports. Two or three rumors of kidnapping attempts began to circulate. One was tied to a '65 case at Renton, Washington, where three girls reported seeing space beings at close range—creatures with "white domed heads," bulging eyes and stony gray faces. In an exaggerated version, the girls were said to have barely escaped capture. A report from South America described a group of one-eyed, powerfully built beings who tried to drag a man into their spacecraft. Neighbors rushed to his rescue, the story said, and after a struggle the aliens fled in the UFO.

During the *Gemini* X mission in July, Astronaut Collins sighted an unknown space object moving in a polar orbit. The Manned Spacecraft Center publicly confirmed the report. A "contactee" seized on this for a warning on a talk show: what Astronaut Collins saw was just one of an invasion space fleet preparing to take over the Earth.

Tales like this got a good laugh, along with stories of ten-foot giants, hairy dwarves with long claws, and a report of a fierce, seven-foot space woman with swarthy skin and a glowing, golden eye in the middle of her forehead.

But some of the claims were not so funny. In sensational magazine articles and paperbacks, a few writers openly branded the UFO aliens as murderously hostile, and warned that our world was in deadly peril.

Ordinarily, the AF would have welcomed reports of weird space beings. Until recently most people had dismissed them as nonsense, and this had helped to take off the pressure. But now it seemed safer to keep silent and not add to the "scare" publicity.

In spite of the wild tales, few of the public seemed worried. So far, there was no sign of any hysteria. Earlier, there had been a few miniature panics—in France, South America and Spain. In the United States, residents of a village had been suddenly frightened when a balloon descended, half obscured by lowering clouds. Scores rushed out with pitchforks, shotguns and other weapons. There were a few tense minutes—until the supposed spacecraft was recognized. The foundation for panic now was much greater, but even with all the excitement and tension there had been no real hysteria.

It was not until late August of '66 that public fear of UFO aliens began to alarm the Air Force. Before this, a series of UFO operations near Washington had caused new attacks on AF censors.

On the night of August 1, high-speed, maneuvering objects

were sighted over Prince Georges County, Maryland. Witnesses included police officers of the county, state troopers and a member of the U. S. Park Police.

During this sightings outbreak, an unusual experience was reported by Dr. Basil Uzunoglu, a physicist and electronics research expert. At 11 P.M. he was driving on the Capitol Beltway, not far from Washington. Suddenly he saw an unknown flying object about 18,000 feet above the highway. As it descended he lost sight of it temporarily, then he was startled to see it hovering above a house 200 feet from the Beltway. He was about to stop and get out for a closer glimpse of the eerie machine, then he changed his mind and raced away. He said later, after reporting to Andrews AFB, he had been shaken by the encounter.

That same night, police investigated the story of a frightening space being, reported by a Jamestown, N.Y., girl. According to the police, the girl was one of a group of young people in a picnic area on the Erie Peninsula. They were about to leave when an unfamiliar flying object appeared, apparently landing not far away. While the rest waited to see if it would reappear, the girl went back to her car. A few minutes later, she told police, a strange, hairy creature tried to break into the car, then climbed onto the roof. When she frantically blew the horn to bring her friends the monster jumped to the ground and disappeared.

Whatever the cause, police said the girl's terror seemed genuine—she was in complete hysterics. During a NICAP investigation some of the group's statements showed discrepancies, and the facts were not determined. But the story caused some alarm in the area, and news stories of the Maryland sightings led to added publicity.

Six days after this, the shaky AF cover-up suffered another blow. It came from one of the top AF authorities on UFOs —Lt. Col. Charles Cooke, now retired. As an Intelligence officer in World War II, he analyzed AF pilots' first-hand accounts of UFO encounters. After the war he became founder and editor of the *Air Intelligence Digest*, reviewing hundreds of documented AF reports. Later he was editor of *FEAF*, the *Far East Air Force Intelligence* round-up, and again he analyzed hundreds of verified cases.

On August 7, the Washington *Star* carried a full-page discussion of UFOs by Colonel Cooke. Indicating the powerful evidence supporting the interplanetary conclusion, he bluntly hit the "myriad explanations by the Project Blue Book staff, widely referred to as 'The Little Boy Blues' or 'The Little Blue Boys,'" which included the usual debunking answers of stars, planets, meteors, birds, reflected lights, mirages, marsh gas, delusions, hoaxes, publicity stunts.

One immediate result was a renewal of efforts by members of Congress to break through the censorship. Rep. Edward Hutchinson had already introduced a resolution, HR 866, for an investigation of Project Blue Book methods. Colonel Cooke's disclosures brought new backing for such a probe.

Shortly after this I had a private talk with an AF officer who strongly opposed the cover-up. For several years, without violating security, he had given me valuable leads and advice.

"This thing's really gotten bad," he told me. "I'm still against the cover-up, but this is no time to stop it. After Hynek exposed those lies at the hearing, a lot of congressmen got steamed up. And now Cooke's put more fuel on the fire. Any day, the AF could get hit with an all-out congressional investigation, and some of the top brass are getting desperate."

"Well, they've had plenty of warning," I said.

"Yes, but it's not all their fault—you know that. The CIA's gotten us into this mess, and now they sit back out of sight while the Air Force catches all the hell."

"What happened to the university scheme? I thought they had Colorado signed up."

"Something's held it up—no contract yet. It could be too late, if Congress goes into action. An investigation would be bad enough, with all the hidden evidence brought out in the open, but now we've got these crazy stories about space monsters and people being kidnapped."

"At least there's no sign of any panic."

"Don't forget about that Orson Welles invasion broadcast. People hadn't been primed with any reports of UFOs or space beings. But when they heard that broadcast about Martian monsters landing they ran wild—thousands of them stampeded that night. In the last few months the public has been exposed to some pretty scary stuff. Even if they don't believe it, some of those things are in their subconscious minds, and a really bad report might set off a wave of fear. It could be ten times worse than the panic Welles caused."

After this private conversation I checked recent scare stories for any possible panic build-up. One delayed South American report described a supposed abduction early in '65. According to the victim's story, he was captured by space beings and flown to another planet in a disc-shaped UFO. During his enforced stay, he said, he saw a huge fleet of UFOs which were being prepared for an invasion of the Earth, and after this he was taken home, unharmed.

Other abduction stories reported that humans were kidnapped so the aliens could learn all about our world before attempting landings here. This was probably the explanation, one writer said, for all the thousands of msyterious disappearances every year—these missing people were still alive, on some unknown planet.

In spite of these ominous warnings no one ran for the hills. Only one scare report, during this uneasy period, received any serious public attention. But this story was fact, recorded by the police of Rio de Janeiro.

On August 20, police officers climbed up a hillside in Niterói, a suburb of Rio, after a woman reported that a UFO had landed there shortly before. Not expecting to find anything, the police made a gruesome discovery.

Near the top of the slope lay the bodies of two men, their

faces covered with lead masks. On the ground were slips of paper with notations in Portuguese. One of them read:

"At 4:30 P.M. we will take the capsules. . . . After the effect is produced, protect half the face with lead masks. Wait for agreed signal."

The police investigation was supervised by Inspector José Venancio Bittencourt of the Rio de Janeiro force. After laboratory tests he said there was no clue to the cause of the deaths.

"There was no medical reason. . . . our lab men have ruled out the possibility of poison, violence or asphyxiation."

The medical examiners set the date of death as August 17, and two witnesses said they had seen a UFO on that day, as it hovered over the area where the bodies were found.

When this dramatic news story was first reported in the United States, the UFO angle was omitted in most broadcasts. A follow-up, aired by several stations, mentioned rumors in Rio that the two men had intended to meet UFO beings, and that the aliens had killed them for some unknown reason.

That evening I had a call from the AF officer who had discussed the build-up of scare stories.

"Thank God those lead-mask murders didn't happen here!" he said. "We haven't had much trouble—some letters and a few calls. But if that had happened here we'd have been in a real jam."

In late September the final police statement came out. Inspector Bittencourt admitted they were completely baffled. Though he did not accept the UFO reports as proof of space-being murderers, some of the Brazilian press claimed this was the official conclusion:

"Deaths caused by beings or persons from the unknown."

Since previous news stories had implied this, the final report probably would not have added to the public impact. But there was hardly time to learn this before it was eclipsed by an Air Force announcement: A new, scientific study of

UFOs, arranged by the AF, would be carried out at the University of Colorado. It was to be headed by the distinguished scientist Dr. E. U. Condon. The new investigation, to begin in November, would be completely independent of the Air Force.

As if a switch had been thrown, the harsh attacks ended. Almost overnight, most of the press switched to praise for this new approach. Except for a few who knew the hard facts, most of Congress fell into line.

In the past twenty months, AF secrecy had been proved and exposed countless times. The false debunking answers had been shown up, and impressive evidence by highly qualified observers had gone on record. Now all this seemed forgotten, the slate wiped clean. After the past months it was hard to believe.

But it was true. The heat was off the AF, and the Condon Project was about to begin. Though I didn't know it then, I was to be deeply involved in this "new, independent study" —the most unbelievable period of my long investigation.

8

Battle
at Boulder

It was on October 7, 1966, when AF Headquarters announced the Colorado University study at Boulder. Naming Dr. Edward Condon as the CU Project director, the AF declared that he would conduct a serious, objective, scientific investigation.

Within twenty-four hours Dr. Condon brushed aside this reassuring picture and revealed himself as a tough-minded disbeliever in UFOs.

"It is highly improbable they exist," he was quoted in the New York *Times* and scores of other papers. "The view that UFOs are hallucinatory will be a subject of our investigation, to discover what it is that makes people imagine they see things."

Just four days before this, Dr. Condon had promised an impartial, careful study. This pledge was written into the AF contract he signed, along with two high CU officials:

The work will be conducted under conditions of the strictest objectivity by investigators who, as carefully as can be determined, have no predilections or preconceived positions on the UFO question. This is essential if the public, the Congress, the Executive and the scientific community are to have confidence in the study.[1]

[1] AF-CU contract F.44620-67-C-0035.

On October 9, Dr. Condon told the Denver *Post* he thought the AF had been doing a good job. "About 95% of the UFO reports are relatively easily identified. With more information, others could probably be explained . . . [which] indicates an appalling lack of public understanding."

That same day, the *Post* also carried a disparaging statement by Project Administrator Robert J. Low: "The project came close to being unacceptable . . . [but] you don't say no to the Air Force. . . . It will probably yield more information about witnesses who report UFOs than physical information [evidence]."

Before this, Dr. Condon and Low had asked for NICAP's evidence and our help in their investigations. An independent inquiry seemed impossible after the long AF secrecy and debunking. But if we refused we would be accused of not having any real evidence to submit. I told Condon and Low we would assist them—*if* they made a full-scale investigation, free of AF interference. Both assured me this was their definite purpose.

After reading the press statements I called Condon and Low.

"Dr. Condon, from what you've told the press you have already drawn your conclusions—without even seeing the evidence."

"That's absolutely untrue," Condon replied. "It's the press that's at fault—I've been badly misquoted."

Low also blamed the press.

"We'd be stupid to risk alienating NICAP. We're counting heavily on your assistance. Frankly, we don't know how to start. Your evidence of course is important, but first we urgently need your subcommittees' help in training our field investigators—which you agreed to."

"That was based on the promise of an unbiased project."

"Those news stories were wrong," Low insisted. "We've had over fifty calls from reporters and newscasters. It's been a madhouse—they were bound to make mistakes. If you come out to Boulder for that conference we planned you'll see we're not biased."

That they had been misquoted three days in a row, with such specific, derogatory comments, was hard to swallow. But I consented to the Boulder meeting, hoping to get the true picture of this AF-financed operation.

One of the biggest puzzles was the strong emphasis on NICAP's evidence, which totaled about 9,300 reports. More than 2,000 had come from veteran pilots, scientists, satellite trackers, FAA tower and radar operators, aerospace engineers and other highly qualified observers. Many times skeptics had been convinced by this verified hard-core evidence. The AF could have been expected to do everything possible to keep these key reports from the CU Project scientists. Instead, the study contract had designated NICAP as a source to be checked—the only independent UFO research organization to be named.

The first hint of the answer came at Boulder, during a conference intermission. Dr. Condon had left for another appointment, and since Low was the number two man I decided to give him a brief rundown on the evidence we would submit.

"The first reports will include some of the most powerful cases. One, for example, involved an attempt by AF jet pilots to force down a UFO near Redmond, Oregon. It was hovering near Redmond Airport—"

"When was this?" Low interrupted.

"September 24, 1959."

Low shook his head. "That's too far back. The witnesses wouldn't remember the details."

"The Federal Aviation Agency has a complete report. The main observers were FAA men at Redmond Airport. The official log nails down every bit of the action, and we've got the witnesses' detailed statements." I gave Low the chief points (cited in Chapter 3), including confirmation by high

FAA officials. "You'll not only have documented proof but the AF cover-up answers."

Low shook his head again. "We just can't waste time on old reports."

"Are you trying to get the truth?"

"Of course," Low said quickly. "But we've got barely a year. We have to concentrate on current reports."

"Mr. Low, this is an extremely serious case. The date's got nothing to do with it, all the evidence is on record. A lot of the earlier cases are just as important, and some are even more serious—AF jet chases where pilots were killed, airliner near-collisions where passengers were hurt—"

"I didn't realize that," Low said earnestly. "I'll talk to Ed Condon about it. Meantime, go ahead and send us the lists."

General discussions took up the rest of the conference time. NICAP's viewpoint was covered by Assistant Director Richard Hall and myself, and Low moderated the question period.

Dr. Condon, a solidly built man of about sixty-five, had little to say. Most of the time he listened silently, with no hint of his reactions. There was one exception, during a short appraisal of UFO books with sensational claims about visitors from space. Dr. Condon made a jocular comment on a paperback which, among other things, related an unusual encounter between a space woman and a young South American. Except for this unexpected display of humor, Condon's expression was normally deadpan.

Most of the project members seemed sincerely interested. But the only one who knew much about UFOs was Dr. David Saunders, senior CU psychologist, who had visited NICAP and discussed the problem.

When the conference ended I still had strong doubts about the project, but I told Low we would train their field men and help toward an objective evaluation.

Just before I left, Dr. Saunders got me aside.

"You can count on most of the project group," he said.

"We'll try hard for a full investigation—as much as the contract allows."

Low joined us before I could ask what he meant. But after returning to NICAP I checked the contract and found this disturbing paragraph:

Because of the continuance of Project Blue Book for the handling of all reports, it is our understanding that the university is under no obligation to investigate reported sightings other than those that the principal investigators [Dr. Condon and Administrator Low] select for study.

By this significant provision, all the massive evidence of UFO reality could be suppressed. Whether or not this was the AF intention, not a single case could be examined by the project scientists unless Condon and Low approved. If this rule should be strictly carried out, thousands of strong cases, including NICAP's documented reports, could be blocked from investigation.

There was only one way to find out, by submitting documented, unexplained reports to Condon and Low—and privately informing Saunders and a few of the other scientists. This powerful ammunition might dent Condon's skepticism —or he might ignore this evidence. Either way, we should soon know.

For the first group of cases I was checking early reports when Gordon Lore, a senior staff member, brought me a Condon news clip.

"Maybe you didn't see this." He pointed to an underlined sentence:

"Most of the early reports," Condon was quoted, "are too old and vague to be any good."

"Thanks, maybe I can use this." I put the clipping in a desk drawer, then told Lore about my argument with Administrator Low. "I can see now why he tried to brush off the Redmond case."

As a test, we began the first list with the World War II

report by Capt. Alvah Rieda, followed by the Mantell case, the disappearance of the AF jet over Lake Superior, the Walesville tragedy, two 1957 airliner near-collisions with UFOs in which passengers were injured and other close-approach scares. In addition, we listed verified reports from all the armed forces, NASA, the FAA and other documented encounters up to 1965, including the names of expert witnesses. (See partial listing in Appendix.)

After sending this first evidence to Condon and Low we began on the next group, covering the main cases in 1965 and 1966 (described in Chapter 7). In the second half of '66 there had been two or three frightening close approaches. One unnerving encounter was reported to NICAP and the AF by a former Army Security investigator, J. J. O'Connor, now a lawyer in Florida.

On September 20, 1966, O'Connor was piloting his private plane near Sebring, Florida. He was flying at 9,500 feet when a huge UFO came down directly above him. As its shadow covered the plane O'Connor hastily reduced power and dived.

When he pulled out, at 3,500 feet, he saw that the object had followed him down. Now really scared, he reached for a .38 revolver he kept in the cockpit. But the size of the enormous craft stopped him—firing at it would be futile, and it could be dangerous. After a few more tense moments the UFO circled upward and went out of sight.

Many of the cases in the first list and the hundreds later given to the CU Project had been checked by experienced investigators in the Los Angeles NICAP Subcommittee (LANS) and other subcommittees at Cape Kennedy, Seattle, in Massachusetts, Texas, the San Francisco Bay area and twenty other sections of the country. Important foreign reports also had been checked by NICAP investigators in several countries. The CU scientists also were given a copy of NICAP's documented evaluation, *The UFO Evidence*, a 184-page report on more than seven hundred verified cases, many reported by top-rated observers and also analyzed by NICAP's staff and scientific and technical advisers. This strong compilation of evidence, along with proof of the cover-up, had convinced many skeptics, but no word of Condon's reaction came from Boulder.

Several weeks later, when Low was visiting NICAP, I told him we had heard nothing from Dr. Condon.

"What did he decide about the Redmond case?" I asked.

"He hasn't told me yet."

"What about that first list of cases?"

Low hesitated. "Ed says we have to concentrate on recent cases. He's not ignoring the others—"

"But they're just too old and vague?" I brought out the Condon press clipping and handed it to him.

Low looked embarrassed. "All right, I'll admit that's Ed's view. He's convinced the early reports are worthless."

"How could he know? He told me at Boulder he hadn't checked any reports. Three weeks before that he told the press that astronomers, FAA operators and satellite trackers had never reported UFOs. We've got hundreds of such reports, with proof. There were some in that first group—has he read any of them?"

"Not yet," Low said unhappily. "I'm sorry, but there's nothing I can do about it. The final decision's up to Ed."

"I'm not blaming you. But many of those cases are vitally important—there's nothing vague about them. Somebody should make Dr. Condon realize he's evading documented evidence. It's bound to backfire—" I stopped short.

"What's the matter?" said Low.

"If you're not investigating any of those reports, just why do you want all of NICAP's evidence?"

"Oh—that's different. We need it to get the full picture. And we may look into a few older cases later—"

"Mr. Low, we're not going to work up thousands of cases unless they're going to be examined. Look, here's our second list. It shows the main evidence in the '65 flap and most of

'66. Tell Dr. Condon we want a definite answer on investigating these cases—they're certainly recent enough. Then we'll decide about going ahead or pulling out."

"Pulling out?" exclaimed Low. "You can't do that. All right, I'll tell Ed Condon as soon as I get back."

Any change in the project director seemed unlikely. But early in '67 Saunders told us they were now testing the ET (Extraterrestrial) hypothesis. I had a cautious hope that a miracle had happened, but it ended abruptly.

On January 25, Dr. Condon made a speech before two scientific societies in Corning, New York. As reported by newspapers, he said that UFOs were not the business of the AF and it did not take the matter seriously.

"My attitude right now is that there's nothing to it," he was quoted, "but I'm not supposed to have a conclusion until we finish. Less than 100 sightings in 20 years are significant enough to be considered. Of these less than 20 are truly puzzling, only because we know so little about them." In regard to secrecy, he said that anyone who believed the AF was concealing facts was suffering from paranoia.

A NICAP member present, who confirmed these statements, saw Condon after the talk.

"Would you accept a signed statement by reputable witnesses?" he asked.

"No, I would not," Condon replied.

In Washington, a newscaster tied the Corning talk to a previous interview by the Rocky Mountain News. On November 5, 1966, Condon had been asked if he thought the AF might be hiding the facts from the project.

"We have to take it on faith that the AF is not trying to deceive us," Condon answered. "I know some people who believe the AF is misleading us," he was also quoted, "but I don't think so. Maybe they are. I don't care much."

After all the other negative Condon comments, this quote and the Corning statements were just too much to take. I called Boulder, and when I failed to get Dr. Condon I gave Saunders the news.

"It's useless for NICAP to go on. I'll have to wire Condon that we're through."

"Please wait—it'll finish the project. Give me two hours to work on it."

Later I learned that the entire group of scientists went to Dr. Condon and warned him the project could not continue without NICAP's aid. Condon was not a man to give in even under pressure; he had a bulldog-like tenacity. But he finally agreed to call me. I told him that his public statements had put us in a bad spot.

"If we kept on we could be called blind or stupid. Some of our Board members have already warned me that we might be discredited."

As before, Dr. Condon said he had been misquoted, but I pointed out that none of the statements had been publicly retracted. After thirty minutes of sometimes blunt discussion, Dr. Condon promised he would make no more UFO speeches.

"That way I won't be misquoted again," he added. He apologized for causing the trouble. "I appreciate your co-operation and I hope NICAP will continue."

When I asked about the ignored reports Condon said everything had been delayed but our evidence would be examined as soon as possible.

"On that basis," I told him, "we'll keep on helping."

Besides case evidence, we gave the CU Project copies of secrecy orders—JANAP 146 and AFR 200-2—and leads to other official documents linked with the cover-up. Among these were the 1947 Air Matériel Command analysis and opinion signed by Lieut. Gen. Nathan Twining, the 1948 Project Sign Top Secret Estimate that UFOs were interplanetary spaceships and restricted policy letters such as the one issued by the Office of the Secretary of the Air Force on Aug. 15, 1960. Labeled a policy letter for AF commanders, it contained this statement entitled: "Air Force Keeping Watchful Eye On Aerospace":

"There is a relationship between the Air Force's interest in space surveillance and its continuous surveillance of the atmosphere near Earth for unidentified flying objects—UFOs."

But the weeks passed with no sign that this cover-up proof had had any effect on Condon or Low, or that any of the key cases had been investigated. Most of the NICAP staff were convinced, as I was, that it was useless to keep on submitting such evidence.

"Maybe there's some other way to wake him up," Gordon Lore suggested. After talking it over we hit on a new approach —concentrating on the hazards the UFOs had created. Even if the objects were only some strange natural phenomena—which we knew was impossible—they had caused some very real dangers. If we could get Condon to see this, instead of insisting on evidence of alien spacecraft, he might possibly realize there was a serious problem.

It had to be handled through Low. Saunders had told me that Dr. Condon was still angry at having to apologize for the Corning trouble and he would probably ignore anything I sent to him directly.

The next time Low visited NICAP I talked with him privately.

"There's one serious problem you and Dr. Condon may not know. It's the risk of mistaking UFO formations for a surprise Soviet attack and setting off World War III."

"With all our Early Warning safeguards? Why, that's practically impossible."

"No, it isn't. The Strategic Air Command has dispatched H-bombers several times when they mistook UFOs for a possible sneak attack."

"You have any proof of that?" said Low.

I showed him our Confidential Report to Congress, approved by Admiral Hillenkoetter, Colonel Bryan, former AF Monitor Fournet and all the other NICAP Board members. The accidental-war warning included this statement:

In 1958, the AF admitted that Strategic Air Command bombers more than once had been launched against Russia when defense radar tracked mysterious objects in seeming formation which never have been identified. The errors were caught, but the hazard is greater today.

As I told Low, the AF admission was given to the president of United Press, Frank Bartholomew, after a top-level conference at SAC Headquarters. It was cleared by the AF, at the Pentagon. The original purpose was to inform the Soviets, through the approved UP statements, that we had a powerful Early Warning system which would detect any sign of an attack and cause quick retaliation. Why the disclosure about UFOs was included has never been explained.

"Well," said Low, "if the errors were caught each time then there's no real danger."

"No warning system's perfect. Remember when defense radar picked up signals that had bounced off the moon? NORAD had a bad shock—they thought this was the start of World War III. They were about to launch in full force when the mistake was discovered."

As added proof of the hazard, I showed Low two sober official warnings. One came from Lyndon Johnson, when he was the Senate Majority Leader. Shortly after he sent NICAP's confidential report to the Senate Preparedness Subcommittee, he released this statement:

"The Western allies must be prepared for every possibility—deliberate or accidental."

The other warning was given by Dr. Marvin Stern, Assistant Director for Research and Development, Department of Defense: "We are not giving enough consideration to the factors of stress and coincidence that might lead to war by accident."

Though unknown flying objects were not mentioned, the UFOs were known to be a major part of the accidental-war danger.

"Well, even if there is such a danger," said Low, "our AF contract doesn't give us jurisdiction."

"The AF says you're independent. Mr. Low, this could be the most important part of your investigation. The AF cover-up has confused a lot of Early Warning radar operators. They've been told UFOs don't exist, so when they pick up high-speed objects heading toward the U.S. they're likely to think it's a surprise enemy attack."

The hazard had increased, as I told him, because of missile submarines. If UFOs suddenly came in from the Atlantic or Pacific, or the Gulf of Mexico, defense radar operators could easily mistake them for sub-launched missiles. UFOs also had been tracked at the speed of intercontinental missiles, adding to the risk of accidental war.

"If your project exposed this," I said, "it could compel the AF to train Early Warning operators so they'd be on guard against such mistakes. UFOs often have certain characteristics the operators could learn to recognize—once they knew the objects are real. If the U.S. took these precautions the Kremlin probably would do the same. The Soviets tracked UFOs, too, and it's fairly certain they've also launched by mistake. Your project could do a great service to the country, and I think Dr. Condon should know this."

"If it's that serious he certainly should know," Low answered. "I'll show him your Confidential Report to Congress."

But a month later I learned the attempt had failed. Condon had decided this was strictly a Defense Department problem, if it really existed.

Before this, a few NICAP members believed the AF had persuaded Dr. Condon it was his patriotic duty to help conceal the truth, until they were better prepared to cope with the UFOs. Though it was possible, I didn't believe it. From what I had learned about him there was only one answer: Dr. Condon was a 100 per cent skeptic, honestly convinced UFOs were nonsense and all witnesses were irresponsible. If he had had even a small doubt of the AF denials he would have been concerned over the possible danger of accidental war. But because of his rigid conviction that he was right, his mind was closed to any possible hazard.

Earlier, I had urged that the project heads confer with the NICAP Board members, at least with Bryan, Emerson, Fournet and others who had proof of official secrecy and evidence of UFO reality. When this was ignored I sent Low a recent statement by a famous Greek scientist, Dr. Paul Santorini, a leading physicist and engineer. During World War II, Dr. Santorini had aided in developing radar, fuses for the atomic bomb and the NIKE missile guidance system. Until 1964, he was Director of the Experimental Physics Laboratory of the Polytechnic.

In March of '67, Dr. Santorini had revealed a long-hidden experience connected with UFOs. In a lecture to the Greek Astronomical Society, he stated there was a "world blanket of secrecy" around UFO reports. In 1947, he said, strange objects flying over Greece had alarmed the government. Fearing they might be Russian missiles, the Greek Army commanders had provided him with a team of engineers to investigate the sightings.

"We soon established that they were not missiles," said Dr. Santorini. "But when Greek Army commanders asked the U.S. Defense Department about the mysterious objects they were quickly pressured into silence, (and) the Army ordered the investigation discontinued." Afterward, the scientist revealed, he was closely questioned by U.S. scientists from Washington. Later, Santorini's private research convinced him the UFOs were surveying the Earth—possibly for an invasion. Secrecy has been invoked, he stated, because officials are afraid to admit the existence of superior machines against which we have "no possibility of defense."

Since Santorini was such a distinguished scientist, I thought Condon might just possibly have Low check with him. But one of the project members privately told me Santorini's statement had been brushed off.

A few days after this development, I was trying to figure our next move when television commentator Frank Edwards came into my office. At that time his program originated in Indianapolis, but he made frequent appearances on major networks. When he was in Washington he usually dropped in at NICAP—as a Board member he had access to the latest UFO information, which he often put on the air.

"How's it going?" he asked. "Is that Boulder outfit still muddling around?"

"It's worse than that, Frank." I told him the main points.

Frank looked incredulous. "Why, that's fantastic. Why don't you quit them cold?"

"Saunders keeps after me to hang on. He seems to have some strong reason for believing he and the other scientists can swing Condon over. I just can't believe it—I think we should call a press conference and blow the lid off."

"Why don't I blast it on the air?" Frank said. "I can always get on one of the big networks. You can help me work it up, and I'll have it plugged in advance as an exposé."

After we talked it over I agreed. "If it's powerful enough it's bound to jolt the head men at CU. To save face they even might have to make some changes. There's still time—the project runs until January 31 of '68."

Frank reached for a pad. "Here's how we'll put it over. I'll bring you on as NICAP's director and explain you've been on the inside at Boulder. You can say there never was any need for such a project—the AF already had proof the UFOs were spacecraft. Then I'll hit it as a scheme to take the heat off the AF, and I'll say they completely misled Condon and Low so they'd think the reports were bunk. That'll lead into all the solid NICAP evidence they've ignored. What's the strongest AF denial of the cover-up?"

I brought out a thick folder. "There must be over a hundred here. This one's pretty strong—it's from a UFO Project Report sent to members of Congress and the press, early in '65—"

Persons submitting a UFO report to the Air Force are free to discuss any aspect of the report with anyone. The Air Force does not seek to limit discussion on such reports and does not withhold or censor any information pertaining to this unclassified program.

Frank grimaced. "The stuff they get away with! Have you given the project proof of the secrecy?"

I showed him a summary with JANAP-146 and other secrecy orders, concealed cases and the names of silenced witnesses, the classified AF Intelligence manual with the sketch of a disc-shaped UFO and other censorship proof. "Now, I don't know how much Condon saw, if anything— he has Low handle practically everything."

"He's still responsible as the number one investigator," said Frank. "Say, why not write Condon and urge him to interview Senator Goldwater and Congressman McCormack —they're on record about the secrecy. Add Colonel Bryan and that Lieutenant Colonel Cooke who spilled the beans in the Washington *Star* article."

"I'll try, but it won't work. We sent Condon the names of over a hundred top-qualified witnesses, and he hasn't checked with a single one."

"All right, if he ignores these people we'll put it on the air. Maybe we can get McCormack or Goldwater to appear, or run taped interviews with them." Frank looked at his watch. "That's enough for a start. Send me any new dope on the project. I won't be able to arrange this for a month or so, but that'll give us time to make it foolproof."

After Frank left I thought over the telecast plan. I had no doubts about the impact. Frank was a professional, a confident fighter with a sense of humor which somehow added power to his delivery. In the seventeen years I had known him I had often seen him handle rude or cocky opponents, using an easy banter which made them look ridiculous. During his long investigation of the UFO problem, he had built up an impressively large audience, through his own program and his frequent network appearances. Regardless of the effect on CU, the program would give the public a candid picture of the project operation.

A few days later, when Low phoned about a routine item, I decided on impulse to test his reaction to the risk of panic.

"That's already covered, in the contract," said Low. "We're going to do a special study, to see why people react to UFOs the way they do."

"You don't need any study. You'd get scared, too—and so would Dr. Condon—if a UFO suddenly came in toward your car, or a plane you were in." I cited reports we had sent them—the Stadvec case, the shooting in Maine, UFO chases of cars, airliner near-collisions.

"Yes, but people tend to exaggerate. You yourself admitted lots of scare stories were fakes."

"Sure, but that doesn't apply to the cases we sent. The foundation's already been built for sudden hysteria—some sensational report, even a wild rumor, might set it off. Ask the AF to let you see their confidential analysis of the Orson Welles broadcast in '38. It caused a terrific panic, and most of those people were average, normal citizens."

"That was twenty-nine years ago," Low replied. "People are more sophisticated today. I can't believe they'd panic over some UFO story."

"All right," I said shortly. "But while you're on, there's something else I want to know. How many AF explanations have you spot-checked?"

"What do you mean?"

"On November 8, 1966, Dr. Condon wrote me a letter giving his guidelines for the investigation. He said the main guide 'would be whatever appears to us most clearly to serve the national interest . . . existing facts, sighting reports, will be as fully tested as possible . . ."

"Yes, I remember," said Low.

"He also said no proper investigator would approach his work otherwise. Here's what I'm driving at—Dr. Condon promised that AF cases listed as explained will be spot-checked if there is any reason to suspect the answers aren't valid. In the evidence we sent you are over a hundred cases with absolutely false answers—the Redmond one you've by-passed, the Walesville case, for example. We can produce hundreds of others. Now—how many have been spot-checked?"

"So far, none," Low answered calmly. "Dr. Condon hasn't found any AF explanations he considers untrue."

"Thanks." I abruptly hung up and then called Frank Edwards.

"That's the damndest thing yet!" he said.

"I almost blew up," I told him. "But after all, it wasn't Low's decision."

"Did he tell you how many NICAP reports they've checked?"

"I didn't ask. I'm waiting to see him face to face for that one."

It was several weeks later when Low dropped in. As soon as we were alone I put it to him. "We've given you over a thousand reports. By the time the project ends, how many will you have investigated?"

"Well, we don't know yet. I told you we couldn't check any large number." I waited, and he finally told me. "Probably four or five." Seeing my grim expression, he added lamely, "We'll do the best we can."

"What will the total be, including NICAP's cases?"

"Around eighty-five to ninety investigations—field checks and evaluations at the university. We're short-handed, we don't have enough money."

Just ten days later we learned that Colorado University was asking for an extra $210,000. I had told Frank Edwards about Low's investigation figures and when he heard about the money request he was disgusted.

"Don, I don't see how they've got the gall!"

"The application says it's for a five-month extension, so they can make a more thorough study. And get this—they say it's partly so they can examine more of NICAP's information."

"That does it!" said Frank. "I'm going to speed up this program. Can you fly out and help?"

"Sure, how soon?"

"I'll call you. Bring out all the hot stuff we talked about, and we'll really hit it. This is going to be a blockbuster."

They were the last words I ever heard Frank Edwards speak. On June 23, he died suddenly from a heart attack.

Losing Frank was a shock. We had been close friends since 1950, when he lived in Washington. We had often worked together, exchanging confidential leads and investigating cases for his Mutual Network program. Two or three times he had cheered me up after a setback. He had always been such a strong, vibrant figure that it was hard to realize he was gone.

After Frank's death I made no attempt to go on with the exposé. Three or four commentators and program stars whom I knew would probably have taken it on. But to get the full impact would require a known UFO authority who knew the whole inside story, as Frank had learned it in the past seventeen years.

On into the summer of '67 we continued the uneasy truce with Dr. Condon. The AF was still debunking and ridiculing UFO reports, and by now I was convinced it was back of the CU efforts to obtain all of NICAP's evidence. If Dr. Condon turned in a negative verdict headquarters could claim the project had investigated all our thousands of reports and found them worthless. To prevent this, we slowed down, holding back most of the remaining big cases, in spite of CU's constant requests for more reports.

Up to September 17, Dr. Condon had kept his word about

avoiding UFO speeches. But on that day his silence ended. In a talk at an Atomic Energy Commission station, Condon ridiculed UFO reports, concentrating on humorous contactee stories. Dr. William S. Bickel, a University of Arizona scientist, told NICAP the speech was funny—but it gave no hint of a serious investigation. Others in the audience of scientists agreed.

When I called Boulder a project member gave us even worse news. Ignoring protests by the majority of scientists, the project heads had ordered a search for negative evidence.

Dr. Condon and Low were immediately given notice: The transmission of NICAP UFO reports was ended.

This notice, as we discovered later, dismayed Condon and Low. With an urgent message, asking us to reconsider, Condon sent his administrator to NICAP.

The discussion which followed was at times so strange it was almost incredible. I had never felt sure about Low's attitude. But in spite of our differences, and occasional sharp words, I did not dislike him. His role of mouthpiece for Condon was bound to be a trial; once or twice I had almost felt sorry for him.

The meeting was held in my office. By this time Richard Hall had resigned. Gordon Lore was the new assistant director, and I had asked him to be present.

At the start, I told Low we had already gone too far.

"We've had too many runarounds. We won't consider going on unless you give us some straight answers."

"All right. You're being frank—I'll try to be, too."

"First, has Dr. Condon ever interviewed a UFO witness?" When Low shook his head I added, "Does he ever intend to?"

"Not at present," said Low.

"The only field trip we know about was after a contactee told Condon a UFO was going to land near an Air Force base. Condon went there—why, I don't know."

"Those contactees fascinate him," Low explained. "But

you're right, he hasn't made any other field investigation. And he has no plans for one. I might as well tell you—if he had to make a conclusion now it would be negative."

Gordon Lore looked startled. "Without even examining any of the evidence?"

Low nodded. "He is honestly convinced there's nothing to it."

"Mr. Low," I said, "Dr. Condon sent you here to urge us to keep sending reports. Exactly why—since he won't examine them?"

"Because we can be accused of reaching a conclusion without examining all of your evidence."

"The project will be accused of a lot more," I said a bit curtly, "if there's a negative verdict and you claim NICAP's evidence *was* examined." Low started to break in but I stopped him. "Some of the Board members and advisers don't believe the project is on the level—"

"Wait a second," Low said quickly. "I don't feel it's your job to find out whether it's on the level or not. Your job should be to submit your best evidence and try to change Dr. Condon's present disbelief."

For a second, Lore and I just looked at him, amazed.

"After all you've admitted about Condon?" I demanded. "There's only one way you'll get us to resume—by Dr. Condon giving us a signed agreement to investigate certain selected cases, and that means a full check, interviewing the witnesses, and giving us copies of the evaluation. We'll agree to keep them secret until the project ends and Condon's report is out."

"Well, I'll try to persuade him," Low said glumly. "It might help if you put it in writing."

As he was starting to leave I suddenly thought of another angle.

"I've been told the AF questioned you before the contract was signed. Just how did they describe the problem?"

I hardly expected an answer, certainly not the one Low gave.

"They said they didn't know how to prepare the public," he blurted out. After my first astonishment, I pressed him for details, but he apparently decided he'd said too much. "I don't remember if they said any more."

For about three weeks, I delayed writing Condon, to see if my message through Low had had any effect. By coincidence, there had been a jump in UFO reports. Early in October, the Royal Canadian Air Force had confirmed that a brightly lighted UFO had glided into the water off Shag Harbor, Nova Scotia, seen by many residents. After a large patch of bubbling water and yellowish foam was seen, Canadian Navy divers searched for the object, but apparently the UFO had moved out of the area. About this same time, Superior Court Judge Charles E. Bennett reported sighting three UFOs near Denver. In Dallas, Astronaut James McDivitt told a newspaper "The UFOs are there," in verifying his sightings. At Vandenberg AFB, an official log confirmed visual and radar tracking of UFOs and attempted jet interception. On October 20 and 22, eleven sightings were reported in Georgia.

Besides sightings, there were other developments which could be expected to draw Condon's attention. On October 17, Congressman Louis Wyman submitted a congressional resolution for a full UFO investigation—without waiting for the Condon report. On November 11, the U.S.S.R. announced a large-scale UFO investigation, to be headed by Maj. Gen. Anatoly Stolyerov. Investigations, the general said, would be made by eighteen scientists and a number of Russian Air Force officers. Reports were to be transmitted to Moscow by a 200-observer network. The general stated they expected to analyze thousands of UFO cases.

On November 14, I wrote Dr. Condon, asking if he would agree to investigate NICAP evidence, as outlined to Low. "We do not ask any guarantee of a positive conclusion,"

I told him. "We do ask a guarantee of an impartial investigation and evaluation of evidence from qualified, honest observers."

Administrator Low was asked similar questions in a separate letter, also dated November 14.

In the replies, sent on December 1, both project officials refused to answer the questions, though they praised NICAP.

"We deeply appreciate the cooperation," said Dr. Condon. "The help you have given us has been of great importance."

Low went even farther: "NICAP's assistance has been invaluable. . . . Your files, because of the high caliber of the field investigations NICAP has conducted, are of very good quality . . . Our working relationships have been excellent. . . . It would be a great pity if they were terminated. . . . Dr. Condon has said to you that our study is being done objectively. It is."

We seemed to have reached a dead end. I was about to ask the Board's feelings in regard to a public announcement when Dave Saunders made an unexpected visit. He knew about Low's visit and the refusal letters.

"But before you do anything I want to tell you something. First, take a look at this." He handed me a photostat of a two-page typed memorandum signed by Low. It was dated August 9, 1966, and addressed to CU officials E. James Archer, dean of the graduate school, and Thurston E. Manning, university vice-president. Outlining some views of the proposed project, it stated:

In order to undertake such a project, one has to approach it objectively. That is, one has to admit the possibility that such things (UFOs) exist. It is not respectable to give serious consideration to such a possibility. Believers, in other words, remain outcasts. . . . admitting such possibilities . . . puts us beyond the pale, and we would lose more in prestige in the scientific community than we could possibly gain by undertaking the investigation. . . .

Under the heading "Comments," Low made his proposal
for handling the project if it were to be accepted:

Our study would be conducted almost exclusively by non-
believers, who, although they couldn't possibly prove a negative result, could and probably would add an impressive body
of evidence that there is no reality to the observations. The
trick would be, I think, to describe the project so that, to the
public, it would appear a totally objective study, but to the
scientific community would present the image of a group of
nonbelievers trying their best to be objective but having an
almost zero expectation of finding a saucer. One way to do
this would be to stress investigation, not of the physical
phenomena, but rather the people who do the observing—
the psychology and sociology of persons and groups who report seeing UFOs. . . .

Saunders was watching my face. "Incredible, isn't it?"

"It's a jolt, though maybe I should have been prepared.
I knew he was negative. But this—"

"It shocked me, too—and most of the other scientists. We
were already sore about the search for negative evidence.
Then when we discovered this—well, it certainly united us
against ignoring the evidence."

"Does Condon know about this?" I asked.

"We're not sure."

"What are you going to do about it?"

"We haven't decided yet. I'll let you know."

At dinner that evening I asked Saunders if he thought the
majority of project scientists believed the UFOs were
spacecraft.

"There's a fair chance," he said. "At least there would be a
strong dissent to any negative conclusion."

"If the majority did back the interplanetary answer, what
then?"

Saunders looked at me soberly. "I think we'd try to persuade Dr. Condon to deliver a secret report to the President,

with the best plan we could figure to prepare the public."

"The AF would scream—that's against the contract."

"I know that." Saunders got a stubborn look. "But there's nothing to keep the majority from giving the President their conclusions, if the AF tries to hide them. He should be the one to decide whether to end the secrecy, or wait."

"I hope it works out—the President should at least have some kind of preparation program ready."

"Even then it will be a hard decision. I'd hate to be in his shoes. I've already done some work on a program, and it's an appalling problem."

"It should have been started long ago," I said. "Then it wouldn't be such a shock in case of a sudden development."

Though I didn't learn it until later, the AF even then was facing serious trouble.

When the Soviet Union announced its full-scale UFO investigation, on November 11, it had worried the Air Force. This was the first time the Soviets had ever admitted concern over the unknown objects. There had to be an important reason for this surprising reversal and the new high-level operation.

The AF was still trying to find the answer when disturbing rumors reached headquarters. If they were correct, then the Soviets had made a startling discovery about UFOs, backed by scientific proof.

For years, the U. S. Air Force had known this dramatic secret and had tried to keep it suppressed. Several times there had been leaks, but by quick debunking—and luck—the full story had been bottled up.

When General Stolyerov stated that important UFO evidence would soon be revealed, Air Force apprehension increased. Some headquarters officers still hoped Moscow would realize the danger of making their discovery public. But early in 1968 a top scientist of the new UFO Commission released the official evidence—the momentous and startling sightings by Soviet astronomers.

9

Giant
Spaceships

The first red-letter day in this dramatic record was July 18, 1967. Until evening, it was an ordinary day at the Soviet Astronomical Station near Kazan. As the twilight deepened, two of the staff astronomers began making routine observations.

Suddenly a huge flying object appeared, moving swiftly across the sky. As it passed above the observatory its orange glow made it easily visible in the dusk. It was an amazing sight—an enormous crescent-shaped craft at least eight times larger than any known airplane. The horns of the crescent were pointed backward, emitting jetlike exhausts.

Flying at incredible speed, the gigantic spaceship was out of sight within seconds. The two astronomers were shaken by the experience. At first they made no report, afraid no one would believe them. But confirmation of the giant spaceships' existence soon came from other astronomers.

On August 8, another huge flying crescent raced over the Soviet Astrophysical Station at Kislovodsk, which is operated by the Soviet Academy of Sciences. The sighting was logged by astronomer Anatoli Sazanov, one of a dozen staff members who saw the monstrous ship. On September 4, October 18 and several other days in 1967, identical spacecraft were sighted over southern Russia and tracked by astronomers.

During February of '68 some of these reports were confirmed at Moscow in an officially sanctioned statement. The most startling disclosures were calculations by the Kazan Observatory astronomers, made after several sightings of the huge spacecraft:

The diameter of the flying crescents was between 500 and 600 meters (between 1,640 and 1,840 feet). Their speed was approximately five meters (3.1 miles) per second, or 11,160 miles per hour.

This officially approved release was made public by Dr. Fritz Zigel, a ranking scientist in the new UFO Investigation Commission, which was part of the All-Union Cosmonautics Committee. Dr. Zigel was also a key figure at the Moscow Aviation Institute.

Some of the Soviet evidence was omitted in Zigel's statement, but this did nothing to reduce U. S. Air Force concern. In a previous public release, the scientist had strongly indicated that UFOs came from a more advanced world. He had also hit at witness ridicule and debunking of evidence—in the United States as well as in Russia. Urging that the secrecy be ended, he had called for a worldwide exchange of UFO information and a joint effort by all scientists to determine the facts.

In his new post, as a close adviser to General Stolyerov, Dr. Zigel could be a real threat to USAF secrecy. If he managed to release convincing Soviet evidence of UFO reality it would be serious enough. But if this included proof that giant spaceships were operating near our planet it was almost certain to set off a wave of fear. The Colorado Project would crumble, and far worse, the AF cover-up would immediately be exposed, increasing the chance of panic.

Just two years before, the AF had faced the same danger, when a giant-spaceship report leaked out.

On the night of February 15, 1965, a Flying Tiger airliner chartered by the Defense Department was cruising over the Pacific, transporting an Army and Air Force group to Japan. The flight was about an hour from Tokyo when the cockpit radar picked up three large fast-moving objects.

At first, the operator and the pilots thought the set had malfunctioned—they had never seen such huge blips on a radarscope. Then a reddish glow appeared in the sky, above and to the left. Staring upward, the captain saw three enormous oval-shaped objects. Descending at high speed, in close formation, they seemed to be heading straight at the plane.

The captain hastily started to turn, then stopped. The three giant UFOs, veering to one side, had abruptly reduced speed. Now they were leveling out at the plane's altitude, still in close formation.

The radar showed they were five miles away, but even at that distance they looked gigantic. For several minutes, the Flying Tiger crew tensely watched the three glowing craft. Though they made no attempt to come closer their formidable size made them seem menacing.

As the giant ships continued to pace the airliner the captain sent a crewman back into the cabin. In a few moments he returned with an AF officer. The Flying Tiger captain had hoped that an emergency message might bring jets from Okinawa, in case of trouble. But the AF man, after an amazed inspection of the huge UFOs, warned him not to try it. Even if the jets arrived in time, they probably would be helpless— and they might cause an attack.

For several minutes more the giant spaceships kept on pacing the plane, while the strain built up in the cockpit. Then the formation abruptly angled upward. Accelerating to 1,200 knots, the ships disappeared in a few seconds.

When the plane landed, AF Intelligence sent a coded report to the Pentagon. It had a powerful impact. The AF officer who had viewed the huge ships had estimated their size, using the five-mile distance as the basis. If he were correct the three spacecraft must have been nearly 2,000 feet in length—possibly even more. Fortunately for the AF, they had descended over the ocean. If they had come down over a large city, nothing could have stopped a panic.

At first the AF thought the story was safely hidden. But a

month later, a signed report was sent to me at NICAP by an AF captain in Japan. After analyzing the case we detailed it in the *UFO Investigator*, NICAP's report to members, but at the suggestion of a psychologist adviser we reduced the size estimate to 700 feet. By the time it was published the '65 sightings outbreak had become almost daily news, and the Flying Tiger encounter was not widely known.

But shortly after this AF Intelligence had another scare, when front-page stories reported the Antarctic sighting of an enormous flying disc. When the Secretary of the Argentine Navy confirmed that motion pictures of the huge flying object had been taken, some AF Headquarters officers feared the censorship was doomed. If pictures of the spacecraft were released to the world press, the results could be disastrous. Perhaps high Argentine officials realized this. Perhaps they were persuaded to withhold the evidence. Whatever the answer, the films were never released, and in the excitement of the '65 flap most of the public forgot them.

For the AF this was a greater relief than most people knew. Since 1953, it had known that giant spaceships were operating near our planet. At least nine times, huge alien spacecraft had been seen or tracked in orbit, or as they descended nearer the Earth for brief periods. Each time it had been an ordeal for the AF censors, as they struggled to conceal the reports or explain them away when attempts at secrecy failed.

During 1953, the AF began experiments with new long-range radar equipment. While making the initial tests, AF operators were astonished to pick up a gigantic object orbiting near the equator. Its speed was almost 18,000 miles an hour. Repeated checks showed that the tracking was correct. Some huge unknown object was circling the Earth, six hundred miles out.

Shortly after this a second enormous object approached the Earth. Tracked by AF radar experts, it also went into orbit, about 400 miles away.

Alarmed Defense Department heads hurriedly set up an

emergency satellite-detection project at White Sands, New Mexico. The scientist in charge of this secret search was Dr. Clyde Tombaugh, discoverer of the planet Pluto, the only noted astronomer who had admitted sighting a UFO. The "sky sweep" was a combined armed forces project, under Army Ordnance Research.

In February 1954, plans for a satellite search were described in an article for the Astronomical Society of the Pacific. Quoting Dr. Tombaugh, it said that special telescopic equipment would be used. The article had been written before the project began, and there was no hint of giant spaceships. The operation was called a search for natural objects. But the press quickly sensed a hidden story. At White Sands, Army Ordnance officials were deluged with questions. Were there actually unknown satellites? . . . Where had they come from? . . . How many were there? . . . Had this ever happened before?

At first, the censors started to cover up, but Dr. Tombaugh persuaded them this was unwise. On March 3, an official explanation, approved at the Pentagon, was released at White Sands.

The armed forces, Army Ordnance stated, were searching for tiny moons or "moonlets," natural objects which had come in from space and were now orbiting the Earth. They had not been tracked or discovered sooner, a spokesman said, because they were following orbits near the equator and the scarcity of observatories there made them harder to locate. Also, special automatic-tracking cameras moving at the satellites' speed would be required, because such fast-moving objects gave off very little light and ordinary telescopic cameras would not reveal them. The armed forces' intention, the spokesman explained, was to locate suitable "moonlets" which could be used as space bases and for launching missiles for the country's defense.

There was no hint that the unknown satellites might be intelligently controlled craft. The official statement implied that they were objects like asteroids and nothing serious was involved.

It was a preposterous explanation. For several asteroids to come in from space and, without any control, to assume the precise courses necessary to go into such orbits, would be impossible.

For the first few days there was fear at the Pentagon that this debunking claim might be publicly rejected. At AF Headquarters there was an added worry. If the "moonlet" cover-up failed, the true spaceship answer might emerge as the only alternative. If it did, this could revive a disturbing article on possible alien migration to our world.

The AF had good reason to fear any such spotlight. For the article had been written by a high AF Intelligence officer— Col. W. C. Odell. Why it had ever been written was a puzzle. Even more mystifying, it had been cleared by AF Security and Review—at a time when the great sighting wave of 1952 was still fresh in many minds.

Entitled "Planet Earth—Host to Extraterrestrial Life," the article began with these words:

Granted that superintelligents in another solar system are looking for a suitable planet for a second home, why would Earth be singled out?

Colonel Odell had avoided melodramatics, but his quiet suggestions had a powerful impact. According to his theory, alien beings from a dying planet were considering and surveying our world as a new home—a planet similar enough to their own so that they could survive here and perpetuate their race. Colonel Odell did nothing to indicate a violent occupation of Earth. But if his evaluation was right, then planet Earth might become—peacefully or not—a "host to extraterrestrial life."

When this surprising article was shown to me at the Pentagon I was amazed that it had been cleared for publication. At the request of AF UFO spokesman Albert M. Chop, I had a New York editor friend read the manuscript. But the AF stipulations disturbed him. Odell was not to be identified as an AF officer. Also the clearance by AF Security and Review was not to be mentioned. What bothered the editor most was this official clearance when the AF was still debunking UFOs in public statements. He finally decided not to risk being involved in some power play at the Pentagon, although the article would undoubtedly get national attention.

In the next few weeks Colonel Odell's manuscript was shown to a few selected members of the Washington press corps. Apparently the AF restrictions worried them too; so far as I know, it was never published, at least not by any national news service or magazine.

But headquarters censors, who had been bypassed by Security and Review, knew Colonel Odell's migration article had not been forgotten. If the growing evidence of giant spaceships became public, the Intelligence colonel's conclusion would probably be tied in, adding to the risk of hysteria.

On through '54, new reports kept the AF on edge. On May 5, two huge objects maneuvered at a high altitude over Washington, tracked by radar at National Airport. The next day Navy radar tracked an enormous machine circling 90,000 feet above the capital. On June 12, another giant ship—or the same one—made a night appearance, hovering at 79,000 feet between Washington and Baltimore. Air Defense immediately scrambled jet fighters, to be ready if the alien spacecraft came down in firing range. For an hour, the gigantic craft held its high altitude, while the AF jets circled helplessly beneath it. Then it climbed swiftly out of sight. Two nights later the same spaceship, or a similar one, returned to the Washington area. This time it remained for two hours, maneuvering between the capital and Baltimore. Again, Air Defense jets were hurriedly scrambled, as the coast went under a full alert. But the alien machine gave no sign of hostility —nor any indication of its purpose.

For almost a month, the story was suppressed. When it leaked to the newspapers, Air Defense admitted the alert but claimed the interceptor pilots had seen nothing. Later, an AF pilot I knew told me the truth about those tense two hours.

"It was like a nightmare, seeing that giant ship. What we'd have done if it came down near us I don't know. Just the idea of trying to attack it gave me cold chills. I talked with two other pilots when we landed—they were just as scared as I was."

During October of '54 a new puzzle was linked with the giant spaceships. In a press statement, NASA said it had picked up strange signals from an unknown orbiting object. Soon after this, a French astronomer publicly revealed that he also had heard signals from an unknown source orbiting the Earth. According to the reports no message could be recognized.

To the AF, the giant-spacecraft reports were specially alarming because of potential panic. While the usual UFO reports had sometimes caused uneasiness, they were far less ominous. But the huge spaceships could be carrying a large number of alien beings. Though there was no proof of this, the public might believe the giant machines could be part of an invasion plan.

To most analysts, in the AF and at NICAP, the odds seemed against hostility. During the long UFO surveillance, most encounters had been devoid of harm. And the giant spaceships had shown no hostility during their infrequent visits. If an attack were intended, why the seven-year wait since the first mass sightings in 1947? The chance of hostility could not be ignored, but in seven years we should have had some indication. Although this was based on human logic, there was reason to believe that the aliens had some far different purpose.

Unfortunately, the cover-up had increased the danger of public alarm, with the growing suspicion that something frightful was behind the secrecy.

In 1955, the censors were hit hard by syndicated columnist Stewart Alsop. Through highly placed sources in government agencies, including the National Security Council, Alsop had learned the true reason for the emergency satellite-detection operations. By this time a project at Mount Wilson had been added to the first one at White Sands. In his nationwide column, Alsop revealed the intensive search for *artificial* satellites. His exposure of the "moonlets" explanation angered top officials at the Pentagon and the National Security Council. In a later column, Alsop reported that NSC Secretary Cutler was so furious that his close friends at NSC were afraid to be seen with him.

To avoid any more serious leaks, censorship on the "sky sweep" was tightened, along with attempts to suppress giant-spacecraft reports. But in 1960 one important case was confirmed despite the censors.

On August 25, a mystery satellite was seen and tracked for several days. It was photographed by the Grumman Aircraft Corporation, and all efforts to debunk the photos were futile.

On May 18, 1961, another mysterious orbiting object was discovered. The announcement came, surprisingly, from the Smithsonian Observatory at Cambridge, Massachusetts, which works closely with the AF in operating a worldwide network of tracking stations.

"The satellite was first spotted at Jupiter, Florida," the Smithsonian told the press. Labeling it "an unsuspected, unpredicted bright satellite," officials said it could be seen with the naked eye under the right conditions. "Satellite tracking stations around the world have been asked to help track it," the spokesman said.

The Smithsonian also alerted its network of high-powered telescopic cameras to spot and photograph the unknown orbiting object.

Later in the sixties the Space Science Board announced a program to speed up a search for extraterrestrial life. In line with this, NASA began preparations for launching an unmanned spacecraft equipped with robot observation and evaluation devices, for an eleven-year tour of our solar system. During this time it is expected to observe and photograph Venus, Mars, Jupiter and the other solar planets, relaying a great mass of information to special stations on Earth. Robot equipment will constantly check all phases of the operation, making necessary adjustments and replacing faulty parts. The most important purpose of this automatic survey spacecraft will be to record any discoveries of inhabited areas and relay photographs to Earth, including if possible photos of the alien beings living on such a planet.

Even before this, some UFO researchers suspected that the giant ships were space-exploration craft, and the eleven-year tour program caused a new study of this possibility.

With a technically advanced race, such huge survey ships would undoubtedly carry superior equipment for photography, mapping, monitoring and recording television and radio transmissions, and probably other devices unfamiliar to us. Almost certainly they would be linked with super-computers for swift evaluations of all the recorded information and photographs.

Even if most of these operations were automatic, such enormous spaceships would hardly be launched on important missions without a crew to monitor the survey equipment and handle emergencies that might arise. The crew might include experienced aliens with the power to make important final decisions, after constantly relaying their discoveries to their home planet. Or they might first have to recommend decisions and actions to the beings controlling their world. This could mean a long delay before the spaceship crew could proceed.

To carry out a long, detailed survey, such as the observation of our world, the huge ships would logically carry flying discs or other types of UFOs for low-altitude observations. The medium-sized machines could have crews, smaller ones could be remote-controlled. Many documented cases on record have proved that large spacecraft frequently launch smaller units and retrieve them with swift precision.

In 1952, the crew of an AF bomber tracked a formation of UFOs at 5,240 miles an hour, during a practice flight over the Gulf of Mexico. Another formation swung in behind the bomber, slowed to pace the aircraft, then raced up toward a large craft which had suddenly appeared on the bomber's radar. Within seconds, the smaller UFOs merged, on the radar, with the giant ship. Evidently this was a prearranged rendezvous, for retrieving the smaller-sized units. As soon as they were taken aboard, the huge carrier ship accelerated to a speed of over 9,000 miles per hour and went off the scope.

The Gulf of Mexico report was released to me early in '53, before the CIA take-over and the increased cover-up. The AF report, given to me with a signed official clearance, admitted there was no conventional explanation. Later, radar engineers calculated the size of the carrier ship, as indicated by its large blip on the bomber's radarscope. The giant craft, they estimated, was at least 1,200 feet long. This is only one of many confirmed reports of huge carrier or mother ships, observed visually or tracked during the aliens' surveillance of our world.

But even with all the detailed UFO evidence, the aliens' purpose has not been discovered.

To some researchers, the most reasonable answer is the aliens' need to migrate to another planet. The inhabitants of Earth will face this urgent problem in some far-off time, as scientists have pointed out. In that far-distant future the Earth may lose its oxygen; it may become frigid as the sun's heat diminishes, or it may become unbearably hot from expansion of the sun. Man may attempt to survive by building underground cities with controlled atmospheres and temperatures. Or he may try to escape to another planet, one not too unlike the Earth.

As already discussed, mass migration is no longer considered a science fiction dream. Some serious planners believe that overpopulation will make it inevitable. As predicted by Andrew Haley, a former high official of the American Rocket Society, the time may come when gigantic spaceships will transport humans to Mars or some other planet where colonies for Earthlings can be constructed.

If we can achieve this, an advanced space race should be able to carry out migration, if existence on their home planet were threatened. It could be a complex and difficult operation, even for a technically advanced race. Years might be required for a complete survey, to make sure they could live without great difficulty on the selected planet. If the planet were already inhabited, the problem of landing without force, adjusting to a different race, might be almost insurmountable. But if no more suitable planet could be found, the aliens might decide they had no other choice.

There is no proof that migration is the answer. If it should be right, what is the most probable source for the aliens and their giant spacecraft? Here, too, the answer is unknown. Some scientists believe they would have to come from outside our solar system. Others believe they may originate from one of our sun's planets—or that the aliens have established a base on one of these planets.

Back in '48, the Project Sign scientists carefully discussed this question. Their opinions were kept secret until April 27, 1949, when AF Headquarters gave this summary to the press:

Since flying saucers first hit the headlines almost two years ago, there has been wide speculation that the aerial phenomena might actually be some form of penetration from another planet.

Actually, astronomers are largely in agreement that only one member of the solar system besides Earth is capable of supporting life. That is Mars. Even Mars, however, appears to be relatively desolate and inhospitable, so that a Martian race would be more occupied with survival than we are on Earth.

On Mars, there exists an excessively slow loss of atmosphere, oxygen and water, against which intelligent beings, if they do exist there, may have protected themselves by scientific control of physical conditions. This might have been done, scientists speculate, by the construction of homes and cities underground where the atmospheric pressure would be greater and thus temperature extremes reduced. The other possibilities exist, of course, that evolution may have developed a being who can withstand the rigors of the Martian climate, or that the race—if it ever did exist—has perished.

Before this, gags and cartoons picturing weird-looking Martians had already become popular, and the AF statement somehow gave them an extra boost. Even now, the idea of possible life on Mars makes many people laugh. But some might be surprised if they knew the sober opinions of certain respected scientists, including planners at NASA.

In 1963, a high NASA official startled members of the Institute of Aerospace Sciences with a statement about the Mars moon Phobos. The official was Raymond H. Wilson, Jr., Chief of Applied Mathematics.

The moon Phobos, Wilson told the scientists, might actually be a colossal space base orbiting Mars. Disclosing that NASA was seriously considering this possibility, Wilson also revealed that the Space Administration had plans for special probes which eventually would bring the answer. Phobos, he said, had long been an enigma because of its peculiar orbit, which appeared to violate natural laws.

In 1959, a Soviet scientist, Dr. I. S. Shklovsky, announced that Phobos was an artificial satellite, basing his conclusion on calculations by the U. S. Naval Observatory. Phobos, he said, was being slowed by electromagnetic drag and tidal friction more than was possible with an actual solid moon. The explanation: Phobos was a hollow sphere, an enormous round spaceship built to shelter a colony which had to escape from Mars when the planet started to lose its atmosphere.

Since Phobos is ten miles in diameter, the Russian's analysis shocked many scientists and set off a fierce controversy. But the recorded observations, which later caused the NASA decision, convinced other scientists and space experts, among them Dr. Fred Singer, chief space adviser to President Eisenhower, Prof. James A. Harder of the University of California, and Wells Alan Webb, both respected Mars authorities.

The Space Administration's decision to investigate Phobos was based on its strange orbit, Raymond Wilson told the aerospace scientists. Phobos, he said, goes around Mars faster than the planet turns on its axis, which could not happen naturally. Phobos, he added, is the only satellite in the solar system to rotate faster than its main body. Its period is about one third of Mars' twenty-five-hour rotation.

If Phobos is found to be hollow, astronauts from Earth are expected to board and enter it as soon as this becomes possible. If it was built to shelter a colony from Mars, it would be sealed to prevent leaking of the artificial atmosphere, and it presumably would be a small world, equipped with everything needed for the colonists' survival. Such a gigantic space station would of course have to be built with sections carried from Mars by shuttle craft.

Phobos was first observed by an astronomer in 1877, almost a hundred years ago. According to Dr. Shklovsky, it may have been built long before this, so the chance of finding life aboard would be small. But the colony members could have made shuttle trips to Mars, building permanent shelters in which they could live safely. These could be underground cities, such as the AF suggested in its 1949 quotation of Project Sign scientists. Or they could be large domed bases on the surface of the planet.

In 1962, evidence supporting the second possibility was made public by Dr. Ernst J. Opik, a top-rank astrophysicist. A huge, unnatural bulge at the Mars equator had been discovered, after months of observations by noted astronomers Trumpler, Muller and seven others equally experienced. Before confirming the discovery, the astronomers had carefully rechecked their observations, using different methods to rule out the possibility of an optical illusion.

"It is a good case," said Dr. Opik, "for suggesting that the equatorial bulge of Mars is hollow, a kind of roof built by the Martians who lived, or still live hidden beneath it, perhaps enjoying the benefits of an artificially conditioned climate and atmosphere."

The NASA Mariner photographs of Mars have been taken from too great a distance to show the reported bulge. But if Opik and the nine astronomers are right, then our astronauts may eventually find a hidden world under a tremendous dome over the Martian equator.

Even closer Mariner photographs may not give the full answer. According to Bart J. Slattery, Chief of Public Affairs, George C. Marshall Space Flight Center, we may have to wait for astronauts' landings:

"We'll know for sure, probably, only when we get there."

Several puzzling observations also are awaiting explanation. In 1949, a tremendous explosion was seen on Mars by Dr. Tsuneo Saheki, the famous Japanese authority on the Red Planet. His suggestion, also accepted by other distinguished astronomers: an atomic bomb had exploded, either by accident or as a test by an unexpectedly advance Martian race.

During Mars' close approaches to Earth, every twenty-six months, mysterious clouds and color changes in the planet's surface have been observed by many astronomers.

One of the biggest puzzles concerns the so-called Mars "canals." For years, many reputable astronomers have reported seeing a geometrical pattern of lines, a network which they insist could not be accidental. Some also have reported fairly large areas, labeled "oases," where the lines intersect. It has been suggested that the lines are canals which carry water from the melting polar caps, and that the "oases" are

Martian cities or pumping stations. Other astronomers reject all this as nonsense, explaining the "canals" as surface cracks —in spite of their geometrical network—and the "oases" as spots where meteors have impacted.

In 1954, when Mars once again approached the Earth, an International Mars Committee was established, with the co-operation of the *National Geographic* magazine. The "Mars Patrol" quickly caught the imagination of the public. Press features and networks revived the question of intelligent life on the Red Planet, quoting well-known astronomers.

Dr. Robert S. Richardson, the Mars expert at Palomar Observatory, said that the new photographs should show whether the canals were real. If they were, then they probably would have been built along "great circle" paths—the shortest distance between points on the surface of a sphere.

"If the photographs show that the canals always lie along great circle paths, it would be an indication they are the work of intelligent beings. It is conceivable," Dr. Richardson added, "that some form of life quite different from ours might have developed on Mars."

Harvard's Dr. Fred C. Whipple, chairman of the Department of Astronomy, agreed on the question of Martian life. "Our kind of life is not likely. But there might be a different form of life on Mars—a kind that we know nothing about."

The unexpected publicity caused a problem at AF Headquarters, since they had no control over the Mars Committee—at least, not officially. And in April, the usually conservative *Reader's Digest* added to their troubles with an article called "Is There Life on Mars?"

Instead of different, strange-looking Martians, the *Digest* said they might be intelligent creatures similar to humans. It agreed Mars had lost most of its atmosphere, but it said that as the oxygen content dwindled the inhabitants could have learned to manufacture oxygen and also control the temperature problem (as the AF had stated earlier in suggesting underground cities).

Describing the long investigations of Percival Lowell, the creator of Lowell Observatory, the *Digest* article cited his conviction that Mars, slowly losing its water supply, was a dying planet. Then came the words which worried the AF censors:

"And presumably the Martians, an intelligent race, would be feverishly hunting around for other planets to which they could migrate. Earth was the closest, most suitable neighbor."

That same month, U.S. newspapers quoted a noted French expert on Mars, Dr. Gerard de Vaucouleurs, one of the Mars Patrol astronomers who were to observe the planet from Mount Stromlo Observatory in Australia. In his original interview by the Australian *Post*, Dr. de Vaucouleurs stated: "There is something remarkable on Mars. If we could one day conclude there was activity displayed by reasoning minds on Mars, what a prodigious upheaval it would cause in human thought!"

In a sober comment, the *Post* added: "This is not only a learned probe for academic information. It is also a hunt for possible enemies from space."

The head of the Mars Committee was Dr. E. C. Slipher of Lowell Observatory, the world's greatest Mars authority. The AF was already concerned about the large number of Mars experts involved—prominent astrophysicists, astronomers and meteorologists from seventeen countries. In the final conference at Washington, Dr. Slipher told newsmen that the "patrol" members would carry out a twenty-four-hour, round-the-world watch on Mars. Frequent news bulletins would be issued—daily if there were important discoveries.

"What if you find proof there is life on Mars?" a reporter asked Dr. Slipher.

"I'll announce it to the world!" he answered.

The news dismayed the AF censors. The daily bulletins could work up a feverish excitement about Mars—at the worst possible time. Every time Mars had approached the Earth since 1948 there had been a big outbreak in UFO sightings.

To let the Mars Patrol bulletins come out this time would be a dangerous risk. Slipher's publicity plan had to be blocked.

How it was done is still a secret—but not a single Mars Patrol bulletin ever appeared.

Exactly as the censors had feared, a wave of sightings began as Mars neared the Earth. Reports poured in from around the country, and abroad. The Walesville tragedy, aircraft near-collisions, frightening car chases made daily news. But nothing leaked out about the astronomers' discoveries until the patrol was over.

Through the *National Geographic* I learned the vital answer Dr. Slipher had relayed:

The canals followed great circle courses.

But not one word of this was made public. In spite of Dr. Slipher's determination to tell the world, this discovery was effectively suppressed.

In July of '65, *Mariner* IV took pictures which showed straight-line "canals" on Mars. This was first denied at Jet Propulsion Laboratory, which controls Mariner operations for NASA. But later the JPL head, Dr. William Pickering, admitted the canals were photographed. Their existence on the films was confirmed by Dr. Clyde Tombaugh, and copies were shown to NICAP by another Mars expert, Dr. Frank Salisbury.

But the controversy still rages. In the end, all the evidence may somehow be disproved. Or it may be correct, and we shall have to face the problem of an advanced race on our neighboring Red Planet.

Meantime, the mystery of the giant spaceships remains. Whether they are from Mars, or some unknown source, is not the crucial problem. Proof of their existence is on record. We urgently need to know the purpose which has brought these formidable ships here, to observe us and our world.

10

Fiasco

As 1968 began, AF Headquarters was still baffled by the Soviet Union's sudden, intense concern over UFOs. AF Intelligence was continuing its search for the answer when another disturbing development occurred.

The Soviet Academy of Sciences, the top-level scientific agency in Russia, had announced it was preparing an official publication with confirmed UFO evidence. To anyone who knew the Academy's previous stand this was incredible: many of its officials and members had openly derided the subject. But the announcement was explicit. The analyzed evidence was to appear as a special UFO section in a USSR book called "Populated Outer Space." It was being edited by the Academy's vice president, Boris Konstantinov.

This was strange enough, but what startled the U. S. Air Force was this added statement: The book would include evidence and discussions by three leading U.S. authorities on UFOs—Dr. James E. McDonald, Dr. J. Allen Hynek and Dr. Frank Salisbury, a well-known exobiologist who had lectured at the Air Force Academy on the evidence for life on Mars.

All three scientists had strongly criticized the AF for concealing or falsely debunking the evidence and its general mishandling of the UFO problem. Their disclosures in a Soviet Academy of Sciences book were certain to be quoted in U.S. newspapers and broadcasts, adding to the attacks on the cover-up.

What worried the AF even more was the continued release of Soviet sighting reports by Dr. Zigel, obviously with official approval and aid from Major General Stolyerov, head of the UFO Commission. After the first reports on the huge flying crescents, Dr. Zigel had released verified evidence of UFO encounters in recent years, along with more details on the giant spacecraft.

In 1964, a TU-104 aircraft flying over Bologoye was suddenly approached by a large disc-shaped craft. The UFO raced under the plane, then turned back and paced it for several minutes. One of the witnesses was Prof. Vyscheslav Zaitsev. He reported that the disc was made of gleaming metal, with a cabinlike structure on top.

On July 26, 1965, another large disc was sighted by astronomers in Latvian S.S.R. Viewed through telescopes, the UFO was estimated to be 100 meters (about 325 feet) in diameter. The flying disc was accompanied by three smaller round objects. For fifteen minutes they rotated steadily around the large UFO, then they separated from it and departed in different directions.

Also in the summer of '65, a geodetic astronomer named Lyudmila Tsekhanovick sighted an alien craft near Sukhumi in the Caucasus Mountains. He reported that the UFO was emitting light from windows or openings in the side toward him.

The chief navigator of Soviet polar aviation, Valentin Akkurstov, reported a close-range sighting during an ice-reconnaissance flight late in '65.

"We dropped down from the clouds and suddenly noticed an unknown flying craft," the chief navigator stated. He said his pilot tried to get closer, but the UFO veered away to keep its distance. After pacing the plane for twenty minutes, it climbed steeply out of sight.

In 1966, a disc-shaped UFO was sighted by V. I. Duginov, Director of the Kherson Hydrometeorological School, and forty-five other witnesses. That same year, radar confirmation of UFO reality was put on record by the chief of the Latvian space-tracking system, Robert Vitolniek.

Except for some uneasiness during close approaches, most

of the Soviet reports were not frightening. But released with them were added details about the flying crescent operations. Several times, Soviet astronomers had reported that the huge spaceships were preceded or flanked by smaller UFOs which kept precise formations, matching the crescents' terrific speeds. No explanations or motives were suggested in the public reports.

At the Pentagon, some analysts believed Moscow was building a foundation for public acceptance of UFO reality, through the more routine reports, before releasing all of its information on the giant spacecraft. It was supposed that another group of sightings would soon be made public, by the UFO Commission or by Dr. Zigel. But instead there was a surprising lull, with no new releases and no new information on the UFO Commission. It was as if silence on the UFO subject had been officially imposed. But no explanation, no hint of the reason, came from Moscow.

Shortly before this, in January of '68, a crisis was developing at Colorado University. During a conference with Dr. James McDonald, I had confidentially told him about the memorandum by Administrator Low. McDonald was shocked, and he was sure that many other scientists, also members of Congress and the public would have the same reaction.

"This is dynamite," he said. "We should use it to make Colorado University live up to the contract agreement. They certainly wouldn't want this to be made public."

"Saunders knows that, but I don't think he'll agree to any threat—"

"I don't mean a threat, or pulling anything behind their backs. Saunders doesn't even have to appear in it. I could write a letter to Low, with a copy to Condon, saying I have a photocopy of the memorandum. I'd come right out and say it's contrary to what they've said publicly, and I'd urge them to change the project and live up to their promises. It wouldn't be necessary to send copies to the university heads—at least not at first. I think it would scare Condon and Low so they'd let Saunders and the other scientists try the program they've been pushing for."

"I hope you're right," I said. "But you'll have to clear it with Saunders. He gave me that memo copy in confidence. I know he wouldn't mind, since you've been helping him."

"I'll check with him and I'll be careful," McDonald promised.

Two days later he put it up to Saunders and Dr. Norman Levine, who also had worked hard for a more thorough investigation. Both men were uneasy, but they finally agreed. McDonald also got their permission to inform the head of the National Academy of Sciences, if he felt it was necessary. Under the AF-CU contract, an Academy panel was supposed to review the Condon report.

If anyone could succeed with this plan, McDonald would have the best chance. He had degrees in chemistry, meteorology and physics. He had been a research physicist at the University of Chicago. In World War II he had served in Naval Intelligence, and afterward he was a member of scientific panels at the National Science Foundation and the Academy of Sciences. He was now the Senior Physicist at the University of Arizona, and for two years he had scientifically investigated UFOs under a grant from the university. During that time he had lectured to numerous scientific and engineering societies and had established important connections in the armed forces—including the AF UFO Project.

On February 5, 1968, McDonald's fateful letter to Low arrived. When Low and Condon read it they were furious. As Saunders later told me, and stated in a book—*UFOs? Yes!* —Condon harshly told him, "For an act like that [allowing McDonald to have the Low memo] you should be professionally ruined!" Dr. Levine, Saunders said, was told his actions were "treacherous." Both men were fired from the project the next day. In a news release Condon charged them with incompetence, but according to reporter R. R. Harkins he said later he meant to say "contumacy"—insubordination.

Just three days later a bulletin brought bad news from Russia.

In an abrupt reversal, the Soviet Academy of Sciences denounced the new UFO Commission as "sensational and unscientific." The Academy also rejected all reports of the huge flying crescents, even those from veteran Academy astronomers. A sharp attack in the Communist Party newspaper *Pravda* indicated a complete turn-around at top Soviet levels, and it seemed certain that the highly publicized UFO Commission investigation was ended—or was now being kept secret.

Regardless, Soviet ridicule of their own giant-spaceship reports relieved the Pentagon censors' fears—one more lucky break for the AF.

The firing of the two CU scientists also seemed a fortunate break; the other project members had given up the fight, and there had been no more publicity.

But a blast at the CU project was already in the works. Author John Fuller had been tipped off by McDonald, and a *Look* article was set for the end of April, with inside-story facts from the two scientists and NICAP.

Unaware of this, the AF continued its quick debunking of public UFO reports. Several strong cases had already been summarily rejected. At Columbus, Ohio, two maneuvering UFOs had been observed by city police, newsmen, deputy sheriffs, press photographers and other convincing witnesses. In a hasty explanation, the AF implied the objects were probably shooting stars. A frightening experience reported by a South Dakota couple received harsher treatment. Robert and Lynn Ballard were driving toward Vermillion when a UFO came down over their car. It touched down briefly on the road ahead, then continued pacing the car. Ballard drove at 100 miles an hour, trying to escape. But the UFO stayed with them for five tense minutes, almost to the edge of the city. Without naming the couple, an AF spokesman said many such UFO chase reports were delusions, or practical jokes.

By mid-April most UFO witnesses had stopped making public reports. Then a well-known U.S. citizen, ignoring the AF tactics, put the headquarters debunkers squarely on the spot.

The citizen was Henry Ford II. On April 16, 1968, he was aboard a Ford company plane, a JetStar, with several other company executives. They were flying at 35,000 feet, en route from San Antonio to Detroit. Near Austin, Texas, the pilots sighted a huge, round object overhead. Because of its size, they first thought it might be an unusually large research balloon. Then they realized it was moving with them. After checking for a few minutes, they found the unknown object was apparently pacing the jet, matching its ground speed of 535 knots (616 miles an hour).

"It looked twice the size of a DC-8," the senior pilot later reported to NICAP, at Mr. Ford's direction. "Our guess was 500 to 600 feet in diameter. There were no protrusions or windows. All the passengers saw it, but no one could identify it."

Mr. Ford separately confirmed the sighting to the Detroit *News*. The UFO, he said, had paced the JetStar for at least an hour. He also revealed that he had asked the senior pilot to contact the Air Force, so they could send up an interceptor. But the pilot had begged off, fearing AF ridicule.

When the story broke, reporters at the Pentagon descended on AF Headquarters. Caught in a serious dilemma, AF spokesmen tried to stall. The Ford company pilots had already knocked down the balloon answer, one of the debunkers' favorite explanations. Calling the report a hoax, or implying that the Ford executives and the pilots had had hallucinations would be little short of insanity. In the end, HQ fell back on its only alternative: The Air Force has no comment.

The Air Force was still evading the Ford report when the *Look* article came out, calling the Colorado Project a "fiasco." Besides revealing what had led to the firing of the scientists, it announced NICAP's complete break with CU.

Some newspapers and broadcasting stations denounced the

project, but the hottest criticism came on Capitol Hill. Congressmen J. Edward Roush, William F. Ryan and other lawmakers demanded a congressional investigation. Roush, a senior member of the House Science and Astronautics Committee, attacked the CU investigation on the floor of the House. According to the Denver *Post*, May 2, 1968, he also told its Washington bureau that the CU probe was an AF "trick" rigged from the start. In addition, as a member of the Government Operations Committee, which checks on possible misuse of federal funds, Congressman Roush asked the comptroller general to investigate the operation.

At a Washington press conference, NICAP made it clear we did not accuse Condon or Low of dishonesty. Both seemed to believe their actions were correct because of convictions that UFO reports were nonsense—convictions resulting from failure to examine the massive evidence.

With the NICAP Board's approval, I sent President Johnson the Low memorandum and other indications of bias, then urged that he create a new, impartial organization, free of any military or other government agency. It was suggested that evaluations be made to him directly and that secrecy be ended. The President was offered the full co-operation of NICAP's Board members and its scientific and technical advisers.

When Johnson was the Senate Majority Leader he had shown a serious interest in the UFO problem and NICAP's investigation. In 1961, he had examined our Confidential Report to Congress and had instructed the Senate Preparedness Subcommittee to evaluate the evidence, which showed the risk of accidental war. It did not seem likely he would overlook the situation at Boulder—if he received the NICAP letter.

The answer came from the AF Secretary's office, signed by Col. B. M. Ettenson. The colonel said he was replying at the President's request, but this phrase is often used in handling White House mail. The President's AF aide could have sent the NICAP letter directly to the Pentagon. Completely ignoring the bias evidence, Colonel Ettenson wrote:

The Air Force awarded the unidentified flying object contract . . . convinced that an impartial, open-minded, independent and objective scientific report would be forthcoming and we expect Dr. Condon will fulfill the terms of the agreement.

This curt brush-off stiffened NICAP's determination. The Condon report was not due for six months. We still had a chance for a public exposé of the Air Force cover-up, which would nullify any negative CU conclusion.

A full-scale congressional investigation would be the best way to reveal the long deception. We had tried before and failed. But the *Look* article and our press conference disclosures had had a strong effect on Capitol Hill. Even though it was an election year, we found encouraging support for a congressional probe.

Working with Congressman Roush, we began assembling our most powerful evidence. When word reached the AF it quickly acted to block any hearings, as it had done before. For a time we feared the AF would succeed, then a welcome message came from Capitol Hill.

Hearings by the House Science and Astronautics Committee had been approved by Chairman George P. Miller. Congressman Roush would be in charge of the proceedings, and prominent scientists who knew the UFO problem would be invited to testify. The first two on the list were Dr. Hynek and Dr. James McDonald. The hearings would be public, beginning at 10 A.M., July 29, 1968.

Elated at this news, we added some important evidence for the hearings. As disclosed in Chapter 1, the AF had concealed Project Reports 1 to 12 for fifteen years, denying they ever existed. After pressure by the Moss Committee, the AF had finally allowed NICAP staff members to make photocopies of the original sighting records, which still bore their

Secret or Confidential labels. Besides this proof of AF censorship, many of these reports were solid evidence of UFO reality, like the cases cited earlier.

One encounter was described by a B-29 crew in Korea. The bomber was on a routine mission when a strange flying object appeared, trailing a fiery exhaust three times its length. Turning toward the B-29, it closed in at high speed. It seemed to be on a collision course, then it swiftly nosed down and raced under the bomber.

An even closer approach was reported to the AF by a pilot in Michigan. He was flying at 3,000 feet when a disc-shaped craft suddenly appeared, coming toward him head on. Until the last moment it flew straight toward the plane, then it shot to one side. It was so close that the pilot could clearly see the polished metal shape. The UFO, he reported, was between thirty and forty feet in diameter.

Among the other long-hidden cases were reports by AF radar operators. At Larson AFB, one UFO was tracked at 950 miles an hour, faster than any known aircraft at that time. Another radar report, far more startling, showed a UFO speed of 3,700 mph. And this was recorded at a time when the Air Force was insisting there was no UFO evidence.

In the Project 3 report, the AF showed it was fully aware of the bad effect from witness ridicule. According to the project record, one group of pilots told the Air Force "they would be very reluctant to report any type of unidentified object to the AF"—and this included *Air Force* pilots. "If a space ship flew formation with me," one pilot was quoted, "I would not report it."

For the greatest effect, we decided to publish a special NICAP report on this evidence, duplicating the photocopies of the actual AF records with their Secret and Confidential classifications. By a speed-up of the printing, we were ready to submit this cover-up proof, along with our other evidence, well ahead of the hearings date.

But our optimism abruptly ended, when we learned the truth about the supposed hearings:

No criticism of the Air Force or the Colorado UFO project would be allowed.

The orders had been issued by Chairman Miller. They applied to Congressman Roush and all the other members of the Science and Astronautics Committee. The invited scientists also had been warned. Anything that might lead to disparaging statements about the AF investigation or the CU project was prohibited.

Although NICAP had played the leading role in securing the so-called hearings, we could not submit any information. Not only was our evidence blocked, we could make no comments on the discussions. No questions from the NICAP staff would be permitted, even if they were devoid of any AF or CU criticism—we could attend the meeting only as silent spectators. Although the discussions were officially called hearings, the meeting was also labeled as a symposium on unidentified flying objects, to remove any idea that this was an actual investigation.

Although the press had been invited, newsmen also were prohibited from asking questions. Some of them knew the inside story and they could have caused trouble. One correspondent, whom I had known for years, expected the muzzling order to cause a row.

"The Air Force must've pushed Miller into that," he told me. "But some of those Space Committee members are sore about it. They were all set to hit the AF and that Colorado Project. I know two who are going to try to buck the order. I'm not going to name them—"

"I think I know who you mean."

"Well, it could set off a fight, and what a story that would be. That's the only reason I'm going—I already know most of the things McDonald and the rest will bring out."

Within minutes after the symposium began, Chairman Miller repeated his warning against criticizing the Air Force.

"I want to point out that your presence here is not a challenge to the work that is being done by the Air Force. . . . Unfortunately there are those who are highly critical of the Air Force, saying that the AF has not approached the problem properly. I want you to know that we are in no way trying to go into the field that is theirs by law, and thus we are not critical of what the AF is doing.

"We should look at the problem from every angle. . . . I just want to point out we are not here to criticize the actions of the Air Force."

The first attempt to bypass the muzzling order was made by Congressman Ken Hechler.

"Is it your assumption," he asked Dr. Hynek, "that the AF . . . has not really measured up to a thorough scientific analysis of UFOs?"

But Hynek refused to answer the question. "The letter that came with the invitation to speak here strongly stated that we should not discuss the AF participation."

Congressman William F. Ryan, while questioning Dr. McDonald, tried to get his opinion of the Colorado Project. Symposium Chairman Roush, following orders, quickly broke in:

"We agreed this was not the place to discuss that. . . . I'm sure Dr. McDonald would be very happy to confer with you privately on this."

Switching to another approach, Congressman Ryan led to McDonald's disclosing the Low memorandum to the National Academy of Sciences.

"You wrote . . . concerning this [Colorado] project?"

"Yes," McDonald replied. "I received a letter . . . saying we must let the Colorado Project run its course."

Congressman Roush interrupted. "I would appreciate it, if we disposed of that."

But Ryan persisted. "I'm suggesting maybe this committee should make an investigation of the University of Colorado Project."

Committee Chairman Miller immediately stopped him. "That is something we don't have authority to do here."

In spite of the silencing order, a surprising amount of open criticism, hitting at the AF and the CU Project, was printed in the official Hearings Record. Most of it was contained in prepared statements which were not read aloud or quoted at the symposium.

One sharp comment on the project at Boulder came from Dr. Garry C. Henderson, Senior Research Scientist, Space Sciences, General Dynamics, Fort Worth, Texas. Dr. Henderson said prominent scientists had ignored careful research methods in dealing with the UFO problem.

"Such an example," he stated, "is the unfortunate selection of the University of Colorado team headed by a respected scientist, with the result that the squirrel-cage atmosphere usually associated with UFO interest has been augmented by built-in bias and confusion, rather than eliminated by one group of scientists' involvement. . . . The public has been led to believe that everything has been done to either prove or disprove the existence of UFOs—rubbish! Available information of a truly reliable nature should tend to increase activity, not place it in neglect, or worse, in ridicule."

Another paper, inserted in the Hearings Record by Rep. James G. Fulton, was prepared by nuclear physicist Stanton T. Friedman, who has worked on nuclear and radiation projects at General Motors, Westinghouse and the Aerojet Corporation. Friedman said that long studies and UFO investigations had convinced him that Earth is being visited by alien-controlled space vehicles. Referring to the AF debunking explanations, he added, "The low percentage of unknowns [unsolved cases] is the direct result of deception on the part of the U.S. Air Force . . ."

Another indication of AF deception appeared in a discussion by Dr. Robert M. L. Baker, Jr., a noted research scientist engaged in NASA, Navy and AF projects. As a Douglas

Aircraft Company consultant he made an eighteen-month study and scientific analysis of the famous Utah and Montana films. Oddly enough, this was requested by the AF, although it had debunked the film images as birds and reflections from aircraft. During his extensive examination, Dr. Baker found that the AF explanations were incorrect. He reported his findings, with all the detailed analyses, to Maj. Gen. H. E. Watson, head of Air Technical Intelligence. But the disproved answers were never retracted. (At the time of the hearings, the AF was still using these false explanations.)

Dr. Baker urged a truly scientific UFO investigation, with a mobile force of highly qualified scientists to secure the best information; a special tracking system; "listening posts" to seek out possible alien messages. Plans should be made, he said, to extract valuable information from an advanced society, if the extraterrestrial answer proves correct. He also urged studies to learn the characteristics of an advanced civilization and to be prepared for the psychological impact on our own culture, in case of "contact."

"The goal of understanding, if attained," he said, "may be of unprecedented importance to the human race."

The AF claims that UFOs do not exist were rejected by Dr. James A. Harder, Professor of Engineering, University of California. A prolonged investigation, he stated, had proved UFO reality. He also stressed the need for learning the technical secrets of these superior spacecraft.

The bad effects of ridicule were emphasized by Dr. Robert L. Hall, head of the Sociology Department, University of Illinois, and a former AF psychologist. As an example, he related the case of an American artillery colonel in Korea. While flying in his observer plane he encountered a typical UFO at fairly close range.

"He was an experienced observer," said Dr. Hall, ". . . [but] when he returned he was so ridiculed he gave up trying to be taken seriously."

The risk of panic, from sudden contact with aliens, needs

to be countered, Dr. Hall warned. Instead of issuing reassuring statements, he said, the public should be given sound information through a careful preparation program.

The most detailed exposé of the AF cover-up was made by Dr. James McDonald. It was done without any harsh attack, through a long statement including over thirty pages of verified reports, with proof that public explanations were untrue—most of them AF debunking answers. Almost every important aspect of the UFO problem was covered, analyzed scientifically with confirmed evidence.

Even Dr. Carl Sagan, the least positive of the symposium scientists, made some important admissions. A frequent adviser to NASA, Dr. Sagan has degrees in physics, astronomy and astrophysics. He is an associate professor of astronomy at Cornell University, and is also connected with Cornell's Center for Radiophysics and Space Research. Interstellar flight at nearly the speed of light is not impossible, even with present principles of science, Dr. Sagan told the symposium members. "If we are being visited by representatives of extraterrestrial life, just sticking our heads in the sand would be a very bad policy. . . . If there are other technical civilizations, any random one is likely to be vastly in advance of us. It is unlikely there is any other civilization in the galaxy that is as backward [as we are]."

The only scientist adamantly opposed to acceptance of the UFO evidence was Dr. Donald H. Menzel, former director of Harvard Observatory. In his prepared statement Menzel explained UFOs as mirages, reflections from windows, TV antennae and car fenders and also as optical illusions—afterimages, or spots before the eyes. Pilots and other trained witnesses, Dr. Menzel said, often make huge errors. Many unidentified objects, he claimed, were only birds, saucer-shaped clouds, or wind-blown hats, spider webs, feathers and seedpods. In conclusion, Dr. Menzel stated: "The time has come for the Air Force to wrap up Project Blue Book. . . .

to put an end to chasing ghosts, hobgoblins, visions and hallucinations."

None of the other scientists accepted Menzel's explanations.

Dr. E. Leo Sprinkle, psychology professor at Wyoming University, was convinced the UFOs were spacecraft from an alien civilization. From his long investigation of the evidence, he believed we may be near the "most exciting and challenging period in man's history." He recommended that a national research center be created to help learn the full implications of the UFO surveillance.

The two remaining scientists who submitted statements, Dr. Roger N. Shepard, psychology professor at Stanford University, and Dr. Frank B. Salisbury, exobiologist at Utah University, also urged more intensive scientific investigations of the UFO evidence.

Considering all the criticisms of the AF and the CU project in the prepared statements, and the prohibiting order by Chairman Miller, it may seem incredible that they were allowed to appear in the official Hearings Record.

If the press had known of these attacks and the massive, powerful evidence put on record, the symposium would have made headlines.

But the press had no way of knowing about this hidden ammunition. Disappointed at the lack of fireworks, they gave the symposium very little publicity.

After the hearing, several legislators kept pushing for a genuine investigation. Congressman Ryan, as quoted in the Denver *Post*, said there should be an immediate probe of the CU project. Earlier, Congressman Louis Wyman had introduced a resolution requiring a full investigation by the Science and Astronautics Committee (H.R. 946). Some of the anti-secrecy lawmakers renewed their efforts to get it approved, using the printed hearing record as a lever. It was hoped that the criticism and UFO reality proof in the prepared statements would force favorable action. But the Pentagon pressure was too great.

Once again the AF, backed by the CIA, had prevented a congressional spotlight on the UFO cover-up. How they had gotten away with it this long was hard to understand—there were determined men in Congress, too. But somehow these legislators, at least the committee chairmen, had been persuaded to avoid a showdown.

One night shortly after the symposium I had a private talk with an Air Force officer formerly stationed at the Pentagon. During UFO investigations in early '65 he had realized the growing secrecy hazards. After I met him through another AF contact we had discussed the problem confidentially. As he is still on active duty I'll simply call him Johnson.

"I know the Air Force and the CIA are in a bad spot," I told him. "But they're only making it worse, trying to keep it hidden."

"I think there's only one answer," said Johnson. "They just don't know what to do."

"That's the second time I've heard that." I explained about Robert Low's statement during our conference at NICAP in October of 1967. "He said the AF doesn't know how to prepare the public."

Johnson looked surprised. "That's odd. The Air Force was counting on skeptics like Low and Condon for a negative conclusion. Why would they tell Low that?"

"I couldn't figure it either, or why he'd want to tell us. And yet, somehow the way he said it—blurting it out—he seemed to be telling the truth. Of course, he could have misunderstood."

"I still don't get it, their telling him—but I think it is the truth." Johnson looked at me gravely. "Because that's what the CIA believes, too. They don't think the public can ever be prepared."

"Not ever? Why, that's—" I stopped. "How do you know this?"

"A CIA agent said it, during a hassle at headquarters. There were three agents there, and he was the senior man. It was when the newspapers were giving us hell, after that 'swamp gas' deal. An Air Force colonel said we'd better start preparing the public before it was too late, instead of trying to keep on fooling people. That's when this senior CIA man broke in.

" 'We've got to keep this thing secret—as long as we can! It's just not possible to prepare the public.'

"He acted kind of mad, and the colonel got sore. 'I'll admit it's a bad mess, but the American people can toughen up when they have to. Just why can't they be prepared? Give me one good reason.' The CIA man got a funny look, then he calmed down.

" 'Sorry, Colonel, I guess I'm a bit on edge today. That's the way I feel about it when things get rough. Forget it— just one man's opinion.' "

Johnson shook his head. "I didn't believe that. Those other agents looked upset—really worried. I think that actually is the CIA opinion."

"It could explain why they fight so hard to cover up. But I just can't believe they've discovered something that bad— so awful people couldn't take it."

"I can't either," said Johnson. "They couldn't hide it from the Air Force, and I'm cleared for Top Secret—I'd certainly know it. And with all the contacts you've got you'd surely have had some hint."

I agreed, but after he left I suddenly remembered there was a higher classification than Top Secret. This had stopped several legislators who were also high-ranking Reserve officers, when they tried to get the facts about UFOs. One, as already mentioned, was Senator Goldwater, who was a major general in the AF Reserve. Another was Senator Kenneth Keating, an Army Reserve general. On June 28, 1963, Senator Keating wrote a NICAP member after failing to get the answers by using his Top Secret clearance. As a high military officer, he said, he was not overawed by AF officers connected with UFO investigations or impressed by some of their statements.

"As you know I have no hesitancy in taking issue with other government agencies as to the dangers facing our country. . . . [but] I am sorry there seems to be nothing I can add to the UFO situation at the present time."

Twice, I had tried to find out about the higher secret classification, through Pentagon sources which had never proved unreliable. Both times I was told that it concerned plans for emergency defense if the UFO aliens proved aggressive. Though they could not discuss details, I realized any such plans would include our most secret space missiles, besides the original Project Saint program for devices to attack unknown satellites which appeared to be hostile.

Since it was AF policy to consider any unknown devices or objects hostile until proved otherwise, this seemed a reasonable explanation. I did not fully accept it—the super-secret protection could hide entirely different information, so important that my sources would have to deceive me. But I did not seriously consider some frightful discovery. As Johnson had said, I was certain there would have been some guarded warning, at least an indication of some grave threat.

But what if I were wrong?

Though I still didn't believe it, I decided to check back on all the disturbing incidents and reports. With some of the NICAP staff, and earlier investigators I knew, I had already searched through this evidence for signs of the aliens' motives. But a recheck might turn up some overlooked clue. Even if it didn't, there would be one valuable result.

By trying to see these sometimes frightening cases through the eyes of average citizens, the scare effect should be clearer.

The final picture could be a badly needed guide for reducing fear of the UFO beings and preparing the millions of citizens—for whatever is to come.

11

The
Crucial Question

At the height of the '66 crisis, with the censorship close to a breakdown, the AF and the CIA were almost forced into these two long-feared admissions:

1) A disclosure of the long official cover-up, believed to be in the national interest.

2) A revelation of the hidden evidence and secret AF conclusions that the UFOs are alien spacecraft engaged in a detailed reconnaissance of our world—the purpose still unknown.

Though the threatened break was averted, censors were shaken by the narrow escape. Another such crisis could make further secrecy impossible, leaving them with the fearful problem of trying to prepare the public.

At such a critical time the mere admission of UFO reality could cause a wave of fear, and the disclosure of UFO-caused accidents and injuries would naturally make it worse. To reduce the chance of panic, officials first would release harmless reports, from the thousands on record. The disturbing cases would probably be made public one or two at a time, the least startling ones at the beginning, with a gradual build-up to the few more serious reports. But eventually the spotlight would focus on the most alarming accidents. If the press dug out some almost forgotten early cases, this could quickly offset the attempts at gradual preparation.

In fear of sudden hysteria, some officials might delay the worst "scare" cases—or even try to hide them indefinitely. But even a small-scale cover-up could endanger the preparation program if this leaked out, as it almost certainly would.

There is only one way to educate the American people and help them accept the UFO problem without a serious risk of panic. The full story must be told: the apparently encouraging aspects and the frightening, though fewer, accident reports. The public must *know* it has been told the truth, with nothing held back.

The evidence which follows was first intended only for a recheck in the search for possibly overlooked clues to any unrecognized danger. But this record has a double importance. It will serve as a guide to the truth in examining any future official admissions about UFOs.

To disclose all the known facts, any official preparation program *must* include the detailed accident and injury cases described in the following evaluation.

The first analyzed accident, in July of 1953, involved a Transocean Airlines DC-6.

Departing from Guam with a crew of eight and fifty passengers, the plane flew to Wake Island, first stop on a flight to Oakland, California. At 7 A.M., after refueling, the DC-6 took off for Honolulu. About eight-thirty, the captain radioed Wake. Conditions were normal, he reported. The plane was cruising at 15,000 feet. This was the last word from the Transocean flight.

When the next scheduled report failed to come, Wake Island operators tried to raise the DC-6, with no success. Then an emergency search was immediately begun by the Navy, the Coast Guard and the Air Force, at the request of the Civil Aeronautics Administration (now the FAA).

Shortly after this the Wake operators picked up mysterious signals on the international distress frequency. No one could decipher them, and the source was never determined.

During the hunt for the DC-6, strange fast-moving objects

with brilliant green lights were sighted by the search pilots and ship crews. This was the first hint that UFOs might be involved.

In 1948 a new type of UFO had puzzled the AF and astronomers. Night after night, the unknown objects flew over New Mexico, then exploded silently with an almost blinding flash of green light. At the New Mexico Institute of Meteoritics, a top scientist said they were some extraordinary kind of missiles. By 1953 the sightings had almost died out. There had been no reports of damage, nor any indication of danger —until the Transocean airliner disappeared.

After several hours of searching, the crew of the S.S. *Bartlett* found twenty-five bodies floating near fragments of plane wreckage. From their condition it was plain that everyone aboard the DC-6 had died instantly.

Engine failure from an ordinary cause was ruled out; it was very unlikely that all four engines would fail at once. Even if they had, the captain would have had plenty of time for a "Mayday" distress signal and a report on the plane's position. Following standard procedure, he would have instructed the passengers to prepare for ditching, while he was gliding down from 15,000 feet. As the airliner neared the ocean he would have reduced speed, selecting the best direction for stalling in with the least damage to the passengers and the plane.

But the wreckage fragments proved there had been a tremendous impact from a high-speed dive—or that the plane had been torn apart in the air.

It was evident from the searchers' reports of green-lighted objects that these strange UFOs had been in the crash area. During the investigation, a check was made on the mystery objects' operations as recorded by the Air Force. The Project Sign reports showed that most of the "green flare" UFOs were sighted over New Mexico, with a few appearing over adjacent states. After a special probe called Project Twinkle, the AF disclosed that some of these oddly silent objects had been tracked at speeds up to 14,000 miles an hour. Air Force ground crews had searched wide areas after the UFOs exploded, but nothing was found.

Though there was no definite proof that the "green flare" objects had caused the Transocean disaster, no other explanation could be found.

Whatever happened, it apparently had been very sudden. One of the unknown devices might have flashed down toward the DC-6 on a collision course. In a frantic attempt to evade it the captain might have dived at high speed, plunging into the ocean before he could pull out. Or the airliner could have been destroyed in midair by some UFO-caused force or explosion.

For weeks, Civil Aeronautics Board and AF investigators checked and rechecked the evidence. No AF report was made public. After many months the CAB said the cause of the crash was unknown. But to scores of airline pilots who examined the detailed report the green-lighted UFOs were the only possible answer.

Another baffling crash, in the United States, involved a Braniff Airways Electra. Eyewitness reports indicated that some deadly UFO device caused the disaster.

On the evening of September 29, 1959, the four-engine Electra took off from Houston, bound for New York. Designated as Flight 542, it carried a crew of six and twenty-eight passengers. Its assigned altitude was 15,000 feet.

The airliner was passing over Buffalo, Texas, when witnesses on the ground saw a sudden fiery glow in the sky. Then they heard a violent explosion.

In a few seconds an eerie whistling sound filled the air as thousands of fragments fell to earth—all that was left of the plane and those aboard.

To investigators, this was the most appalling airline disaster they had ever known. Braniff's chief of operations, R. V. Carleton, told newsmen he had never heard of such a terrible accident.

"I've investigated lots of crashes, but I've never seen one where the plane was so thoroughly demolished, the wreckage so widely scattered and the people so horribly mangled. And there was nothing among the wreckage which indicated a fire or bomb aboard the plane."

None of the witnesses had seen the airliner disintegrate. At first the fiery glare was supposed to have blinded the observers. But investigators quickly realized the reported sequence was wrong.

The mysterious explosion which destroyed the Electra had come first. It would take almost twenty seconds for the sound to travel down from 15,000 feet, but the fiery blast would be seen instantly.

A Buffalo resident, W. S. Webb, said he had seen a small, bright object flash across the sky. Two or three other witnesses reported the same or a similar object, which resembled a small fireball.

By this time it was obvious that some external force had shattered the Electra, but no ordinary fireball could have caused such tremendous destruction even if one had hit the plane—which was a highly remote possibility.

The investigators were still baffled when an Air Force pilot, Maj. R. O. Braswell, made a startling report. As the Braniff airliner approached Buffalo, Major Braswell had been piloting an AF C-47, heading for Lufkin, Texas. He was flying at 6,500 feet when the red glare from the explosion suddenly appeared.

"It was colored like a large red fire and it looked like an atomic cloud," he reported. "It was a massive thing, about five degrees above my plane. The base was at an altitude of twelve to fifteen thousand feet. [The Electra had been cruising at 15,000.] The top was about sixteen thousand feet."

If the atomic-cloud description was correct, this could explain how the plane had been destroyed. Even a small A-bomb, used as a missile warhead, would have been capable of blowing the plane into bits.

At first it seemed too grimly fantastic to consider, even as possible retaliation for AF attacks on UFOs. The AF jet chases had been going on a long time. Why the sudden decision to strike back? There was a possible answer—the AF capture attempt at Redmond just five nights before. It had been the most determined AF capture operation on record. But why select an airliner for such a terrible warning—why not an Air Force plane?

For the Civil Aeronautics Board as well as the airline, investigating the Electra disaster had been a shocking experience. Even the slightest official hint of a possible UFO link, with the gruesome details still fresh in many citizens' minds, would have seemed a grave mistake. The CAB public report, which said the cause was unknown, was not released until months later. By then most of the public had forgotten the story, at least the worst elements.

But airline pilots who knew all the evidence did not forget, especially those who had almost collided with UFOs. Pressure and ridicule had kept some reports hidden, but several determined captains had disclosed their frightening encounters.

In one case, Capt. Edward Bachner made an official report to the Civil Aeronautics Board. He was piloting an American Airlanes coach plane, with eighty-five passengers aboard, when a strange flying craft descended nearby. Turning sharply, the UFO came straight toward the air coach. Bachner dived under it, barely averting a head-on collision. His hasty maneuver threw many of the passengers from their seats, injuring ten of them and bruising several others. For a minute or two there was panic in the cabin, then the crew calmed down the passengers. While they were giving first aid, Captain Bachner radioed the nearest airport and then made an emergency landing.

On March 9, 1957, the Civil Aeronautics Board received a "flash" message from Miami Air Traffic Control:

"Douglas 6A PAA Flight 257. To avoid unidentified flying

object traveling east to west, pilot took violent evasive action. Object appeared to have a brilliant greenish-white center with an outer ring which reflected the glow from the center. . . . Above description fits what seven other flights saw. . . . Miami reports no missile activity. . . . Original reports of possible jet activity discounted."

In a follow-up report to the CAB, Pan American Capt. Matthew Van Winkle said when he first saw the UFO he thought it might be a jet—since he was off course, avoiding a storm, an AF interceptor pilot might be checking on the plane's identity. Then he saw the light was too brilliant. It seemed to be reflecting from the shiny rim of some unknown flying object.

To avoid colliding, Captain Van Winkle hauled the controls back, putting the plane into a steep zoom. By the time he leveled off he had climbed 1,500 feet. When he nosed down from the zoom many of the passengers were hurled from their seats, and several were injured. As in many of the near-collision cases, the captain had to radio ahead for ambulances and doctors to meet the plane.

After the story broke in the papers, the AF tried to discredit the veteran PAA captain. Ignoring the confirmation by seven other airliner crews, it implied he had been alarmed by a shooting star many miles away.

Similar cases have been kept under wraps. Some of them were terrifying. More than one airline pilot, and probably many passengers, will remember those dangerous encounters for a long time. Reports like these have always worried the AF. Since they might alarm air travelers, some airline companies have been persuaded to muzzle their pilots.

Despite the potential danger during close UFO approaches, the AF has constantly refused to answer pilots' questions about such emergencies. While one captain was being interrogated by AF Intelligence officers, after a UFO maneuvered close to his plane, he asked what he should do if it happened again.

"Should I make an emergency landing or radio for jets—or what?"

"We can't answer that," one of the officers told him.

"Why not?" the captain demanded. "You got me in here to report that UFO and I've co-operated. I'll tell you right now, that was a rough experience. The first officer and I were both scared. If the passengers hadn't been asleep all hell would have broken loose. Why can't you advise me what to do—off the record if necessary?"

But the Intelligence officers refused to suggest any emergency steps. When the captain told me about it, some months later, he was still angry.

"Somebody ought to spread the word to the passengers," he said. "I'd do it myself if I wasn't afraid of losing my job."

"If you do run into a UFO again, there's one thing you could try." I told him about Capt. William Bruen of National Airlines. One night as he was approaching Washington a UFO suddenly appeared near his plane. Bruen quickly turned off all his lights, but the object stayed alongside, dimly visible in the dark. On an impulse, the captain switched on all lights, including the powerful landing beams. The intruder instantly pulled up and streaked away.

"I'll remember that," the captain said, "but I hope I never see one of those things again."

At one time, even the FAA was helpless to advise or assist airline pilots in regard to UFOs. In February of 1959, three unknown flying objects were sighted over Pennsylvania and Ohio by the crews of six airliners. Twice, one of the UFOs separated from the others and came down toward an American Airlines plane, Flight 713. Capt. Peter W. Killian started to make a hasty turn, during the first approach, but the object stayed at a safe distance, apparently observing the airliner. After rejoining the other UFOs it made a second, closer approach. This time Killian held his course. By the object's glow he could tell it was huge, much larger than the plane. He had already warned the passengers, through the intercom. Only one had showed any sign of panic, but Killian knew that could swiftly change if the strange craft came any closer. He was preparing for a hurried evasion when the UFO pulled up and rejoined the others.

Answering a radio call from Killian, two other American Airlines captains reported that they too were watching the three objects. One of Killian's passengers was an aviation expert—N. D. Puncas, manager of a Curtiss Wright plant—and when they reached Detroit he tipped off the newspapers.

"I saw those three objects in a clear sky," he told newsmen. "They were round, and in precise formation. I've never seen anything like it."

After the story broke, the UFO sighting was confirmed by a United Air Lines captain, A. D. Yates, and flight engineer L. E. Baney. Two other United crews, Flights 937 and 321, also verified Killian's detailed account and agreed that the objects were no known aircraft.

When the AF refused to comment I called the FAA. The official I reached was obviously on edge. After trying to stall, he told me the FAA would not investigate the reports.

"Why not?" I asked. "Killian's plane was on a federal airway and the UFO was close enough to endanger it on that second pass. If he'd tried to get away and the UFO turned at the same time they might have collided."

The FAA man made no reply, but I persisted.

"FAA is supposed to safeguard airline passengers and crews as much as it can. Why doesn't it tell the pilots what to do in a tight spot like that?"

"FAA's responsibility ends when a UFO report is forwarded to the Air Force. Beyond that, no comment."

Though the other airline crews had confirmed Killian's report, his forthright statements had received the most publicity. To debunk this serious case, the AF said Killian had merely seen stars through broken clouds. The captain quickly knocked this down—the clouds had been *under* the plane and the sky was clear above it. Switching answers, the

AF said Killian had failed to recognize an aerial refueling operation. Then to discredit him completely, a HQ spokesman hiding behind anonymity implied the captain was drunk.

Overnight, the ridicule spread to Killian's family. Several people in their community started taunting his wife, and his children were mocked at school. In a cold anger, Captain Killian went on the air and blasted the Air Force.

Within twenty-four hours the AF put the heat on American Airlines and Captain Killian was silenced. In his fifteen years with American he had built up a spotless record. But under AF pressure he was forbidden to defend himself in a broadcast, a press interview—or even in a discussion with friends.

After this vicious slander by the AF, some FAA officials began to rebel against Air Force control. Apparently this feeling of guilt for not going to Killian's aid spread to top levels. It was climaxed seven months later by the official release of the FAA logs at Redmond. The AF's denunciation of the FAA intensified the agency's stubborn resistance, and on through the sixties it gave out several significant UFO reports the AF tried to conceal.

But the Pentagon's attempt to ruin Killian was a victory for the censors. Most airline pilots stopped reporting UFO encounters, fearing they would get the same treatment. Hundreds of dramatic and sometimes startling reports are still being withheld by these embittered pilots.

This is one of the big factors in the censors' fight against trying to prepare the public. Both the AF and the CIA know that many embittered pilots are only waiting for a chance to hit back. An admission of UFO reality would start a flood of airline pilot reports, setting off another torrent from thousands of other serious and competent witnesses.

In the Air Force itself there have been accidents caused by UFOs, and others in which evidence strongly indicated that the aliens were involved. Since military orders make it easier to conceal such cases there may be some accidents in which a UFO connection was not suspected outside the AF. But enough are recorded in AF files, and at least partly admitted at headquarters, which must be included in any honest preparation program.

One mysterious accident occurred in midevening on April 1, 1959. Shortly before 7 P.M., an AF C-118 transport plane took off from McChord AFB in Washington, for a routine training flight. About 8:19 P.M. the tower at McChord received a frantic radio message from the pilot:

"We have hit something—or something has hit us."

After this hasty distress call the pilot said he would try to return to the base. But soon after this the C-118 crashed in the rugged Rhodes Lake area, killing the pilot and his three-man crew.

Before the crash, witnesses in the area sighted the lights of unknown flying objects. Some reports were confirmed by Chief of Police Fred Emard, at Orting, Washington. Witnesses said two glowing objects were following the plane before the disaster.

As quickly as possible, the AF cordoned off the crash area. Newsmen were told that information would be given out only by AF Headquarters. But the pilot's emergency call had already been made public at McChord AFB by Col. Robert Booth, CO of the 1705th Training Group.

"Evidently there was a mid-air collision," he told the press. He would not speculate on what had hit the C-118.

At the Pentagon, the AF quickly put out a different explanation, to refute Colonel Booth's admission. For some unknown reason, HQ said, the pilot had flown too low and had hit the top of a ridge. At McChord, this hasty answer was privately denounced by close friends of the pilot. He was an experienced night flyer, familiar with the terrain. If anything had forced him to make an unexpected descent he would have put on his landing lights, so as to avoid anything jutting up in his path. He also would have radioed McChord immediately, so Search and Rescue teams could reach them promptly if he had to make a crash landing.

The AF investigation report on the C-118 accident has been kept secret since 1959, but in any genuine preparation program it will have to be revealed in full detail. If the AF secretly concluded that a UFO caused this disaster, this must be admitted. If the AF has proof that a UFO was not involved, in spite of the sighting reports, this too must be made public, to remove the case from the list of accidents believed caused by aliens surveying the Earth.

This same procedure should be strictly followed with all accident and injury reports linked with UFOs.

High on the list are the fatal UFO chases by AF pilots.

One of the strangest cases on record occurred in 1953. Though it has received considerable publicity, some of the follow-up developments are not generally known.

On the night of November 23, 1953, an F-89 all-weather interceptor was scrambled at Kinross AFB, to check on a UFO flying over the Soo locks. The jet had a crew of two —Lt. Felix Moncla, the pilot, and Lt. R. R. Wilson, the radar observer. Guided by an AF GCI (Ground Control Intercept) radar station, Moncla followed the unknown machine out over Lake Superior, flying at 500 miles an hour.

Minutes later, a GCI controller was startled to see the blips of the jet and the UFO suddenly merge on the radarscope. Whatever had happened, one thing was certain: The F-89 and the UFO were locked together.

As the combined blip went off the scope the controller hurriedly radioed Search and Rescue. Moncla and Wilson might have bailed out before the collision. Both had life jackets and self-inflating life rafts—even in the cold water they could survive for a while.

All night, U.S. and Canadian search planes with flares circled low over the area. At daylight, a score of boats joined the hunt, as the pilots crisscrossed the lake for a hundred miles.

But no trace was found of the airmen, the jet or the UFO.
The search was still on when Truax AFB gave the Associated Press this official release:

"The plane was followed by radar until it merged with an object 70 miles off Keweenaw Point in upper Michigan."

In view of AF secrecy this was a surprising admission. The statement appeared in an early edition of the Chicago *Tribune*, headed JET, TWO ABOARD, VANISHES OVER LAKE SUPERIOR. (Photocopy in author's possession.) Then AF Headquarters killed the story.

Denying the jet had merged with anything, the AF said that radar operators had misread the scope. The reported UFO, it stated, had been an offcourse Canadian airliner which the F-89 had intercepted and identified. After this, the AF speculated, the pilot evidently had been stricken with vertigo and the jet had crashed in the lake.

The Canadian airlines quickly denied any flights in the area. Expert pilots also hit at the AF explanation: Moncla could have switched on the automatic pilot until the vertigo passed; also Wilson could have taken over temporarily.

As customary, the AF sent two officers to the families of the lost airmen to give them official messages of sympathy. According to letters which a relative of Moncla sent me, here is what followed. Explaining the accident, the AF representative told Moncla's widow that the pilot had flown too low while identifying the supposed Canadian airliner and had crashed in the lake.

By some headquarters mixup, a second AF officer was sent to offer condolences to the Moncla family. When Moncla's widow asked if her husband's body might be recovered, the officer said there was no chance—the jet had exploded at a high altitude, destroying the plane and its occupants.

For over a year, the AF stuck to the Canadian airline story, despite the denials. Then a Headquarters spokesman, Maj.

William T. Coleman, switched answers. The F-89, he wrote inquirers, had intercepted a Royal Canadian Air Force plane which was on a routine flight. When NICAP queried the RCAF, its chief of staff informed us there had been no such flight.

Later, while I was attempting to force this case into the open, I received a letter from Felix Moncla's mother, thanking me for trying to learn the truth.

"I suppose the Air Force has its reasons for not letting us know," she wrote, "but it is sad for a mother. God bless you for trying to help."

In its official answer, the AF still repeats the disproved RCAF explanation. The crash report, classified in 1953, has never been released.

One more fatal case, where a UFO chase was indicated, involved Col. Lee Merkel, Commander of the Kentucky Air National Guard. In January of 1956 Colonel Merkel crashed and was killed shortly after an unknown flying object was reported. Whether he was pursuing the UFO or had made contact with it was never settled—here again, the AF investigation report was never released. Also included in the secret reports which must be revealed is the tragic Walesville case, since the truth has been officially buried since 1954.

In 1958, the crew of an AF transport had a frightening encounter over the Pacific. The plane was flying at night, between Hawaii and Japan. Without any warning, there was a blinding flash, like an explosion, near the transport. Then the plane's radar picked up a UFO pacing the plane. The captain fired a challenge rocket, and a red flare came in answer, followed by a second, blue-green explosion, then a final red flare.

No damage was done, and the UFO soon went off the radar, but the alarmed crew stayed on watch the rest of the night. In a verbatim copy of the AF Intelligence debriefing, confidentially given to me by an AF source, the captain said he was convinced they were "shot at." The Intelligence debriefing officer, a lieutenant colonel, added another, more ominous statement:

"The entire crew, including Captain ———, were aware of the incidents in which multi-engined Air Force transports have disappeared while flying between —— and ——. The crew believed that what happened to them was related to the previous disappearances."

Several AF planes had vanished between Japan and Guam, and the inked-out words evidently were the names of these locations.

The Air Force refused to comment when asked about the 1958 encounter. But in a preparation program it will have to divulge this case and also reveal anything it learned about the missing transports.

Besides the mysterious "green flares," the puzzling "red spray" incidents will have to be disclosed.

One night in 1949, a new type of UFO descended near the airport at Albuquerque, New Mexico. It approached at 500 feet, then abruptly dropped to 200 and exploded with a shower of reddish spray. At first it was feared this might be some kind of gas, but it caused no ill effects. This was repeated on three more nights, at the same time and location, proving the "red spray" UFOs were under precise control. The incidents were confirmed in the AF Project Grudge Report, with no opinions as to the purpose.

Two years later, new light was thrown on the riddle by the pilots of an American Airlines DC-4. On November 2, 1951, the airliner was cruising at 4,500 feet, east of Abilene, Texas. At 7:15 A.M. a brilliant green object raced past the DC-4. In their brief glimpse, the pilots could see it was projectile-shaped. It had a white trail, like exhaust vapor, and it was holding the same course and altitude as the plane.

Just after it streaked past, the missile-like UFO exploded, hurling red balls of fire in every direction.

"It was like a Fourth of July roman candle," the first officer reported later. But it was no joke. If the device had exploded a moment sooner some of the red balls would have struck the plane. There was no way of knowing how the missile had been launched, or if it had been intended to destroy the DC-4. But one thing was now certain—the so-called red spray was far more dangerous than the Albuquerque observers realized. Apparently the red balls had disintegrated before reaching the ground near the airport.

Unfortunately, several unsolved AF plane accidents have been called proof of alien hostility without any evidence that UFOs were involved.

From February 8 to 12, 1955, there were three disasters, still unexplained. On February 8, a new B-57 jet bomber was being tested for the AF by a Glenn Martin Company pilot. After taking off from the Martin plant at Baltimore, the new bomber mysteriously exploded over Bel Air, Maryland, killing the pilot. By coincidence, two Canadian Air Force Sabre jets crashed near Chatham, New Brunswick, about the same time. Both pilots were killed; and the cause of the crashes was unknown. Next day, two USAF Starfire jet fighters crashed near Goose Bay AFB in Labrador. At the Pentagon, an AF spokesman said they had collided, but the U. S. Northeast Air Command Headquarters immediately denied this.

"The planes went down within five minutes of each other and almost seven miles apart," the Northeast Command stated.

On February 12, an AF Stratojet bomber exploded while on an Arctic training flight. The plane was at 35,000 feet when the sudden blast occurred. Two crew members were killed. The others, Lt. Col. K. G. McGrew and Capt. L. E. Epton, were thrown out, unconscious, as the bomber disintegrated. Luckily, both revived in time to open their parachutes. They had no explanation for the explosion—it had come without any warning.

In all of these disasters there was no evidence of any UFO link, as far as I could determine. But coming together in this short period, with the causes a mystery, they were cited by two or three doomsday writers as proof of alien hostility. The strange accidents also led to press stories spotlighting another baffling case, a few months before.

On October 12, 1954, test pilot George Welsh was making some final checks on an F-100 Super Sabre jet, for the North American Aviation Company. He was flying over California when the F-100 was suddenly and completely destroyed. For three months the NAA had tried to find some explanation, with the help of AF investigators. It was obvious that the test pilot had been killed instantly, by the same mysterious force which tore the fighter apart.

On February 9, 1955, in the midst of the new crash headlines, NAA told the press that the F-100 had encountered some terrific force which was totally unknown.

"Aerodynamic phenomena never before experienced by man caused the F-100 disaster," the company solemnly stated.

In reporting these strange aircraft accidents there is no intention to claim proof they were caused by UFOs. But since some broadcasts and press stories suggested that aliens were responsible, these cases should be discussed in any official disclosure of UFOs. Naturally they would be presented with emphasis on the lack of any UFO evidence. Unfortunately, it is hard to disprove that aliens were involved in mysterious cases like this, even when it seems certain there was no such link. This is one more reason why the officials concerned fear to end the cover-up.

Since 1957, the Air Force has had full proof of the UFO aliens' ability to interfere with electrical circuits, evidently by controlling and directing EM (electromagnetic) waves. Time and again, UFOs have stalled cars and put out their lights. Also they have interfered with aircraft electric equipment, including navigation instruments and radio aids. These malfunctions can be serious, especially for aircraft flying by instruments in thick traffic or in landing approaches. But there is another EM effect which could be more dangerous—blacking out large areas including big cities.

Before the great Northeast blackout, on the night of November 9, 1965, there had been several cases on a smaller scale. One had occurred just six weeks before, at Cuernavaca, Mexico.

On the evening of September 23, 1965, a glowing disc-shaped object appeared near the city, witnessed by Governor Emilie Riva Palacie and most of the local residents. As it came in over Cuernavaca, at a low altitude, the lights dimmed and electrical equipment began to fail. When the UFO stopped and hovered all the lights went out. For a few minutes the city remained dark, then the disc climbed swiftly out of sight and the lights came on again. Besides Governor Palacie, the observers included Mayor Valentin Gonzales and a military zone chief, Gen. Rafael Enrique Vega.

Earlier cases were reported in several countries. The first power outage recorded in the United States was at Tamaroa, Illinois. On November 14, 1957, a hovering UFO blacked out a four-mile area for ten minutes. Eleven days later, all city lights failed in Mogí Mirim, Brazil, as three unknown machines flew overhead. At Rome, on August 3, 1958, part of the city was darkened briefly by a luminous round object. On January 22, 1959, the same type of UFO passed over Salta, Argentina, and the lights went out.

On up into 1965 there were other confirmed UFO-EM reports, but nothing approaching the tremendous Northeast blackout, which covered an area of 80,000 square miles with a population of over twenty-six million.

Luckily, most of the millions caught in New York and other cities did not know of the UFO-caused blackouts. Also, they were unaware that UFOs were over Greater New York before and during the blackout, otherwise their reactions might have been far different. The UFO appearances were later proved by verified reports and a photograph taken from the

Time magazine building, evidence which was given to the Air Force and the Federal Power Commission.

The first report of a strange object, seen at the beginning of the blackout, was made by the Deputy Aviation Commissioner of Syracuse, Robert C. Walsh. Just after the power failed at Syracuse, a fiery round device was sighted from Hancock Airport by several witnesses, among them Walsh, who had just landed. In appearance it resembled a fireball—a huge one, as Walsh described it. But its performance proved it was not any type of fireball. When first seen it was ascending at a moderate speed, from a fairly low altitude—a fireball would have streaked past and struck the ground. A few minutes later Walsh and other airport observers saw a second "fireball" as large as the first, which by now had disappeared.

About this time a flight instructor, Weldon Ross, was approaching Hancock Airport for a landing, and he saw the second fiery object. It appeared so close to the ground that at first he thought it was a building on fire. Then he realized it was in the air, a round-shaped object about 100 feet in diameter. Apparently its speed quickly increased, for it soon vanished. Both Ross and his passenger, a computer technician named James Brooking, were startled by the "flame-colored globe," as Ross called it.

After landing on the darkened field, Ross reported the sighting to the tower and Deputy Commissioner Walsh. The unknown fiery object, he calculated, was directly above the Clay power substation, an automatic control unit through which electric power ordinarily flowed from Niagara Falls to New York.

At approximately the time when Walsh saw the first "fireball," witnesses in the Time and Life Building spotted an odd glow in the sky above darkened Manhattan. It appeared to come from a round object hovering over the city. This was twenty minutes after the lights began to go out. Several photographs were taken by a *Time* magazine photographer, one of which appeared in the November 19 issue.

During the first hour other witnesses sighted one or more UFOs, according to reports from New Yorkers and observers in New Jersey and Pennsylvania. Of the few which could be checked out in detail, several appeared to confirm the presence of UFOs.

One of these was a report by pilot Jerry Whitaker and his passenger, George Croniger. About forty-five minutes before the blackout started, the two men witnessed a UFO chase over Tidioute, Pennsylvania. Two unknowns, which they called "shiny objects," were flying at a higher altitude than their plane, and racing behind them were jet interceptors. One of the UFOs, Whitaker said, put on "a burst of speed" and swiftly pulled away from the jets. While he and Croniger were watching this, they lost sight of the other UFO. Presumably it escaped in the same way.

Soon after the blackout engulfed Manhattan it spread to parts of six other states and a section of Canada. New York City, with millions caught in the rush hour, was hit the hardest. Some 600 trains, with over 600,000 passengers, were trapped in the subways. Thousands were stranded in elevators. Bridges and tunnels were jammed, and with all the traffic lights out, as well as all other lights, traffic was badly snarled on many streets.

At La Guardia Airport, some flights operated, but Kennedy International had to close down, sending dozens of incoming flights to other cities.

When the blackout first hit New York, word was flashed to Washington and to President Johnson at his Texas "White House." Fearing a panic, the President told the Office of Emergency Planning not to announce a national emergency. On through the night, reports were relayed to the President at five-minute intervals. Power company experts still had no explanation. It was impossible for the highly touted grid system to break down—but it had.

Though it seemed almost a miracle, there was no wave of panic. Many people were still trapped in the subway, and some were hysterical. But most of them kept under control, though tension built up as the hours passed. It was after midnight before the last passengers were taken off and guided along the dark tracks to subway stations and exits.

During the blackout, New York broadcast stations stayed on the air, using battery-powered transmitters or emergency equipment. News also was phoned to cities outside the stricken area. Almost all the commentators said there was no alarm in Manhattan. At Washington, ABC commentator Edward P. Morgan relayed a New York statement that the situation was "a marvel of calm and co-operation." While this was a wise procedure, the newscasts were not entirely correct.

Some of the thousands trapped in dark elevators were close to terror. Where there were elevator doors on all floors, rescue workers could open the door above the stalled car, descend by ladder and open the roof, so that passengers could climb out. But with the "blind" express-car shafts this was impossible. Rescue workers had to cut through the walls and into the elevators to get the passengers out. In many cases people were trapped for hours. Some were in shock or emotionally out of control before they were brought out.

According to a CBS newscast, St. Patrick's Cathedral was swamped with people who apparently feared enemy attack or a supernatural event.

Some hospitals with insufficient emergency generator systems had to use candlelight or have automobile headlights aimed to shine in through first-floor windows. Ship or boat traffic in New York harbor or in the Hudson or East rivers was subjected to possible hazards when the radar and navigational aids failed.

On through the night, hungry and weary people waited for the ordeal to end, trying to sleep in stalled commuter trains, in railroad, bus and subway stations, in building lobbies—

even on sidewalks. Among the hundreds of thousands a few gave way to hysteria, but the great majority caused no trouble. In other blacked-out cities it was about the same. Parts of eight states were without power—Connecticut, Massachusetts, Maine, New Hampshire, New Jersey, New York, Pennsylvania and Vermont. There were some disorders, some looting. In Massachusetts, Governor Volpe ordered out National Guard units as a precaution. But in general the public reaction was surprisingly moderate.

Most people supposed some ordinary trouble, a mechanical breakdown, had caused the blackout. Not many knew that the huge power grid had been declared invulnerable. A vast interlocking network linking twenty-nine utility companies, the grid had hundreds of automatic controls and safety devices. Dozens of power experts had told Congress and the press that a serious breakdown was impossible. When the great blackout hit the Northeast they were stunned.

Several power company officials, quoted on the air, admitted the cause was a mystery—something completely beyond their understanding. In Manhattan and other stricken cities, some radios in stalled cars were turned on intermittently for the latest news. If the UFO sighting reports had been broadcast after the mystery admissions, there might have been some alarm.

At Washington, several of the AF night staff were uneasy about the grid experts' statements. When the blackout ended with no hints of a UFO tie-up the AF monitors relaxed. But their relief did not last long.

During the night, President Johnson had ordered a full investigation by the Federal Power Commission. At AF Headquarters it was expected that the FPC would concentrate on the technical problem, but several early newspapers spotlighted the UFO angle, revealing that unknown flying objects had been sighted before and during the blackout.

AF denials of verified sightings were quickly released. Most of the press accepted them. But some editors and newscasters, recalling the earlier '65 reports which were still unsolved, rejected the AF debunking claims.

By the end of the day, UFOs had been openly and seriously suggested as the cause of the strange power failure. This unexpected development worried the AF. With most of the blackout sightings now made public, it would be impossible to withhold this evidence from the Federal Power Commission. If President Johnson's order were fully carried out, the FPC would have to investigate these UFO reports.

It could mean the end of the secrecy.

12

Behind
the Blackout

One of the first UFO sighting disclosures was made by the Syracuse *Herald-Journal*. Describing the strange objects seen near the Clay power substation, it strongly suggested that UFOs had caused the blackout.

The Indianapolis *Star*, stressing the long record of UFO interference with electrical circuits, also tied this to the Northeast power failure. "The answer is fairly obvious—unidentified flying objects. It is one angle the multi-pronged investigation should not overlook."

To the AF censors the Syracuse report was the most disturbing. Normally, all the electrical power for New York City and most of the state flowed south from Niagara Falls generators and on through the Clay substation. On November 9, Secretary of Defense Cyrus Vance, the Office of Emergency Planning and most grid experts had agreed that the break was somewhere in this area. During November 10 and 11, commentators repeated the Syracuse report, focusing more attention on the possible UFO answer. Power company experts made the situation worse, admitting the cause of the blackout was still a mystery.

"We have no explanation," said Charles Pratt, head of the huge Niagara-Mohawk plant, the main power source for the northeast states and part of Canada. "There were no severed transmission lines, defective generators or faulty circuit-breakers."

In New York, a Consolidated Edison spokesman compared the power cutoff with a giant water-main break. "The interconnected power networks lost vast amounts of electricity, like a huge short circuit into the ground. We are at a complete loss to explain it."

The chairman of the Federal Power Commission, Joseph C. Swidler, was equally baffled. Heading the investigation, he began a check of the evidence, aided by top power experts. After two days, he made this somber statement: "The Northeast blackout may never be fully explained, and there is no guarantee it will not happen again."

By this time, company heads knew they were in trouble. When the power grid was first proposed it was explained as beneficial to the consumers as well as the utilities. With the power plants hooked together electricity would feed back and forth, flowing to where it was needed to maintain the proper voltage. The Federal Power Commission and a congressional committee had been assured that the hundreds of automatic safety devices would prevent any cascading chain reaction effect or a transmission line failure. Now the grid had failed almost completely, leaving their promises open to doubt, even outright attack.

The FPC also was in trouble. After checking all the grid plans and equipment it had told the White House and Congress that the system was fully protected from any serious breakdown. Now they might be accused of incompetence or careless supervision.

Adding to the FPC problems, some editors and newscasters were still suggesting that EM interference by UFOs had caused the big blackout. One commentator linked this with a statement by a Canadian power expert. Some unknown cause, the engineer said, apparently had created a strange reaction in the grid control circuits. It was, he said, "like a nervous breakdown in the electronic brain controlling the widespread grid system."

On November 14, the Premier of Canada warned the FPC that he might pull out of CANUSE (the Canadian-United States Eastern interconnection), to protect the country against any further U.S. power failures.

That same day, NBC commentator Frank McGee broadcast a new UFO report. Just before the blackout began, he said, a pilot had sighted a round, glowing object near the Niagara Falls power plant. The story was picked up by the Associated Press and carried in numerous papers.

Next morning, the New York *Journal American* ran a feature article on the Syracuse report, with UFOs blamed for the grid disaster. It was also quoted on the air, building up the suggestion of a deliberate act by beings from a more advanced world.

Suddenly the UFO discussions ended—eclipsed by a news flash from Washington.

The great blackout, stated the FPC, was now explained. The mystery which had baffled all the top power experts had a simple explanation: a broken relay, a circuit breaker, in a Canadian power plant.

The billion-dollar grid system had been knocked out in spite of the hundreds of safety devices—according to the FPC. The supposedly broken relay was located at the Adam Beck No. 2 Plant in Ontario. Somehow, during the five-day search for the answer, it had been overlooked.

After all the grid experts' statements this was an incredible explanation.

It also was false.

The Adam Beck Plant relay was *not* broken. It was tripped by some unexplained surge of electricity.

Proof that the relay never broke was later revealed in a special report by the industry publication *Power*, which had close ties with the utilities. The report was written by the executive editor, J. J. O'Connor, after a thorough investigation by *Power*.[1]

The following details from the *Power* report give a startling picture of the catastrophe which struck the grid system.

On the late afternoon of November 9, Adam Beck Plant 2 was in normal operation. Through five transmission lines its generators were providing current to the city of Toronto. The power loads were well within safe limits. But suddenly a relay tripped, as though from an unexpected overload. By tripping, the relay disconnected one of the five Toronto lines.

Ordinarily, this would have been a routine operation. The actual reaction, described in the *Power* report, sounds like a fantastic nightmare.

In just four seconds, the Canadian-U.S. grid disintegrated.

The other Toronto lines instantly tripped off. As though there had been no safety controls a tremendous surge of electricity flashed through the lines to the south. In a violent chain reaction, the Clay substation and a St. Lawrence River plant were knocked out. Then the entire CANUSE network split into four parts.

Until the disaster struck, twenty-nine utility plants were connected with the grid system. In a few cases, automatic devices separated plants from the network or engineers hastily cut them loose. But at most generating plants the enormous surge of power came too swiftly.

Never before had the operators known such chaos. At some points, the cascading current reversed, dangerously increasing the pressure on the grid. More of the steam-driven generators were forced to cut out, and skyrocketing steam pressure blew open boiler safety valves. With the current off, pumps, air compressors and other auxiliaries failed. Plants without standby emergency equipment were unable to restart for hours. Meantime, complaints from stricken areas and demands for restoration of the lights poured in on the helpless operators.

[1] Copy of the *Power* special report in author's files.

In most details, *Power's* picture of the breakdown is correct. But certain important information is missing. The grid's supposed invulnerability is not mentioned, and *Power* skirts around the failure of the extensive safeguard system. Even more curious, it does not actually answer the big question:

What caused the great blackout?

According to *Power*, there was no outside interference. The trouble source was solely within the grid—the tripping of a "simple relay" at Adam Beck No. 2, followed by a series of "improbable events." The load on the line, *Power* stated, was "well within carrying capacity." In spite of this the relay tripped, setting off the violent reaction which wrecked the network in four seconds.

If this was the truth then one hard fact stands out:

The vaunted safety system was a dangerous fraud.

But this was preposterous. It would mean the utility companies had deceived the government, operating under the constant risk of a huge blackout, hoping there would be only minor power failures. The Federal Power Commission almost certainly would have discovered the conspiracy, and company heads would be exposed to White House and congressional attack, public indignation and probably legal action. To follow such a dangerous course would be little short of insanity.

Besides this, the grid safeguards had already met the threat of a large power failure. Over several years there had been a few smaller-scale blackouts, and the safety devices had kept them from spreading. These same safeguards would have confined the November 9 trouble to a fairly small area, if some ordinary power increase had tripped the Adam Beck relay. Instead, scores of other circuit breakers had tripped in those four tense seconds, as the strange surge of electricity swept through the grid system.

There was only one true explanation—an unpredictable, overwhelming EM interference the safety devices were not built to handle.

For some years, there had been verified evidence that UFOs could cause power failures. The same type of electrical interference could have been directed at one or more strategic parts of the Northeast network, causing the uncontrollable, tremendous surge which led to the disaster. The targets could have been the Clay substation, the St. Lawrence plant or the enormous generator system at Niagara Falls, according to the UFO reports.

Though a UFO connection was not proved, the evidence was too strong to be ignored or debunked if it were all brought into the open, along with the reports of previous UFO-caused blackouts.

The increased press suggestions of a UFO link were seriously worrying the AF when it learned, through the FPC, of the Adam Beck development.

The official Canadian message to the FPC actually reported the tripping of the Adam Beck relay and all the others in the swift breakdown. To the AF this was an immediate danger, certain to lead to speculation about the strange surge of power, especially with its source still unknown.

To avoid this, and also to shift attention from the UFO explanation, the "broken relay" story was invented. Since this could have been construed as blaming Canada, the Premier must have been convinced it was best for both countries not to disclose the true situation.

The false explanation disturbed some U.S. utility heads. To the press and the public, it might seem they were only pretending to be baffled, that they knew the grid was at fault. But the criticism was relatively mild. Apparently most people were unaware that the grid was supposed to be invulnerable and a broken safety device seemed a reasonable answer.

Even though they had not been negligent, the utilities began to search for ways to strengthen the grid, in case such an emergency happened again. Not only the companies but the FAA, industries, hospitals and some apartments and office buildings rushed plans for standby emergency equipment—generators driven by diesel or gasoline engines—with special attention to high-rise elevators where thousands of people had been trapped.

Announcements of all these improvements, combined with the broken relay story, rapidly reduced UFO discussions. But the lull ended abruptly as new blackouts occurred.

On the night of November 26, 1965, two sections of St. Paul, Minnesota, lost electric power and lights. Residents of one section reported lighted UFOs were overhead, and the power company had no other explanation for the blackout. The second failure was blamed on the wind, which supposedly blew two power lines together.

On December 2, parts of Texas, New Mexico and Mexico were suddenly hit by a grid failure. Almost a million people were affected, from El Paso to Juárez. There was an unverified report of a UFO over the area. The chain reaction blacked out stores, homes, hospitals, airports and also defense bases—Fort Bliss, Holloman AFB, White Sands Proving Ground and Biggs AFB.

On December 5, some 40,000 homes in East Texas were darkened by another power failure.

The number of December blackouts was higher than normally would be expected, and the December 2 case was a more massive failure. No UFO link was proved; the power company gave a routine explanation.

During December there was also an unusual outbreak of foreign power failures. One occurred at the Zwolle plant in East Netherlands, another in Saudi Arabia. On December 26, Helsinki and three other cities were blacked out in Finland. That same day, a grid chain reaction in Buenos Aires stopped trains on five subway lines and four commuter branches. Thousands of people were trapped in elevators. Lights went out in all buildings. Adding to the tension, all communications failed, leaving millions with no idea when the ordeal would end. After the blackout, a newscaster tied in the great Northeast power failure and the suggested UFO connection, a practice which became more frequent as other foreign incidents occurred.

In the first half of '66, foreign and U.S. blackouts continued, hitting cities in Italy, Peru and England, and areas in Wyoming, Utah, Nebraska and Colorado. The U.S. power failures occurred during the increased tension of the UFO crisis, as sightings were reported all over the country. None of the blackouts was positively linked with a UFO, and there may not have been any connection. But broadcasts on this possible answer increased the pressure on the censors.

By now it was clear that the FPC, as well as the AF, was determined to keep the evidence under wraps. This was confirmed to me by Dr. James McDonald, who had made an intensive check on the Northeast blackout. Because of his standing as a highly respected scientist he was permitted to interview certain FPC officials.

"They admitted they had the Syracuse and Niagara Falls reports," he told me, "also most of the others on that night. But they wouldn't discuss the UFO possibility. The Air Force may have convinced them that UFO reports are nonsense, or at least that they had no connection with the big blackout. No matter what they believed, I think they were convinced the facts shouldn't be given to the public, and that's why they agreed to the 'broken relay' story. At any rate, it was obvious they were covering up."

When the Colorado Project was announced most of the public blackout discussions ended. But some legislators kept trying for a full investigation. One of them was Congressman William F. Ryan (D N.Y.). In the 1968 hearings he put Dr. McDonald on record about EM interference by UFOs, then led to the Northeast blackout.

In answering Ryan's questions, Dr. McDonald made it clear that the problem was serious. There were too many cases of UFO-caused blackouts, he stated, to be ignored. Then he charged that the Federal Power Commission was evading the evidence connecting UFOs with the Northeast power failure.

"The FPC had many dozens of sighting reports for that famous evening," he told the congressional committee. "There were reports all over New England in the midst of that blackout."

McDonald also emphasized that the Adam Beck relay had tripped under an overload from some unknown cause.

"The pulse of current which tripped the relay has never been identified," he said. But he added that the UFO sighted over the Clay substation was suspected of being involved in the blackout.

Since the 1968 hearings Congressman Ryan and other legislators have tried to secure a full investigation. But high-level pressure has bottled up all attempts at a congressional probe.

In any program to prepare the public the AF would have to reveal the evidence that UFOs caused the Northeast blackout. After all the official denials this would be bad enough. But to admit that the aliens' purpose is still unknown would make the problem far worse. This is one of the big factors in the censors' determination to continue the cover-up.

When this recheck of the evidence was completed there was still no sign of any horrible hidden menace which could set off uncontrollable panic. Even without such a threat there were enough disturbing cases to be a problem in preparing all the millions of citizens.

Like other investigators who had spent years in analyzing the evidence, I had learned of these incidents gradually, in between hundreds of reports describing harmless encounters. Naturally, this reduced the impact. But now, viewing the evidence in concentrated form, I could see how it would affect the censors.

To the AF, these disturbing reports would be a big hazard in any preparation program. Besides this, the long cover-up could finally backfire; many citizens might distrust the belated AF admissions. When all the risks were added up, they could seem so formidable that both the CIA and the AF might actually believe preparing the public *was* impossible.

But sooner or later the secrecy is bound to break down, and even a partly prepared public would be better than a sudden, forced admission of UFO reality. The American people have come through before when faced with a national crisis. They would probably come through again even if some UFO reports sounded like bad news. There would be some alarm at first, some tense days. But the majority probably would react without absolute panic if given the truth, if the AF told them the purpose behind the long surveillance.

But the AF cannot tell them. After all these years, it still does not know the answer.

If communication had not been blocked repeatedly we probably would have learned this crucial answer—the aliens' intentions toward our world. But almost from the start certain well-known scientists and high-ranking officers have shown a strong fear of advanced space beings, fear of their technical superiority, fear that communication might speed up some operation against our world.

Lt. Gen. James M. Gavin, like General MacArthur, issued a public warning: "We are likely to encounter beings inimical to Earth's existence." Agreeing with the generals, several leading scientists warned that communicating with otherworld beings could bring disaster. Among this group were four previously quoted—Dr. Albert Hibbs of Caltech's Jet Propulsion Laboratory, Dr. Otto Struve, former Director of Project Ozma, Dr. Thomas Gold, Professor of Astronomy at Cornell University and Dr. Carl Sagan, a frequent adviser to the National Aeronautics and Space Administration. The Brookings Institution report prepared for NASA also played a part in preventing communication attempts. Discussing the impact of the space age, it added a sober reminder that "societies sure of their own places have disintegrated when confronted by a superior society," as in the case of the American Indians.

In the years since then it has become increasingly important to learn all we can about the UFO surveillance, in the event that the aliens land on Earth.

The ban on radio or television communication is still in effect. But there is another way—an important method still under wraps—to get the crucial answers.

This procedure involves a unique but practical operation which includes suggestions by linguists, anthropologists, educators, psychologists, communications specialists and experts in various other fields. It will avoid the forbidden radio and television transmissions, also any direct contacts, during the early vital phases. It can bring us detailed information on the UFO beings, without any hostile actions on our part and with almost no risk of aggression by the aliens. The plan has been developed without publicity to prevent opposition and possible interference.

The full details of this unusual, far-reaching plan will be given to you later, but here is the vitally important first step:

To observe the alien beings—*without their knowledge.*

We urgently need to know what they are like in appearance. Are they similar to humans? Do they come from one of the many planets which, according to some leading scientists, must have life like that on Earth? Or are they so different that meetings would be frightening—to them as well as to us —making adjustments between humans and aliens almost impossible?

The special operation can give us the answer to this vital question. It can tell us the motives behind the long UFO surveillance, whether landings are intended and what developments we can expect. Through this unique operation we should be able to learn the truth about the blackouts, the fatal jet chases, the UFO-caused injuries and other serious incidents. After the first phases we probably shall have the chance to correct any false impressions caused by the lack of communication.

Meantime, we should try to condition ourselves—as much as possible—for whatever the answers may be.

In the roundup which follows you will learn the opinions of scientists who have carefully studied the problems of other-world life. In a discussion quoted from the Air Force Academy report you will find a surprising suggestion about space visitors, supported by interesting facts. You will also learn about some bizarre "contactee" stories, claims of meetings with spacemen (and women), which will help you separate fiction from fact.

Although there is no verified picture showing what the UFO aliens are like, you will see the possibilities, including a probability accepted by some scientists.

Unless there is some unexpected move by the UFO aliens we probably will have to wait for the special operation to bring us the final answers. But this roundup may help you to be at least partly prepared if the unknown space beings land upon our planet.

13

The
UFO Beings

"There are at least one hundred million inhabited planets. On many of them the inhabitants will be far superior to us."

When Dr. Harlow Shapley, former Director of Harvard Observatory, made this announcement he startled most of his colleagues as well as the public. Stating a belief in other inhabited worlds, once attacked as blasphemy, still was avoided by most astronomers. To admit a belief in more advanced beings seemed a serious risk, but Shapley had a solid foundation—an intensive two-year evaluation of the problem with the aid of other scientists.

Since then most noted astronomers have agreed there must be an enormous number of inhabited planets, probably far more than Shapley's minimum estimate. Dr. Otto Struve says there may be a billion in our galaxy alone. Most of these scientists also accept a second evaluation by Dr. Shapley and his researchers. The other-world beings, Dr. Shapley stated, would logically be divided into three goups. The first, because of a longer development period, would be much more advanced than Earth's inhabitants. The second group would be at about our level. The third-group aliens would not have progressed to our state of civilization.

From all the recorded, verified evidence the UFO operators would have to be in the highly advanced first group. Precise UFO maneuvers, often at great speeds, have been reported by military and airline pilots, NASA spacecraft trackers, FAA tower and radar operators and many other qualified observers.

One significant case which proves the alien astronauts' technical ability is the Gulf of Mexico encounter partly described earlier. As detailed in an official AF report, three groups of UFOs were sighted by the crew of a B-29 bomber, during a night practice flight over the gulf.

The first two groups were seen by several of the crew as they streaked across the sky. The bomber's three radars showed the UFOs' speed was 5,240 miles an hour. The third group abruptly slowed to the B-29's speed, trailing it for ten seconds.

Suddenly a giant spaceship showed upon the radarscopes. It was immediately apparent that this was a carrier or mother ship appearing for a rendezvous. The UFOs behind the bomber raced up toward the huge craft, accelerating to match its speed. Tracked by the B-29 radars, the smaller objects swiftly merged with the mother ship. The instant they were aboard, the gigantic carrier speeded up to 9,000 mph and disappeared from the radarscopes.

The UFOs were retrieved at a speed of over 5,000 mph. To control this operation would require absolute precision and perfect timing. Undoubtedly it was automatic, but to create and control such intricate retrieval equipment would take a very high order of intelligence and technical skill.

In the official report cleared to me before the CIA takeover, the AF confirmed all the details and admitted it had no conventional explanation.

To construct and operate UFOs, especially the giant spacecraft, the aliens must be centuries ahead of us. Aerospace genius William Lear, after sighting a UFO from his executive plane, said they must be thousands of years more advanced. The RAND document on UFOs agrees that older civilizations will be extraordinarily advanced. Even the AF has accepted the theory that man is average in development and that some space races must have greater technical ability. (Stated in a HQ release on April 27, 1949.)

But on the question as to what alien visitors could look like there is very little agreement. Adding to the controversy are humorous cartoons of weird space creatures and newspaper or broadcast coverage of outlandish "contactee" claims. Most of the UFO occupant stories are obvious hoaxes. But there are a few reports, by citizens of good reputation, which investigators have not rejected, though this does not constitute absolute proof.

On May 24, 1962, the Argentine Government officially reported that a UFO had landed in La Pampa. This was after hundreds of sightings in five provinces, many confirmed by police and local officials. In the La Pampa case, a government broadcast said that reputable witnesses had seen a disc-shaped UFO land near a ranch house. Two figures described as "robotlike" were reported to have emerged from the machine.

A few moments later the supposed robots turned and saw they were being observed. Whatever their original intention was, they abandoned it and hurriedly re-entered the UFO. The disc quickly took off and disappeared.

After an investigation, an Argentine Air Force officer said he had confirmed that a UFO had landed—the ground was scorched in an eighteen-foot circle where it had touched down. He also confirmed that the witnesses had been frightened by two strange figures which moved like automatons.

In several reports similar mechanical-looking figures have been described. Most of these encounter claims appear to have been hoaxes, but robots cannot be ruled out. Before long, NASA will have some remarkable exploration robots, and an advanced space race could already be using such devices.

However, there is another, more disturbing possibility. If any of the robot reports was correct, witnesses may have seen a special breed of space explorers, similar to the fearsome "Cyborg" which NASA is considering for long voyages.

Cyborg (cybernetic organism) is the goal of a program under NASA contract. Using chemical "mind changers" and surgery, some future astronauts would be transformed into semi-robots. But this fantastic plan is strongly opposed by some medical men and scientists, among them Dr. Toby Freedman of North American Aviation.

"This surgical tempering," says Dr. Freedman, "would produce a weird being who accomplishes his space mission by trading most of his physiological systems for electronic ones, whose mouth is sealed, lungs collapsed, body wastes recycled through himself, neural pathways partly severed and all his emotional feelings dissected out. He would be so fantastically changed he could never rejoin the human race."

Such "closed-cycle" astronauts would be a mating of man with machine. Artificial units would replace their hearts and most other main organs. They would need no food or water —they would have built-in energy suppliers. Eventually even their brains might be replaced.

Cyborg, the emotionless semi-robot, would be used on long journeys which could break down a normal astronaut. There is no question that it can be done—by us or an alien race. Aliens may even have surpassed Cyborg with some biological-mechanical horror. If some of these semi-robots landed on Earth they would not only cause alarm but they would probably be taken for typical specimens of their race —which could be humanoid. In the same way, our Cyborgs could terrify human-like beings on another planet.

In place of Cyborg, Dr. Freedman and his associates have suggested "Optiman," a superman created by a speed-up of his functions.

"His outward appearance would be normal," Dr. Freedman explains. "But he has been adapted to the oxygen requirements of a Himalayan Sherpa and the heat resistance of a walker-on-coals. He needs less food than a hermit, has the strength of Sonny Liston, and runs the mile in three minutes while solving problems of sensor analysis in his head."

But even Optiman could create a false, though not fearful picture of Earth's inhabitants.

Some people may see no need for Cyborgs or the Optiman, because of a belief that man is tops in evolution, or that he was created in God's image and represents the highest level of life. As a result, an upright figure, two arms, two legs, and other standard equipment of *Homo sapiens* are often pictured as the ultimate in development, along with two eyes for binocular vision, two ears for binaural hearing, the efficient arrangement of fingers and thumbs, and the extensive range of the human mind and imagination.

Some people, including respected scientists, insist that aliens could never approach our supposed high stage of development. The late Dr. Willy Ley, well-known writer on space subjects, set off a small storm with a published statement that spacemen will look "just like the man next door."

Scientists almost unanimously rejected the possibility that all space explorers would be human-like. Since then an increasing number have not only agreed that beings on millions of planets probably resemble us but that eventually we may meet members of some of these races. However, other scientists who have studied the problem of extraterrestrial life believe the odds are against such meetings.

One of the recognized authorities on space problems is Professor Zdenek Kopal, a U.S. citizen born in Czechoslovakia. Professor Kopal was a Research Associate at Harvard University from 1940 to 1946, an Associate Professor at the Massachusetts Institute of Technology from 1947 to 1951, and since then Professor of Astronomy at the University of Manchester, England. In the past ten years he has been a member of the Lunar-Planetary Committee of the U.S. National Space Board, playing an important role in the preparations for lunar landings.

Like Shapley, Melvin Calvin and other noted scientists,

Dr. Kopal fully agrees that there must be a great number of inhabited planets. In a recent book, *Man and His Universe*, he discusses this and other fascinating aspects of space exploration and the question of other-world life.[1] Dr. Kopal makes it clear, however, that even if there are many worlds at our stage of development we may never meet beings from such civilizations.

"In our Galaxy," he writes, "we might find a cross-section of planetary life at all stages of evolution—from hundreds of millions of years behind our level to hundreds of millions of years ahead of us. A thousand, or ten thousand, years of evolutionary difference is just nothing on a cosmic scale."

It is unlikely, says Dr. Kopal, that we would encounter a similar civilization, one with which we could develop intellectual understanding. Since we would gain little from a far-advanced civilization—or from one far behind us—there would be no reason to attempt a meeting.

But what if we were to be visited by extraterrestrial beings intelligent enough to have discovered our existence?

"The chances are overwhelming," Dr. Kopal answers, "that we might find ourselves in their test tubes or other contraptions set up to investigate us as we do insects or guinea-pigs. Perhaps they would ignore us altogether; but if so, why would they have made the long journey through space to visit us?"

Like Hibbs, Gold and other reputable scientists, Dr. Kopal emphasizes the possible danger in encountering a superior race.

"It has been amply demonstrated that an impact of a more advanced civilization upon a less developed one brings peril rather than advantage to the weaker partner. Human history is replete with examples of the brutality of such encounters —not the least being the European colonization of America and of other parts of the world during the 16th to 19th centuries."

Dr. Kopal and the other scientists are extremely serious in

[1] William Morrow & Co., Inc., 1972.

their warnings because they are convinced we could be in grave danger. But there is certain important information they may now know—strong evidence that technically superior beings once visited our planet without harming any of Earth's inhabitants.

Actually there are three segments of this remarkable evidence, all indicating that aliens visited and explored our world long ago. My knowledge of the first segment came through the Office of Naval Research, in a confidential discussion with a Navy captain and a commander. Since that time the detailed record has been confirmed by the Navy Hydrographic Office.

In the early part of the sixteenth century a Turkish naval officer, Admiral Piri Reis, acquired a map used by Christopher Columbus in his 1492 voyage to America. In 1513, the admiral created a world chart based on the Columbus map and Greek maps which dated back to the time of Alexander the Great.

Evidently the significance of the Columbus map was not generally realized; after the admiral's death it was almost forgotten. In 1933, a Turkish naval officer, puzzled by certain aspects of the Piri Reis world chart, submitted a copy and also a copy of the Columbus map to the U. S. Navy Hydrographic Office. To get an expert opinion, the chief engineer had the maps examined by a retired sea captain, A. H. Mallery, an authority on old charts who had previously aided the Hydrographic Office.

Captain Mallery, realizing the importance of the discovery, urged the Navy to make a full evaluation. After a long study and technical tests, Hydrographic Office engineers, assisted by Mallery, reached these startling conclusions:

On the voyage to America, Columbus had a map showing parts of the South American coast, including the Antarctic. The original map went back at least 5,000 years, possibly much farther. To produce such amazingly accurate charts would have required an aerial survey and highly skilled cartographers.

Some of the coasts shown on the Piri Reis map had been buried under ice for centuries. To verify the coastlines the Navy secured the aid of an expert on seismic soundings—Reverend Daniel Linehan, Director of Weston Observatory, Boston College. After extensive soundings down through the deep ice, the seismologist found that the coastlines were identical with those shown on the Piri Reis map. This proved the original map was made more than twenty centuries before, when the land was not covered by ice.

Later, the Piri Reis map was compared with photographs taken from NASA satellites. Both showed the identical effect from the curvature of the Earth, distortion of the areas farthest from the center.

Only one explanation was possible. The ancient chart on which the Piri Reis map was based had been made with photographs taken at a very high altitude, approximately that of the satellite. Either the aerial survey had been made from an alien spaceship, or from a spacecraft built by some advanced Earth civilization which later vanished without a trace.

While discussing the Piri Reis map with the two Naval Research officers, I brought up the question of a lost Earth civilization.

"It's just impossible," said the captain. "Even our best aircraft today couldn't get anywhere near that altitude. So they would have to have had at least a start in space operations. To build and maintain even small spacecraft or satellites would take a huge industry. Also they'd have other industries, like ours today. But we've never found a sign of such factories, fuel plants or laboratories—modern industrial equipment simply never existed."

Under these circumstances an alien spacecraft survey appears to be the only realistic answer.

The second segment of evidence is contained in the Air Force Academy analysis of UFOs, drawn up in 1968. Though ancient legends are the foundation for the AF discussion, the analysts had sound reasons for examining this material. There is a curious similarity in the so-called legends, though the countries where they originated—in Europe and Asia—had little or no contact with each other.

The Academy evaluation points out that in those ancient times the observers were unprepared to describe accurately any technical developments:

"Not only were the ancient observers lacking the terminology necessary to describe complex devices (such as present-day helicopters) but they were also lacking the concepts necessary to understand the true nature of such things as television, spaceships, rockets, nuclear weapons and radiation effects. To some the most advanced technological concept was a war chariot with knife blades attached to the wheels."

After this comment on possible misinterpretations, the AF Academy analysis continues:

"Nevertheless, let us start with an intriguing story in one of the oldest chronicles of India . . . the Book of Dzyan . . . legends which were finally gathered in manuscript form when man learned to write.

"One of the stories is of a small group of beings who supposedly came to Earth many thousands of years ago in a metal craft which orbited Earth several times before landing. As told in the Book, " 'These beings lived to themselves and were revered by the humans among whom they had settled. But eventually differences arose among them and they divided their numbers, several of the men and women and some children settling in another city, where they were promptly installed as rulers by the awe-stricken populace.

" 'Separation did not bring peace to these people and finally their anger reached a point where the ruler of the original city took with him a small number of his warriors and they rose into the air in a huge shining metal vessel. While they were many leagues from the city of their enemies, they launched a great shining lance that rode on a beam of light. It burst apart in the city of their enemies with a great ball of flame that shot up to the heavens, almost to the stars. All those who were in the city were horribly burned and even those who were not in the city—but nearby—were burned also. Those who looked upon the lance and the ball of fire were blinded forever afterward. Those who entered the city on foot became ill and died. Even the dust of the city was poisoned, as were the rivers that flowed through it. Men dared not go near it, and it gradually crumbled into dust and was forgotten by men.

" 'When the leader saw what he had done to his own people he retired to his palace and refused to see anyone. Then he gathered about him those of his warriors who remained, and their wives and children, and they entered into their vessels and rose into the sky and sailed away. Nor did they return.' "

"Could this foregoing legend really be an account of an extraterrestrial colonization, complete with guided missile, nuclear warhead and radiation effects? It is difficult to assess the validity of that explanation . . . just as it is difficult to explain why Greek, Roman and Nordic mythology all discuss wars and conflicts among their "Gods." . . . Could it be that each group reported their parochial view of what was actually a global conflict among alien colonists or visitors?"

Several scientists, including Thomas Gold and Carl Sagan, believe Earth was visited in ancient times. Dr. Sagan says our planet may have been visited 10,000 times during its long existence. Others scoff at the suggestion and dismiss the "legends" as storyteller nonsense, in spite of the strange similarity in various countries.

But there is more than legends in the AF Academy report to support the belief in early space visitors. This is the third segment of evidence—evidence with a solid foundation impossible to explain away, as the Academy report proves:

"Evidence of perhaps an even earlier possible contact was uncovered by Tschi Pen Lao of the University of Peking. He discovered astonishing carvings in granite on a mountain in Hunan Province and on an island in Lake Tungting. These carvings have been evaluated as 47,000 years old, and they show people with large trunks (breathing apparatus?). . . . Eight thousand years ago, rocks were sculpted in the Tassili plateau of Sahara, depicting what appeared to be human beings but with strange round heads (helmets?)."

In several parts of the world there are similar carvings, also peculiar flat areas which from the air suggest launching and landing bases. One of these is in the Palpa Valley, near the ancient city of Nazca, Peru, where there is a level strip thirty-seven miles in length and one mile in width. The purpose has never been really explained.

Another possible space base is described in the conservative Washington *Star*, after a recent discovery in Asia, when a Soviet archeologist found a Stone Age drawing suggestive of a "cosmonaut."

"The figure," said the *Star*, "was carrying something resembling an air-tight helmet with antennae on its head and some sort of contraption for flight on its back.

"The Tessalit frescoes near the southern border of Algeria show exactly the same characteristics: big helmets, contraptions for flight, and antennae.

"Who were these figures? What were they doing with space flight or even its accoutrements, before our ancestors had the wheel?

"It is instructive to recall that roughly halfway between two sites is the Middle East locale of the earliest civilizations . . . There also are found the ziggurats, great stepped platforms, man-made mountains reared above the plain. Were they really launching pads? It is humiliating to think that, just as our history was beginning, the better kind of human got out of here while he could and took his knowledge with him.

"The alternative is no better. That all those ages ago, superior creatures from another part of the galaxy discovered our planet, explored it at widely scattered points, and reported back that the place wasn't worth a colony."

North of Damascus there is another curious construction which could have been used for spacecraft operations. It is called the terrace of Baalbek and it is built of huge stone blocks, some of them over sixty feet long, weighing about 2,000 tons apiece. There is no explanation as to how it was built.

Besides the suggested space-base areas there are enormous structures in Egypt and other countries which also defy explanation. Some, like the Great Pyramid, are made of very large stones which were quarried at a distance, smoothly shaped and dressed, and then somehow were transported to the building sites. In some cases they were raised to considerable heights and precisely fitted into place—all by manual labor, according to some archeologists. The Great Pyramid, for example, is almost 500 feet high, yet the heavy blocks of stone are supposed to have been pushed up ramps by Egyptian workers without any mechanical aid. In some of the strange ancient structures, walls and terraces the stone blocks are gigantic, weighing over a hundred tons, and these too are supposed to have been quarried and put into place solely by manual labor. The archeologists' explanation is incredible; even with today's modern construction equipment it would be difficult to duplicate such colossal buildings and stone platforms.

The preceding three segments of evidence should be considered separately, though they may be connected.

The Piri Reis map stands out as proof that Earth was surveyed from a spacecraft thousands of years ago.

The AF Academy report makes several important points besides discussing possible space visitors. Some of these have been presented in earlier chapters. In addition, the report contains a strong warning for scientists who claim UFOs cannot be spacecraft because their reported speeds and maneuvers violate our laws of physics.

"We should not deny the possibility of alien control of UFOs on the basis of preconceived notions not established as related or relevant to the UFOs." (Air Force italics.)

The discussion of the *Book of Dzyan* legend may have a special value. It was implied that the supposed space visitors were like humans in form; there was no indication of any disturbing difference. The Academy analysts make no attempt to link the possible visitors with the UFO aliens. But if this account is based on an actual landing, then at least once members of an advanced human-like race visited our planet. If it happened once then conceivably it could happen again. We have no way of knowing whether space explorers—or some of them—would try to seek out their own kind. But if the *Book of Dzyan* legend is true, such a meeting is not completely impossible.

The mysterious buildings, monuments and ruins dating back to ancient times are not proof of early space visitors. But this answer should not be carelessly rejected—so far, no other explanation stands up under a genuine technical analysis.

Besides the ancient legend reports, the Academy evaluation cites evidence in more recent centuries.

"Many documented sightings occurred throughout the Middle Ages," the report states. "In Lyons, France, three men and a woman supposedly descended from an airship or spaceship and were captured by a mob and killed." From the phrase "three men and a woman" the analysts evidently had reason to believe the supposed beings were closely similar to humans.

Many people naturally refuse to accept the early reports. But the Academy analysis contains official accounts of UFO operations during the present surveillance which cannot be disproved. The following case includes the reported sighting of two alien beings. Those who already know of this famous incident may find an added interest in the AF confirmation:

"We will examine one such case now. It is the Socorro, New Mexico, sighting made by Police Sergeant Lonnie Zamora. Sergeant Zamora was patrolling on 24 April 1964 when he saw a shiny object drift down into an area of gullies on the edge of town. He also heard a loud roaring noise which sounded as if an old dynamite shed located out that way had exploded. He immediately radioed police headquarters, and drove out toward the shed. Zamora was forced to stop about 150 yards away from a deep gully in which there appeared to be an over-turned car. He radioed that he was investigating a possible wreck, and then worked his car up onto the mesa and over toward the edge of the gully. He parked short, and when he walked the final few feet to the edge, he was amazed to see that it was not a car but instead was a weird eggshaped object about fifteen feet long, white in color, and resting on short, metal legs. Beside it, unaware of his presence were two humanoids dressed in silvery coveralls. They seemed to be working on a portion of the underside of the object. Zamora was still standing there, surprised, when they suddenly noticed him and dove out of sight around the object. Zamora also headed the other way, back toward his car. He glanced back at the object just as a bright blue flame shot down from the underside. Within seconds the eggshaped thing rose out of the gully with "an earsplitting roar." The object was out of sight over the nearby mountains almost immediately, and Sergeant Zamora was moving in the opposite direction almost as fast when he met Sergeant Sam Chavez who was responding to Zamora's earlier radio calls. Together they investigated the gully and found the bushes charred and still smoking where the blue flame had jetted down on them. About the charred area were four deep marks where the metal legs had been. Each mark was three and one-half inches deep, and was circular in shape. The sand in the gully was very hard-packed so no sign of the humanoids' footprints could be found. An official investigation was launched that same day, and all data supported the stories of Zamora and Chavez. . . ."

In an odd exception to AF debunking policy, headquarters later admitted that Sergeant Zamora had observed "an un-identified vehicle" as he reported. But the statement avoided any reference to the two humanoids. The official admission was signed by Maj. M. M. Jacks, a spokesman attached to the Office of the Secretary of the Air Force.

In another peculiar policy reversal, HQ accepted the report of a Kansas citizen named William Squyres, who sighted an oval-shaped UFO hovering close to the ground. According to the witness, vegetation was being blown around by the object's propulsion system. (This was verified afterward by the AF.) Squyres said he could see a human-like figure silhouetted by a bluish glow in the forward section of the machine, just before the UFO took off. This case was listed in AF Special Project Report 14.

A few other witnesses of good repute have reported seeing humanoid beings near landed UFOs or inside machines maneuvering slowly at low altitudes. In one case investigated by the chairman of NICAP's North Dakota subcommittee, witnesses at separate locations described human-like figures inside a lighted UFO. In night sightings, or where the sup-posed beings are not close enough for definite details, there is always a chance of error even though the witnesses are known to be reliable. Some of these reports might prove to be correct, but the evidence so far is not conclusive. However, such reports should not be classed with the mass of wild tales and usually ridiculous "contactee" claims.

The most notorious "contactee" was the late George Adamski, who reported meeting golden-haired, godlike beings in the desert, flying in UFOs—and meeting one spaceman friend at a favorite restaurant, where the alien especially enjoyed hamburgers and apple pie. A woman at Silver Spring, Maryland, broadcast a story about spacemen who frequently landed near her home and dropped in for break- fast. Contactee Sid Patrick told newsmen he had had a long talk with a spaceman named Ziena, who was dressed in a very conservative blue suit and who spoke excellent English. On his planet, said Ziena, there was no sickness, no police, no vice, no schools. "We live together as one—and we have very strict birth control."

Another of these contact people was a man who called himself Mel Noel. On frequent trips to Mars, he reported, he met many of the 80 million inhabitants—delightful people over six feet tall, with platinum skin and pink hair. He was selected, he said, to help arrange round trips for State De- partment and military officials who would assist in preparing the U.S. public. (I was told I was on the list, but something must have slipped up.)

The reason I am telling you some of these tales is to help you weed out the bizarre stories and see the facts. Many of the press unfortunately lump all "spaceman" reports together, causing many people to reject all of the UFO evidence. This is not hard to understand when you consider some of the crazy concoctions:

The report of a zebra-striped being who could change color like a chameleon . . . the claim that an alien has been kept in an incubator several years, while linguists teach him Eng- lish . . . the story of a huge being who always wore rubbers and spoke Latin. . . .

Most of this nonsense is harmless, aside from misleading some of the public. But a few of these reports are potentially dangerous, like the story of the twelve-foot being with six arms and hypnotic eyes which instantly paralyzed humans. In South America, there have been reports of attacks and kidnap attempts by bearlike hairy dwarves. At the time, these had serious effects on some of the local population.

In the United States, during the sixties, there was a nationally publicized story of a supposed abduction by UFO beings. This was the famous case involving Betty and Barney Hill, a dramatic example of how fear of UFOs, under certain circumstances, can almost get out of control.

Five years before the case became widely known Mrs. Hill wrote me at NICAP. After reading her strange letter I arranged for a confidential investigation. But before giving you the details I shall quote the AF Academy's brief summary of the Hills' disturbing experience:

"On a trip through New England they lost two hours on the night of 19 September 1961 without even realizing it. However, after that night both Barney and Betty began developing psychological problems which eventually grew sufficiently severe that they submitted themselves to psychiatric examination and treatment. During the course of treatment hypnotherapy was used, and it yielded remarkably detailed and similar stories from both Barney and Betty. Essentially they had been hypnotically kidnapped, taken aboard a UFO, submitted to two-hour physicals, and released with posthypnotic suggestions to forget the entire incident. The evidence is rather strong that this is what the Hills, even in their subconscious, believe happened to them. And it is of particular importance that after the "posthypnotic block" was removed, both of the Hills ceased having their psychological problems."

The Hills' description of the aliens was similar to descriptions provided in other cases.

Though the Academy summary is basically correct, the hypnotherapy did not end the Hills' sometimes frightening problems.

When Mrs. Hill wrote me, on September 25, 1961, neither she nor her husband had any conscious knowledge of what might have happened during the two lost hours. But both remembered that a UFO had descended toward the highway, and something about it had caused them to speed away from the scene. When they arrived at their home, in Portsmouth, New Hampshire, their recollections were blurred, but on the following nights Betty Hill began to have disturbing dreams, apparently linked with whatever had happened during the lost hours.

Neither Mrs. Hill nor her husband desired any publicity, but it was plain that Mrs. Hill hoped for advice from NICAP. Since this did not sound like the usual contactee hoax I arranged for a check by special adviser Walter Webb, a lecturer on astronomy at the Hayden Planetarium in Boston. Webb found that the Hills had a good reputation, and he was convinced they had had a close encounter with a UFO, which somehow was causing increased fears and nervous tension.

Interviews by Webb and two engineers who were aiding NICAP led to consultations with a local doctor who recommended examinations by Dr. Benjamin Simon, well-known Boston neurologist and psychiatrist. Using hypnosis, Dr. Simon began to delve into the Hills' apparent simultaneous amnesia. Little by little, a weird story began to emerge—a sometimes terrifying story which the Hills evidently believed to be true. Though Dr. Simon felt that some strange psychological reactions were back of the story, he agreed with Webb's opinion that the Hills had had an experience with some unusual aerial phenomenon—something powerful enough to cause their intense emotional buildup. Here is the summary of the Hills' story, as told to Walter Webb and as brought out in the hypnotic sessions during which Dr. Simon taped his questions and the answers by Betty and Barney.

On the night of September 19, 1961, the Hills were returning from a vacation in Canada. Around 11 P.M. they were on U.S. Route 3, heading for Portsmouth, when they saw a large, bright object descending. After a few minutes they could see it was some kind of craft with flashing lights. As it came down toward them Barney stopped the car, took his binoculars and walked into a field for a better view. By this time he could tell that the approaching machine was round and larger than a jet airliner. It had two rows of lighted windows, and when he focused the binoculars on them he had a shock. Figures in black uniforms were staring down at him, creatures with strange eyes.

By now the big disc was only a hundred feet from the ground. Fear that he and Betty were about to be captured suddenly hit Barney. In a panic, he ran to the car and sent it racing down the deserted highway. Some minutes after this the Hills heard an odd beeping sound, as if something were pelting the lid of the trunk. Then they both began to feel numb and drowsy. Apparently their conscious minds blacked out; the details of this period were not clear. But under repeated hypnosis they recalled that the car was stopped and that several of the black-uniformed beings were surrounding them.

The aliens' bodies were humanoid, but their faces were frightening. Their heads were oddly shaped, with only holes for ears. Adding to their ugly appearance, their mouths and noses were compressed so they hardly showed from the side. But the worst feature was their long slanting eyes, which extended around to the sides of their faces, giving them a sinister look.

During the hypnotic sessions, both Betty and Barney said their captors had told them they would not be harmed. But it was obvious that they had been terrified at least part of the time. Whenever Dr. Simon started to discuss the supposed beings both of the Hills showed sudden fear and tension.

In their taped answers, Betty and Barney described being taken aboard the disc-shaped craft and then having to submit to long physical examinations. Even though the space beings did not mistreat them it was a severe ordeal. After the examinations they were taken down to the highway and released, with post-hypnotic suggestions that they would not remember what had happened.

Before the meetings with Dr. Simon were over part of the story leaked out and was published in a Boston newspaper. Unfortunately, this triggered a wave of fake abduction stories. The psychiatrist and the Hills had been avoiding publicity, but they decided the full story should be made public to correct wrong impressions. A well-known journalist, John Fuller, had learned about the case in a confidential talk at NICAP. It was arranged that he should prepare the record, using Dr. Simon's taped questions and the Hills' answers.

Fuller's book, *The Interrupted Journey*,[2] was syndicated in many newspapers and it received a surprising amount of serious attention, compared with the usual treatment of "contactee" stories. Dr. Simon's conclusions were made quite clear. The Hills, he said, actually believed this had been a true experience, but in his opinion the supposed abduction was a psychological reaction to an encounter with some unknown aerial activity or phenomenon.

Despite this, an unexpected number of people believed that the abduction report was true—or at least that it could have happened.

For a time, the hypnotherapy treatments seemed to have reduced the Hills' emotional tensions. But for Barney the effect apparently was too strong, for the pressure gradually increased. In February of 1969 he died of a cerebral hemorrhage. Though probably there were other factors, reliving what he believed a real experience was at least partly the cause of his death at forty-six.

One phase of the Hills' reports is still a puzzle. After questioning by Dr. Simon, Betty and Barney separately drew sketches of one of the space creatures, while they were under hypnosis. According to Dr. Simon's conclusions (which I personally consider correct) these sketches were imaginary pictures created by their subconscious minds. When the Hills

[2] Dial Press, Inc., 1966.

were shown the sketches, after coming out of the hypnotic state, they both were upset by the repulsive faces they had drawn.

In 1968, artist David Baker interviewed the Hills at length and later drew several other sketches, after Dr. Simon had placed Barney under hypnosis so he could be questioned again about the supposed aliens. These sketches show actually hideous faces, and again both the Hills were emotionally disturbed when they saw them. What caused the subconscious minds of these two people to create these pictures from their imaginations has never been fully explained. One thing is certain. If any such creatures ever landed on Earth they would frighten most humans, regardless of their intentions.

In the search for possible clues to the UFO aliens' appearance, some scientists views have been examined. A few of their ideas are as eerie as wild hoax reports. Dr. Carl Sagan suggests we might encounter a space creature with a "radar eyeball"—an evolutionary development enabling him to see through his planet's foglike atmosphere. Other speculations include beings with four arms or four legs, or both. Dr. Herman Muller believes that space beings' organs and appendages may be so different they will startle us—and ours may dismay them.

"Aliens might be amazed," he says, "at the arrangement of our sensory and other organs—they would be so different or varied."

Dr. Richard S. Young, NASA exobiologist, has listed seven phases of evolution we may discover. Among them are primitive life, intelligent life, life chemically different from ours, and life with slightly different metabolisms, energy systems and physical compounds. Following through on this, some scientists think we may meet beings with whom we could never exchange information because they communicate only by telepathy.

Besides aliens' possible physical appearance, scientists have speculated on disturbing motives we might find behind operations by advanced beings. Dr. Freeman Dyson of Princeton's Institute for Advanced Study says we should be on guard against unpleasant surprises: we could discover beings with wisdom and serenity—or a race with murderous impulses. Prof. Jeremy Bernstein of the Stevens Institute of Technology says it is naïve to expect that extraterrestrial life will be benign. Using our world as an example, he states: "The more technological our own civilization becomes, in many ways the worse it becomes . . . one could imagine terrible civilizations with a very high degree of technology."

The guesswork and speculation are almost endless. But what it all adds up to is ignorance about space beings— dangerous ignorance when it concerns the UFO aliens.

In contrast, the UFO beings must have amassed a tremendous amount of information about humans during their long surveillance. At the 1965 military conference on communicating with extraterrestrials, several of the panel scientists discussed this probability.[3] Dr. William O. Davis, former AF physicist who had been involved in the UFO problem, was convinced space visitors would learn our languages before taking steps toward actual contact. By now the aliens must know what we look like, through television and radio programs, and also how we react to many different situations. How they interpret this we have no idea—they could be badly misled about our world.

In 1963 the Space Science Board emphasized the great impact which finding other-world life will have on all of us. "The discovery of life on other planets will have an enormous and lasting effect on people of every race and culture," said the Board. It also stressed that finding other intelligent life should be our main goal.

In the years since then there has been only one tiny official step even remotely connected with space-being communications. This is the Navy attempt to reach an

[3] Details in Chapter 4.

understanding with dolphins, a program headed by Dr. John C. Lilly. The Navy has even placed a dolphin in school, to bring it up in association with young children. This is not meant as ridicule. The project is a serious one, and Dr. Lilly has already achieved some success. This has a special importance, according to the scientist. Learning how to communicate with dolphins might help us in contacts with space beings. But, even if this should later prove true, it is of no help now.

We urgently need a full-scale communication program, to learn the facts and to correct our grave mistakes and blunders. But the opposition by Hibbs, Gold, Kopal and other respected scientists is still a powerful influence against such an attempt. One of the strongest recent warnings came from Dr. Kopal, in *Man and His Universe*:

The risks entailed in an encounter with another civilization would vastly exceed any possible interest—let alone benefit, and could easily prove fatal. Therefore, should we ever hear that "space-phone" ringing in the form of observational evidence which admits no other explanation, for God's sake let us not answer, but rather make ourselves as inconspicuous as we can to avoid attracting attention!

But it is already too late. Beings from a more advanced world are here now. It is impossible to hide from them.

There is only one sensible course left—to launch a careful but practical program to learn all we can about the UFO aliens and then to attempt communication and contact.

The special plan already mentioned, which avoids radio and television transmissions in the first phase, has been carefully prepared to overcome the main objections. Until it is approved as an official project I shall call it by a name which seems to fit it best:

OPERATION LURE.

In the fall of 1968 the basic Operation Lure plan was far enough advanced for a confidential discussion with members of Congress who opposed the UFO secrecy. In this critical election year, however, there was little chance of putting it over. Most legislators would naturally avoid such a controversial subject. It seemed wisest to wait until the election excitement was over and the new Congress had settled down, and then to start mustering the strongest possible support.

But at the end of October the situation suddenly changed, offering the chance of an even earlier breakthrough.

For over two months, the AF had been worried by a developing situation which could end the UFO cover-up. To combat this potential danger it had worked out a plan involving the Colorado Project. Unexpectedly, this AF scheme backfired. For several weeks, control of the censorship was seriously endangered.

If the story had become known to the press it would have been front-page news. It could have killed the Condon report.

14

Burial
Attempt

The key figure in this Air Force dilemma was none other than Richard M. Nixon, the Republican nominee for President. But the basic problem back of this AF predicament had begun long before.

For years, there had been ill feeling between Nixon and Condon. When Nixon was a member of the House Committee on Un-American Activities, Condon had appeared for questioning. During the session there had been sharp exchanges between the two men. Later, when the scientist's security clearance was challenged, it was obvious that he blamed Nixon. The bitterness between them had never ended.

By 1968, not many people remembered this, but the AF had not forgotten. If Nixon were elected, legislators who had proof of the official secrecy—among them McCormack, Karth and Goldwater—might tell him the inside story. As Commander-in-Chief of the Armed Forces, he could order the Condon report held up until the project was thoroughly investigated.

Soon after Nixon's nomination the AF had put hard pressure on Colorado University to rush the report through, so it could be released before the election. But it was impossible to make the deadline.

The report was supposed to have been compiled by the

administrator, Robert J. Low, but he had been assigned other duties after *Look* published the so-called "trick" memorandum. His replacement had little knowledge of UFOs and even less about the project's work. Less than a hundred cases had been evaluated by CU investigators, out of almost 15,000 available reports. However, many of the analyses and discussions were lengthy, and there were also chapters on public opinion polls and other angles which swelled the size of the report though they had little to do with the actual investigations. The new editor had the formidable job of assembling this mass of unfamiliar material and completing the 1,500-page document in record time.

Early in October, Pentagon sources who were privately fighting UFO secrecy tipped me off to the speed-up. From then on they kept me informed of the developments, with factual details which since then have been fully verified.

On October 31, 1968, the huge CU Project Report was delivered to the Air Force, and headquarters officers began a hurried review.

In the opening sections, Dr. Condon denied that UFOs were anything but illusions, failure to recognize ordinary objects, and fabricated reports. Many witnesses, he declared, were inept, unduly excited or otherwise unreliable. He also denied any threat to national security, any defense problem and any evidence of AF secrecy. Since Condon's views as a UFO agnostic were fairly well known, these conclusions were no surprise to the AF officers. The reviewers also assumed that the project members shared Condon's beliefs. But when they got to the case analyses they had a shock.

Instead of solidly backing Condon, case after case showed strong evidence of UFO reality. In nearly 30 per cent, scientist-analysts conceded that the objects sighted could not be explained with ordinary answers. The high rating of the case witnesses was an added blow—most of the observers were astronauts, military and airline pilots, and other well-qualified specialists.

It was Case 2 which handed the AF men their first jolt.
The action had taken place near Lakenheath, England, involving a dramatic UFO chase which was tracked by USAF-
RAF radar control centers. Although this encounter had
occurred back in '56, the incident was still being kept under
wraps as unusually important evidence.

Under the AF-CU contract, headquarters had promised
not to withhold any information from the project, but CU
had not been given a hint of this case. The first lead was a
full report from a principal witness at one of the radar control
centers—a USAF sergeant, now retired, who had been a radar
traffic control specialist more than sixteen years. When the
project revealed its knowledge of the case, AF Project Blue
Book finally admitted the encounter, with a detailed account
which confirmed the sergeant's report.

About 10:30 P.M., August 13, 1956, an unknown lighted
object was observed from the tower of an RAF base. It was
also tracked by three Radar Air Traffic Control Centers. An
RAF Venom jet fighter was scrambled to intercept, and the
pilot closed in on the UFO, guided by RATCC's Station A.

Seconds later, the pilot radioed control that his guns were
locked on the object (by radar).

Instantly, the UFO whipped around behind the interceptor. The amazingly swift maneuver was confirmed by the
USAF sergeant, who had been watch supervisor at Station A
that night. He also described the pilot's frantic attempts to
shake off his pursuer.

Despite the pilot's hasty maneuvers, the UFO stayed close
behind him, matching every turn. At control, operators could
tell from his tense voice that he was badly frightened.

When the jet ran low on fuel another Venom was scrambled. The first pilot radioed a quick warning as the second
plane took off, admitting he was completely helpless against
the UFO.

The second jet was hardly airborne when it developed
trouble and was forced to land. An American T-33 pilot tried

an interception but the UFO raced out of the area. A minute later a C-47 pilot reported that the unknown craft had just streaked under his plane, and RAF tower operators had a blurred glimpse as the UFO went past. From the visual reports, it was estimated to be flying at more than 2,000 mph and possibly as high as 4,000.

In the CU Report, separate evaluations were made by two project scientists familiar with radar. Quoting from official logs, the first analyst stressed the UFO's amazing acceleration and high-speed turns. Three radar stations, he emphasized, had tracked the UFO simultaneously—proof that an unknown object was over the area. The CU analyst's final conclusion was enough to startle any Air Force reviewer:

It was highly probable that a genuine UFO was involved.

But the second scientist's conclusion hit even harder. Citing the report as the most unusual radar-visual case on record, with its evidence that the UFO was intelligently controlled, the analyst stated that a mechanical device—origin unknown—was the most probable answer.

Finding such conclusions in the CU Report was almost unbelievable—and this was only the beginning. One of the most powerful cases was Number 46. It was even more disturbing than Case 2, because of an incredible contradiction.

Although it was one of the earlier reports, it had given the AF unusual trouble, but after repeated debunking efforts HQ believed it had been forgotten. Discovering this case in the CU Report was an unpleasant surprise for the reviewers.

On the evening of May 11, 1950, a bright metallic UFO was sighted from a farm ten miles southwest of McMinnville, Oregon. The witnesses were Mr. and Mrs. Paul Trent, owners of the farm. (The CU investigators deleted names in most of the cases, but the Trents were already identified in public records.)

As the object slowly approached, Trent ran inside and got his camera. The UFO's domed superstructure was clearly visible when he took the first picture. A few seconds later the strange craft tilted slightly. Trent shot another picture before it speeded up and disappeared in the west.

As the investigating scientist confirmed, Trent did not seek publicity. At first he thought the UFO was some kind of secret U.S. machine, and he was afraid he would "get in trouble with the government." But after he showed the pictures to friends a McMinnville newspaper learned of the incident. Following a careful check of the negatives, the paper ran the photos, declaring them authentic. Shortly afterward, Los Angeles and Portland papers also published the pictures and key points of the story. Then *Life* analyzed the negatives and printed the photos as evidently genuine. (Details of the case became known to me at the time, and later to NICAP. In 1967, I urged Adminstrator Low of the CU Project to evaluate the report.)

During the investigation by the CU Project photographic expert, the scientist was impressed by the Trents' obvious sincerity, as he stated in his report.

Numerous McMinnville residents, including bankers, vouched for the Trents' integrity. However, to make a full evaluation, the CU expert carried out extensive tests, made possible by the clearness of the photographs. These included a complete photometric analysis, with sketches showing the geometry involved, the light intensity, measurements of background objects and other significant factors. Details of the analysis, with technical formulas, were included in the CU Report, enabling independent photographers to check every step.

In his summary the investigator said the photographs were consistent with the witnesses' testimony—there was no evidence of a hoax.

The most direct conclusion, said the analyst, was that the photographs confirm precisely what the Trents reported. The photographs, the CU expert added, indicated a bright, shiny object at a considerable distance from the witnesses.

The UFO's size, he stated, was on the order of tens of meters in diameter.

The term "tens of meters" means that the UFO's diameter was a minimum of two times ten meters, or 65.8 feet. Generally, the term has been interpreted to mean at least three to four times ten meters—giving a diameter between 98.6 and 131.2 feet. The UFO possibly was even larger.

In his final conclusion, the CU analyst came close to stating that the UFO was an alien spacecraft.

The geometric, psychological and physical factors, he said, appear consistent with the witnesses' report, indicating that the witnesses sighted a strange flying object, metallic, silver-colored and tens of meters in diameter.

By itself, this would have jarred the headquarters reviewers. But there was something else that made it much more damaging.

In Section II of the CU Report, Dr. Condon mentioned the McMinnville pictures, after asserting that the project had examined the UFO photographs with great care. Then came the incredible statement which stunned the AF men:

In this case, said Dr. Condon, the UFO images turned out to be too fuzzy, so that worthwhile photogrammetric evaluation was not possible.

To the AF reviewers, Dr. Condon's denial was even more dangerous than the analyst's conclusions. It would be almost a miracle if some newsmen did not spotlight this at a press conference and demand an explanation. And if Richard Nixon were elected they would be in a tighter spot than ever.

Until now, there had been a hope that he would be too busy after inauguration to look into the UFO situation. Also, the chance of ridicule by the opposition would logically deter him from any early checkup on the "flying saucers." But if this powerful evidence of UFO reality became public, along with Dr. Condon's denial of the detailed McMinnville analysis, he would have strong reason to act. Not only that, he probably would have bipartisan support from legislators who knew of the censorship.

The obvious way out was to delete the damaging conclusions and evidence. It would require Dr. Condon's approval, possibly that of the university heads. Trying this would be risky—the AF had promised there would be no interference with the CU study.

It seemed certain, however, that Condon had not known of the McMinnville analysis and conclusions or he never would have made such a denial. It also seemed likely he had not known of the Lakenheath "probable genuine UFO" conclusion.

The speed-up was evidently the answer. With all the rush to get the report out, it would be difficult for Condon to check everything in the huge manuscript.

But even if this was the explanation, it was hard to believe any of the scientists had taken advantage of the haste and confusion to insert these cases, hoping they would slip by without Dr. Condon's knowledge. Remembering how Saunders and Levine had been fired, after they let the Low memorandum become public, none of the investigators would have risked it.

If the AF reviewers had known the inside story of the project, the answer would have been clear. By the middle of 1967 several of the project members believed the alien spaceship hypothesis was the most probable explanation. In the October meeting at NICAP, Low had admitted a serious split in the project, and as Saunders later told me a near-majority of the scientists were planning a protest against the ignoring of strong UFO evidence.

While trying to solve the riddle the AF reviewers finally came close to the truth. The project members involved had sincerely believed their conclusions were correct and they had included these cases, intending to argue for their inclusion in the finished report. The Air Force analysts had good reason to believe Condon was unaware of many important cases.

Though he was named as a principal investigator in the AF contract and was considered Number One, he had never made a single field investigation. All the investigators' reports and analyses were turned in to Low, and, as some scientists often complained, they seldom had a chance to discuss the evidence with Condon. Including certain hot cases in the CU Report was their last opportunity to get his attention. While it was improbable that he would change his opinions, they would have a chance to argue for a minority report. (In Dr. Condon's December '67 letter to me he had stated he would not repress any scientists' contrary opinions, though he hoped there would be complete agreement.)

Whatever the explanation, the AF reviewers knew they were in a bad spot. Before deciding whether to send the report back to Boulder, they dug deeper into the voluminous document. The more they read the worse the problem became.

In Section III, Chapter 6, three unexplained astronaut sightings were analyzed by a principal investigator of the CU Project. Since this scientist earlier had worked closely with the astronaut program, his evaluations had special importance.

Two reports were made by Astronaut James McDivitt— sightings from *Gemini IV* as it orbited the Earth.

(The detailed McDivitt reports were in my files and at NICAP before the CU Project was even established. In 1967, we urged the project to investigate this evidence.)

On June 4, 1965, Astronaut McDivitt sighted a strange, cylindrical object from Gemini IV. He could see "two big arms sticking out" like antennae. The object appeared to be nearby and closing in, and at first McDivitt thought he might have to change course to avoid a collision. When he saw it was not coming dangerously close he took a still picture, then exposed several frames of black and white movie film. Later NASA released one photo showing an oval-shaped object with a faint trail. Attempts by NORAD to explain the unknown as a man-made space device, or a part of one, were ruled out.

The CU investigator made no attempt to explain away the UFO. In his evaluation he stated that McDivitt's description suggested a spacecraft with an antenna.

The second unknown sighted by McDivitt was too far away for details to be observed. The third sighting analyzed was reported by Astronaut Frank Borman, who described a "bogey" flying formation with his spacecraft, Gemini VII.

In the CU scientist's analysis he emphasized the astronauts' ability, their excellent eyesight, their careful, accurate observations which placed their reports at the highest level of credibility. The three unexplained sightings, he admitted, were a challenge to analysts.

In Case 11, a veteran Canadian airlines captain described how his DC-8 jet was paced for two minutes by some unknown craft. On the night of December 29, 1966, the Canadian Pacific airliner, Flight 421, was flying at 35,000 feet en route from Lima, Peru, to Mexico City. South of the equator an object with two white lights descended toward the plane, then leveled off at the jet's altitude.

"There appeared to be a solid shape between the two lights," reported Capt. Robert Millbank, a pilot with twenty-six years' experience. "There was also a strip of light . . . much like the cabin lights of an aircraft."

For two minutes the UFO held its position off the left wing, observed by all the crew of the DC-8. Then it dropped back, disappearing behind the airliner. (The details given to the CU Project duplicate an earlier report by Captain Millbank, relayed to NICAP.)

In an attempt to explain away the encounter the CU investigator suggested the UFO might have been only a Gemini booster fragment falling to Earth. But this far-fetched idea, that experienced pilots and crewmen had imagined all the rest, proved ridiculous in the light of the evidence. The UFO had been in sight for seven minutes. It had flown parallel to the DC-8, keeping the same altitude for two minutes. During this time it had been observed intently by all the crew and each man had seen the group of windowlike lights.

Though the investigator tried to bolster his far-out suggestion, his final evaluation showed a far different conclusion:

The apparent two-minute pacing, the analyst admitted, was a puzzle. Besides this, he said, Captain Millbank's sketch of the UFO suggested some kind of craft. Quoting the captain's belief that the object was a craft with speed and maneuverability beyond our knowledge, the investigator agreed that the evidence added up to the intriguing possibility of an intelligently controlled device.

Another surprising admission, by a different CU investigator, appeared in Section III, Chapter 1.

Some cases, he said, involve such unusual testimony that if it is taken at face value there could be only one explanation—some kind of strange vehicles were present. As an example he cited Case 6 in the CU Report, which had been previously investigated by NICAP.

The Case 6 incident was a frighteningly close encounter with a UFO. One evening in the spring of '66 several lights reported as UFOs were sighted over a high school at Beverly, Massachusetts. Three women watching near the school saw one object descending toward them. It was disc-shaped, the color of dull aluminum, and about the size of a large car. The witnesses could see a bright light on top.

As the UFO came down above them two of the women, terrified, ran to get out from under the unknown machine. The other woman, almost paralyzed with fear, did not move. When her companions looked back the disc was less than thirty feet above her. She was standing with her hands clamped over her head—later she said she thought the object was going to crush her.

The UFO stopped about twenty-five feet above the ground. Then it tilted slightly and climbed up over the high school.

The three women ran to their nearby homes and called their neighbors. Several came out into the street, joined by police. In the excitement, some of the watchers mistook bright stars for UFOs, after the flying disc vanished. This was established in a NICAP investigation, and the senior scientist of the CU team which later checked the case agreed with this conclusion. Like NICAP, he also put the three women's report in a separate category, treating it seriously.

In his detailed analysis he admitted he could find no ordinary answer.

The evidence in this case obviously impressed the senior investigator. In another part of the CU Report he added this significant comment:

The 1966 incident at Beverly, Massachusetts, could be explained only by the alien-vehicle hypothesis if the witnesses' testimony is accepted at face value.

Publicizing any "scare" case had always worried the AF, and this one could cause extra trouble if it remained in the CU Report. The senior investigator's repeated references to strange alien vehicles could double the fear effect.

In between the disturbing reports were some cases listed as explained. A few were practically duplicates of earlier AF debunking answers; others appeared to be correct. But these were small comfort to the reviewers—the "hot" unexplained cases stood out in sharp contrast.

One report startled the AF men because they thought it was still under cover—Case 21, Section III, Chapter 5.

On the night of May 13, 1967, a UFO was tracked by radar as it approached the airport at Colorado Springs. Since NORAD Headquarters is in this area, any unidentified aircraft or UFO gets quick attention. If advisable, AF interceptors are scrambled for a swift check on the "unknown."

Though there were intermittent rain and snow showers, there was still fair visibility. But the UFO remained invisible, even when strong "blips" on the radarscopes showed some solid craft nearing the airport. The blips were not "ghost echoes"—the operators were experts and they knew they were tracking something real. The flight characteristics were those of an F-100 or F-104 jet interceptor.

The airport tower operators were still vainly trying to see the mysterious UFO when a Braniff airliner landed. Almost instantly the unseen craft pulled to the right, tracked by the tower.

As shown by radar, the UFO flew over the airport at about 200 feet. This is the normal procedure for an aircraft overtaking another one, or if the pilot is practicing an instrument landing approach without actually touching down. According to the radar track, the UFO came within $1\frac{1}{2}$ miles of the control tower, but the tower operators could not see it, even with binoculars.

To the CU radar expert who investigated, this was the most baffling radar case on record. He admitted he could find no explanation.

But for the Air Force it was far more than puzzling. Their own radar experts had reached the same conclusion. Some unknown high-speed craft had maneuvered over the airport —absolutely unseen. Could the technically advanced UFO aliens have devised a means for making their spacecraft invisible? It seemed fantastic, but what other answer was there? If it were true, they could be in serious trouble in case of UFO attacks. Even though jet fighters could be "locked on" to targets by their radar, and their guns or airborne missiles could be operated automatically, fighting an unseen enemy could be highly difficult and unnerving. While the CU analyst did not spell this out, some alert newsman might realize the possibility and tie it to this CU conclusion.

There were several other unexplained recent cases in the CU Report—less serious but potentially important:

Case 8. In the summer of '66, a responsible federal official witnessed a touch landing on a hillside between Minot, North Dakota, and the Canadian border. At one moment the UFO was only 200 feet from his car, affecting the electrical system. It was daylight, and he could clearly see the device—a round, metallic craft with a domed top. Several rocks were displaced by the UFO's landing and takeoff. The report was investigated by both the AF and CU, and the sighting could not be explained.

Two unsolved reports involved EM interference—which Dr. Condon had brushed off in his opening sections. One incident, Case 10, was reported by a nuclear physicist—the sighting of a UFO with a brilliant glow, which he suggested might be linked with nuclear energy.

Just after the AF reviewers finished with the 1966 to mid-1968 cases, one of my Pentagon sources brought me up to date. Since Dr. Condon had indicated that early reports were practically worthless, the headquarters officers had expected all the years from 1947 to 1966 to be a blank in the CU Report. It was true that a huge number of important cases were buried, but several hidden reports somehow had been included in the project compilation.

The most powerful case in this group concerned a dramatic encounter by a Strategic Air Command jet bomber crew. As in the Lakenheath case, the CU Project learned of it by accident. During a conference of AF base officers at Boulder, a colonel revealed that he had had a puzzling UFO experience in the fall of 1957. Attempting to follow up this lead, the project tried to obtain the AF records. When AF Project Blue Book denied it had the report, CU investigators tried the headquarters of NORAD, the Aerospace Defense Command and the Strategic Air Command. All three told the project no such case was on record. Instead of giving up, a senior CU investigator secured the details from the former SAC pilot, who was then a major, the co-pilot, and a third officer in the crew—a radar specialist. All three remained deeply impressed by the experience, and in spite of the time lapse they recalled the main details.

In the early morning of September 19, 1957, the B-47 was returning to its SAC base in Texas, after a training flight. Over the Dallas-Fort Worth area, the major (I'll call him "G") and the co-pilot sighted a white light ahead. The pilot warned his crew to be ready if he had to take sudden evasion. But the UFO shot in front of the plane, faster than any known aircraft, before he could turn. To Major G the object appeared "as big as a barn."

Shortly after this, the UFO was again sighted ahead of the bomber, this time visible as a huge red glow. The pilot went to full power and flew over the unknown craft. The UFO swiftly disappeared, but as the B-47 turned back it reappeared below the plane. With permission from Ground Control, Major G dived at the "target." Before he could close in on it the UFO again swiftly disappeared, visually and from the radarscopes. As the B-47 was low on fuel, the pilot abandoned the chase.

The importance of this case is indicated by the senior investigator's two separate discussions, in Section III, Chapter 1, and in Case 5, Section IV, Chapter 1.

Stressing that the pilots and crew were highly trained observers, who had never before seen anything like the UFO, the analyst admitted he could find no ordinary answer.

Another early encounter, strong evidence of UFO reality, was listed as unidentified in Case 1482-N. During a night flight on June 23, 1955, the pilots of a Mohawk Airlines plane saw a UFO with lighted windows race overhead. The strange craft, only 500 feet above them, was elliptical in shape, about 150 feet long. After it sped out of sight it was observed briefly by two Colonial Airlines pilots and another aircraft crew.

The UFO also was seen by control tower operators at Albany Airport, as it was speeding along Victor 2 Airway. It was tracked, minutes later, still on Victor 2 Airway, by radar at Boston. From the recorded times after the Mohawk sighting, the speed was computed as between 4,000 and 4,800 mph.

This intriguing case, stated the CU investigator, could not

be explained by any ordinary answer. He strongly recommended that it be given further examination.

(In Dr. Condon's opening sections, he had ruled out further UFO studies as unjustified.)

Like several other cases in the CU Report, the Mohawk Airlines incident had been reported to NICAP by one of the pilots, before the CU Project examined the evidence.

Another such report was given to me, long before the CU Project checkup, by Capt. W. J. Hull, Capital Airlines, whom I knew personally. On November 14, 1956, Captain Hull and his co-pilot sighted a rapidly maneuvering UFO about sixty miles from Mobile. For several minutes the pilots watched the strange machine execute chandelles, abrupt stops and "lazy eights." Then the UFO disappeared at fantastic speed. A second encounter over Chesapeake Bay, on August 30, 1957, also was reported to me by Captain Hull. In CU Report 14-N, an analyst admitted the two sightings could not be explained and listed them as unknowns.

When the AF reviewers came to Case 47 the conclusion had a sharp effect—the CU analyst had rejected the AF answer. This was the famous Great Falls, Montana, case involving motion-picture photographs of two UFOs, taken by the manager of a baseball team. The two gleaming objects had been explained as reflections from two AF jets. The CU investigator, stating this explanation strained credibility, labeled the report "unexplained." (This also was the conclusion by NICAP, which investigated the case long bfore the CU Project.)

But this rejection of an AF explanation was overshadowed by a more serious discovery—two CU reports of Air Force cover-ups.

In the fall of '67, a report was relayed to the CU Project that six UFOs had followed an X-15 high-altitude experimental plane during a flight from a West Coast AF base. The source, which the project considered reliable, suggested that motion pictures showing the UFOs were in AF possession.

When project members queried the base, Operations denied the report. Indications of official secrecy were increased by a responsible base employee (called Mr. A in the report) who privately confirmed the UFO sighting by pilots and control tower operators.

When the base director of information evaded the CU investigators they called the Pentagon. Supposedly the director was told to clarify the situation, but the only result was an assistant's denial of any such UFO report. At the project's request, Mr. A tried to follow up. But, as he told CU investigators, the director of information ordered him to "stay out of that."

The CU analyst bluntly stated that the project attempts to investigate met with AF evasion.

The second evasion case was listed in Section III, Chapter 1. According to the project's information, jet fighters at an AF base had been alerted for a UFO chase. The interceptors, armed with rockets, had rolled out to the runway when the takeoff order was held up. A base officer who checked with the fighter defense squadron told CU investigators there had been an alert and jets had been deployed to the runway, but the UFO question was uncertain. To determine if a UFO had caused the alert, the project queried AF Headquarters. But HQ officers denied the alert, and the CU investigators found themselves at a dead end.

Adding to the implications of secrecy was a project explanation for witnesses' withholding UFO reports. Among the reasons were:

Fear of ridicule, fear of being involved with security or military restrictions—and fear of JANAP-146 and its penalty restrictions.

When the reviewers finished the evidence of UFO reality and the censorship cases they were badly shaken. To ask CU to change all this damaging material would be a big risk. If Dr. Condon had not known of the "hot" cases and conclusions it would probably set off an explosion. If he fired any of the scientists the press would be sure to find out and play up the reasons.

The AF reviewers were still trying to decide when Nixon was elected President. Sending back the report now would be too dangerous. Any scientist firings at Boulder, tied to this important reality evidence, would cause an outburst on Capitol Hill. President Nixon would almost certainly order a full-scale probe.

But the decision left the AF in a serious predicament. It was impossible to pigeonhole the CU Report—headquarters had announced it would be released through the press after an independent review by the National Academy of Sciences.

Until HQ officers saw the report they had not worried about NAS. Most of its members knew nothing about the UFO facts, and many believed the sighting reports were nonsense. If the CU evaluations had been wholly negative, as expected, there would have been no problem. But the panel scientists could hardly miss the positive evidence of UFO reality and the glaring contradictions.

The NAS president, Dr. Frederick Seitz, had been informed by Dr. McDonald that the CU study was ignoring important evidence, and as proof he had submitted verified reports by highly rated witnesses. He had also sent Dr. Seitz a copy of the Low memorandum. If Seitz gave the review panel this information from a respected scientist the members might check the CU Report more carefully. Adding up the powerful cases and conclusions of UFO reality could cause panel scientists to prepare a strong criticism of the report and send it back to the Air Force.

Strict review rules, however, had been imposed to prevent any actual investigation of the evidence. The NAS was quasi-official, an advising agency to the government, and this official service was often paid for by federal funds. While its review was supposed to be entirely independent, NAS did not object to the rules.

The NAS panel was directed to examine merely the methodology, to approve or disapprove of the way the project had been run. It could not interview any witnesses. It could not examine any of the thousands of verified cases omitted from the report, though NAS heads knew this massive evidence was available at NICAP. Panel scientists were not allowed to consult members of Congress who knew the facts. They could not interview any of the CU Project investigators. The entire report was on a take-it-or-leave-it basis.

But what if panel scientists felt an obligation to the public? After all, the review would be paid for by the taxpayers. Even if it meant criticizing brother scientists they might rebel against the restrictions and refuse to accept the report.

For over a week the AF wavered. Then on November 15, seeing no way out, it sent the report to Dr. Seitz. While HQ officers waited for the outcome several new sightings, reported by the press and on the air, increased their uneasiness.

On November 22, fishing boat crews in the Gulf of Mexico were alarmed by a UFO's close approach. One boat skipper, P. L. Mallette, said the device beamed a bright light at crew members before it shot up out of sight.

On November 26, verified incidents in North Dakota and Florida made the news. At Bismarck, North Dakota, two round-shaped UFOs were seen by FAA control tower operators and a Capital Aviation pilot-instructor in the area. Traffic controller Jack Wilhelm reported one UFO's high-speed maneuver as beyond the capability of any known aircraft.

Over Lake Cyprus, Florida, that same evening, four UFOs the size of large AF transports were encountered by pilots of two Cessna aircraft. As three of the unknown craft were pacing the planes, one pilot turned on his landing lights, then quickly banked toward the UFO. The strange object shot straight upward and disappeared. Its estimated speed was over 2,000 mph. (Case investigated by aerospace engineers, members of NICAP's Cape Kennedy Subcommittee.)

Sighting reports were still coming in when NAS returned

the CU Report. Braced for at least some criticism, AF censors were almost astonished by the verdict.

The NAS panel scientists unanimously accepted Dr. Condon's conclusions and praised the project for its "creditable" UFO study. Fully agreeing with Condon, the panel said there was no evidence that UFOs were superior, unknown machines. Most reports, it agreed, were mistakes—failure to recognize conventional causes. There was no official secrecy, it stated, and no need for further UFO study.

For the scientists to have missed all the powerful UFO evidence and the damaging contradictions was impossible—if they actually read the full report. Either they had read only Condon's two opening sections, or they had deliberately ignored everything disproving his conclusions.

Whatever the answer, the censors' first ordeal was over. But the biggest hurdle, a much bigger danger, was still ahead.

Before Nixon's inauguration the CU Report had to be released to the Washington press corps. In this group were hundreds of veteran newsmen—wire service editors, newspaper correspondents, network commentators. Because of the AF build-up of the CU Project's importance, newsmen would expect several days to go through the 1,500-page report.

Even then, many newsmen with only moderate knowledge of the subject would overlook some vital material. But some press corps members knew too much about UFOs. Given time to read the report carefully, they would spot the convincing evidence and conclusions, also the serious omissions and incredible debunking explanations in other cases.

Among the omissions were the Transocean crash and the Braniff 1959 disaster; the AF attempt to down a UFO near Redmond, Oregon, proved by FAA logs and traffic controllers' reports; the 1958 AF transport encounter, where the captain reported they were "shot at" by a UFO; and other serious and significant cases. Cases of UFO-caused injuries were left out or denied, including airliner near-collisions in which passengers were hurt.

The Walesville tragedy, mentioned briefly, was not in the regular case list but with no explanation was put under Class II—Radar Returns. Accepting the AF debunking answer with no CU investigation, the report omitted the F-94 pilot's description of the *mysterious*, terrific heat. Quoting an AF crash report, a CU analyst explained the increased temperature as evidently caused by engine trouble, which caused a fire-warning signal, after which ". . . both crew members ejected successfully." The fact that the jet did not catch fire until it crashed is left out. The brief CU coverage—a half page compared with several full pages on trivial incidents—tersely admits the tragedy: "The aircraft crashed at the 'Walesville Intersection,' and was destroyed. The aircraft struck a house and an automobile, fatally injuring four persons. . . . No UFO was involved" (Case 19-B).

Scores of other serious UFO cases were left out, and thousands of other reports were omitted because of this decision by Dr. Condon: The excuse for omitting this massive evidence was Dr. Condon's opinion that studying old cases would be a waste of time.

As a result, over 98 per cent of the UFO evidence was ignored, including many unexplained top-witness reports. Not one of the Michigan cases in March 1966 was examined—and these were the ones causing the crisis which led to the CU Project. Of the hundreds in '65, only three were listed. The great sighting wave of '52 and its "hard-core" reality evidence, was almost completely evaded, as was the significant "flap" in 1957.

Besides omitting massive evidence, the CU Report ignored the UFO-caused hazard of accidental war, EM interference with electric circuits, and the high probability of UFO links with blackouts.

And all this was just part of the vital information evaded, debunked or ridiculed in the CU Project Report.

To turn the Washington press corps loose on this unbelievable evaluation would be to invite disaster. The newsmen would expect a Pentagon press conference to follow—customary with important issues. After discovering the incredible flaws and contradictions, they would almost certainly demand a full-scale discussion. There would be barbed questions AF spokesmen could not evade. For the public information officers this was a risk they dared not take. It could be their Waterloo.

The only way to avoid it was to rush the report through without a press conference, giving the newsmen time for only a hurried inspection before the scheduled release hour.

Once they had decided on these steamroller tactics, the AF PIOs waited a few more days, knowing the press corps would be busier as Inauguration Day approached. On January 8, to pave the way, they released the NAS panel's verdict, stressing that this was a careful, serious review by the nation's top scientists. After planting the panel's praise of Dr. Condon and the project study, the AF gave newsmen copies of the enormous report—for release the next day.

The effect was just what the PIOs had expected. Faced with the impossible job of reading the huge document overnight, reporters and broadcasters begged for an AF press release summary. Instead, PIOs tipped them off to the first two sections by Condon. These, the AF men said, covered all the main points—everything they needed.

When the day ended the AF censors were fairly sure the scheme would work. There still could be trouble; some prominent newsman who knew the inside story might rush through the report and pick out enough hot cases and discrepancies to set off a bomb. But the odds were against it; a veteran columnist or well-known commentator would hesitate to attack and risk his reputation without knowing everything in the report. At any rate, the die was cast.

The next twenty-four hours would tell the story.

15

Backfire

By the evening of January 9, AF Headquarters knew the steamroller had succeeded. Combining Condon's conclusions with praise by the NAS, newspapers and networks told the nation that distinguished scientists had proved UFOs nonexistent. Incredible as it may seem, not one of the glaring contradictions, the "hot" cases, was mentioned by the wire services or the networks.

Though Condon's report got the headlines, some sharp dissents went on record. Congressman William Ryan attacked the conclusions on the floor of the House, urging an investigation of the project. The American Institute of Astronautics and Aeronautics revealed a two-year objective, scientific investigation and rejected the CU Report. At the same time, Dr. Hynek publicly denounced the project conclusions. National columnist Roscoe Drummond urged a new, unbiased study, citing "too many unexplained UFOs." The report also was criticized by scores of papers, among them the Detroit *Free Press*, the El Paso *Times*, the Knoxville *Journal*, the San Diego *Tribune*, the Dayton *Daily News*, and the Chattanooga *Post*. The New York *Daily News* said the study "has been under fire from the start as allegedly rigged to bring in the verdict the Air Force wanted."

But none of the critics cited the "genuine UFO" conclusions or startling contradictions, since they had not had time to search through the 1,500-page report. As a result, most of the press and networks paid little attention.

Within days, the initial publicity was followed by a 965-page paperback edition of the report. Though the CU study had been financed by the taxpayers for a total of $523,000, the AF allowed Colorado University to publish a hard-cover copy and the Bantam paperback edition and keep the royalties.

The introduction, by Walter Sullivan of the New York *Times*, contained a surprising admission about Dr. Condon and the AF:

Dr. Condon, Sullivan said, had once tangled with the House Committee on Un-American Activities and that Richard Nixon, then a committee member, was connected with the challenge of Condon's security clearance. Because of the ill will between the two, Sullivan added, the AF was anxious to get the Condon Report published before Nixon became President.

If the AF had learned of this disclosure in time it almost certainly would have had it deleted, along with another candid admission by Sullivan.

The AF expected charges of "whitewash," Sullivan said, if the CU Project report agreed with the AF claims. It sent the report to the National Academy of Sciences, the newsman added, believing that approval by a NAS panel would reduce public criticism.

At least one serious error was made by Sullivan. The "full-fledged" CU study, he said, investigated "hundreds of cases." Actually, only fifty-nine were investigated, and not all in detail. The rest, less than forty, were evaluated without full-scale checking.

Belittling UFO witnesses, Sullivan said the CU Report proved the fallibility of airline pilots, radar operators and other "sober observers." Referring to long-ago belief in ghosts, he implied that some witnesses may have been conditioned to believe in UFOs.

In the report itself, Condon first said most persons making UFO reports seemed to be normal, responsible individuals.

But this picture quickly changed. Besides being inept, said Dr. Condon, some witnesses embellish their reports, and multiple witnesses often compare notes and change their stories, perhaps unconsciously, until they agree. Even the astronauts' reports were not of great value, he indicated; their spacecraft windows sometimes were smudged and all their tasks often kept them so busy they did not have time to concentrate on observations.

Statements by some project scientists added to the ridicule of witnesses. Eyewitness testimony was declared inherently unreliable. Single-observer reports were mostly ruled out, with the implication that many witnesses could not be trusted without confirmation. One project member suggested that some witnesses might be looking for fame, notoriety, attention or money.

At first, some responsible witnesses started to lash back at the CU Project, but the build-up of ridicule was too much. For weeks, UFO observers grimly kept silent. The AF and the CIA believed they had won, that the UFO subject was buried forever. But the corpse surprisingly came back to life, as some witnesses began to brave public derision.

One of the first public reports was made by Police Chief Lavern Janzen of Westhope, North Dakota. About ten o'clock, March 10, 1969, Janzen was cruising in his police car when a brilliant glow suddenly lighted the area around him.

"The whole damn car lit up," Chief Janzen later told the chairman of NICAP's North Dakota Subcommittee, Donald E. Flickenger. Then he saw a domed UFO with a greenish-blue glow hovering about 700 feet above the police car. The disc had a reddish band around the middle, and it appeared to be rotating. A light beam, almost blinding, came down from the bottom of the object.

"At first I was real scared," said Janzen. "I thought of using my service revolver, but decided against it because it wouldn't have been much help anyway."

While the UFO was above him there was heavy interference on his radio, the chief reported. After ten or fifteen minutes, the unknown device "took off to the south with a high burst of speed and disappeared."

On the afternoon of March 17, a group of oval-shaped UFOs was encountered by pilots Herman Slater and Ben Ripley, who were flying a Cessna 150 over Arizona. Above Mount Buckskin they sighted approximately twenty-five objects about three times as large as an average car. The pilots reported that the UFOs were "undulating in precise unison, as though remote-controlled." Flying at 300 mph, the strange machines passed beneath the plane, then vanished between Phoenix and Lake Havasu City.

Soon after this, a delayed report was received from NICAP Subcommittee Chairman Julian Hennessey in London. On the night of February 25, a UFO with a powerful red light was observed by the crew of an Iberia Air Lines flight. The unidentified craft followed the airliner from Majorca to Spain. It descended close to the ground, then climbed away and went out of sight. The UFO pacing was confirmed by Capt. Jaime Ordovas, co-pilot Augustin Carvajal and flight engineer José Cuenca.

In the next three months, witness reports increased. An airline pilot revealed a sighting in California. An FAA employee described a UFO seen at Knoxville Airport. Additional reports came from observers in Florida, Kentucky, Michigan, Missouri, Tennessee, Virginia and other states, along with details of encounters in Canada, New Zealand and Australia.

By May, the UFO encounter by an AF KC-135 tanker crew, over Southeast Asia, had become known in the United States (reported in Chapter 1). The buildup of public UFO reports was already worrying the AF, and it intensified its efforts to keep pilot reports under cover—not only AF cases, but sightings by other military airmen, airline pilots and FAA personnel.

One dramatic case which was unknown by the public for two and a half years involved FAA traffic controller James V.

Beardsley and the crews of three aircraft. The detailed report was brought to light by NICAP in 1972, revealed by Controller Beardsley.

On the afternoon of June 5, 1969, Beardsley was aboard an American Airlines 707 jet—Flight 112, from Phoenix to Washington. Since his purpose was an official "familiarization flight," to observe pilot procedures as linked with FAA traffic control, he was directly behind the captain, on a "jump seat." Across from him was the flight engineer, who was seated behind the co-pilot.

The 707 was flying east at 38,000 feet. Eight miles behind was a United Airlines flight, and a few miles back was a National Guard plane. All three were on the same course.

The American captain had gone back into the cabin when four unknown objects suddenly appeared ahead.

The co-pilot hastily called the St. Louis FAA Control Center. A controller told him they were tracking "unknowns" near the airliner. The UFOs were still heading toward the 707. Though they were not coming at terrific speed they were only a few seconds away.

"They were in a square formation," Beardsley told NICAP. "The larger one was about eighteen to twenty feet long, seven or eight feet thick at the center, and twelve to fourteen feet across at the rear. The others were smaller and sharp-looking at the front, like darts. All four had the color of burnished aluminum."

"The one in the lower right-hand corner was on a collision course with us," Beardsley stated. "All of a sudden they [the smaller ones] looked like they went up to the large one."

After this quick maneuver, the UFOs passed at a safe distance.

"They were still separated, about twenty feet apart, as they went by," Beardsley reported.

A few seconds after the formation passed, a pilot in the United plane came on the air.

"We see it too!" he exclaimed.

Then the National Guard pilot excitedly joined in. "Damn, they almost got me!" Later he described the UFOs' approach. As with the American Airlines flight, the formation had come straight toward him. Then at the last moment the UFOs had performed a swift evasion maneuver.

Because of the usual ridicule, all the witnesses kept still about the encounter. Beardsley filed an official FAA report, but it remained unknown until 1972, except to the Air Force.

After the report became public, debunkers tried to explain away the UFOs as daytime meteors. All the pilots involved had seen hundreds of meteors, and the objects' speed was too low to fit this explanation, aside from their swift maneuvers. Like hundreds of other pilot sightings, this case remains unexplained in spite of the debunkers.

By the middle of '69, the CU Report had lost some of its harsh effect, due to blunt criticisms by Dr. Hynek, the AIAA and Dr. James McDonald. The RAND document on UFOs, which had now leaked out, also helped to increase scientific interest.

Before this, most scientists had accepted Condon's conclusions. But now some started to dig into the huge report, and they had several surprises. One was especially startling, Dr. Condon's discussion of an alleged sexual encounter between a space woman and a young Brazilian farmer named Antonio Villas-Boas.

According to a book by Coral Lorenzen—*Flying Saucers: The Startling Evidence of the Invasion from Outer Space*—Villas-Boas was plowing a field when a UFO landed nearby. Humanoid crew members forced him to go aboard, undress and take a physical examination. Quoting the book, Dr. Condon went on:

"'. . . in walked a small but well-built and completely nude woman.'" After a description of her "voluptuous, distinctly womanly figure," Dr. Condon continued: "'The woman's purpose was immediately evident. . . . A very normal sex act took place, and after more pettings she responded

again. . . . The howling noises she made during the togeth-
erness nearly spoiled the whole act (for Villas-Boas) for they
reminded him of an animal.'" Afterward, the young Brazilian was put out of the UFO, which then took off and
disappeared.

In Mrs. Lorenzen's opinion, said Dr. Condon, the aliens
were trying to learn whether they could interbreed with humans before deciding on colonization of the Earth.

Citing a less erotic story, Dr. Condon described a hunter's
alleged meeting with alien beings and also robots which
belched out puffs of strange smoke to make him lose con-
sciousness. After a harrowing night, the hunter reported, he
escaped, on the verge of collapse.

On the basis of these reported incidents, said Dr. Condon,
the project found no convincing evidence that UFOs were
spacecraft visiting Earth from another world.

To most of the scientists reading the report, it was incredible that these weird tales could have the slightest influence
on Condon or any project members. Why hadn't they ignored
these wild stories and concentrated on the hundreds of sane,
factual reports by responsible observers?

But Condon had an answer to that. "Past anecdotal records," he said, were of little value, except perhaps to discover
discrepancies. An example of this brush-off policy was the
project's handling of the Gulf of Mexico case—the B-29
bomber crew's report of sighting UFOs and tracking them
as they merged with a larger object, evidently a carrier ship.
The sighted UFOs, said a CU analyst, were meteors. The
radar tracking was some peculiar effect "at present only poorly
understood" (CU Case 103-B).

Another Condon statement also disturbed these scientists.
If a UFO report could be explained plausibly in ordinary
terms, he said, the project accepted the explanation, even if
there was not complete proof.

In "explaining" several cases, analysts stretched plausibil-
ity to the breaking point. An example was Case 1, an expe-

rienced meteorologist's report of an unknown powered craft, its speed between 100 and 200 mph. The CU answer: Probably airborne debris, such as a nearly deflated child's balloon, or a piece of paper.

An even more preposterous explanation was given in Case 304-B, the Odessa, Washington, near-collision report by two AF pilots in an F-94 interceptor (see Chapter 1). The huge UFO with lighted windows, which maneuvered violently around the jet, was labeled: Probably a lighted balloon.

In several cases, analysts conjured up answers even they could not explain. One report, by Capt. James Howard and the crew of a British airliner, described a group of UFOs that merged with a larger object which then disappeared at high speed. The CU Report answer: Some almost certainly natural phenomenon so rare it has never been seen before or since (Section III, Chapter 5).

At one point, Dr. Condon said attacks on those with different UFO opinions should be avoided. But the report often reversed this, calling many sightings "rubbish," and warning that even reports by credible observers must be viewed cautiously. Discussing witnesses' poor perception, one scientist first described a cat's reactions to clicking sounds and then to seeing a rat. From this, he proceeded to humans' perception errors in mistaking various things for UFOs, such as insects, kites, birds, possibly even debris blown off the moon.

In focusing colleagues' attention on the report, Dr. Hynek hit at the mass of "trivial and irrelevant discussions, practically padding," including four public opinion polls, a treatise on statistics, a so-called history of UFOs centered on man's fears in ancient times, and other special contract items totaling $112,950.

After reading the report, more and more scientists began to support Hynek's forthright criticism: "By what right do we ignore such evidence and call witnesses deluded—or just plain liars?" (See list of scientists in the Appendix.)

One outspoken scientist began calling the CU Report

"The CUR," and it caught on with several others. If Dr. Condon ever heard of this it may have increased his reactions to critics, a fury sometimes reminiscent of the attacks on Giordano Bruno, a philosopher of the sixteenth century.

"In space," Bruno wrote, "there are countless constellations, suns, and planets. . . . There are also numerous earths circling around their suns. . . . No reasonable mind can assume that heavenly bodies which may be far more magnificent than ours would not bear upon them creatures similar or even superior to those upon our human Earth."

For this, Bruno was burned at the stake by the Inquisition. While Dr. Condon did not recommend going this far, his anger did lead to his suggestion of public horsewhipping for teachers who allowed students credits for reading UFO material and also for publishers of "pseudo-science" UFO articles and books. Possibly this surprising denunciation played a part in some scientists' closer look at the CU Report.

During 1969 and since, several airline pilots have had frightening close encounters with UFOs. Some have given me confidential reports, following a practice confirmed in the AF Academy UFO analysis:

It is of interest that NICAP even today still receives reports from commercial pilots who neglect to notify either the Air Force or their own airlines.

On one occasion, an AF jet raced toward a UFO which was pacing a 727 jetliner. Later the 727 captain privately gave me the details.

"It was after midnight. We were at 31,000 feet when this thing came down about 200 feet off our right wing and started pacing us. It was round-shaped, with a dome in the middle, and we could see a faint glow around the rim.

"I'll admit it shook me up, but I wasn't about to panic as long as it didn't come closer. I had the first officer switch on the landing lights so we could see the UFO better. The next second an AF jet showed up in the lights, diving toward the UFO.

"It scared the hell out of me. I didn't dare make a move—we might have had a three-way collision. Luckily the UFO shot straight up and the jet went streaking after it. I don't know what happened—I didn't see them again.

"But all of a sudden I got boiling mad. That AF pilot could have warned us—he'd know our radio frequency. I got so sore I was going to tell the newspapers or go on the air and blast the Air Force. But after I landed I got talked out of it. The company could have been hurt by the publicity, and I might have been out of a job. The Air Force would have denied the whole thing, anyway."

In November of '69, AF censors found themselves faced with a new and serious threat. The American Association for the Advancement of Science, impressed by scientists' attacks on the CU Report, announced a symposium on UFOs, to be held at its annual meeting.

The AF and the CIA, also Colorado University heads, were alarmed by the AAAS plans. It was almost certain that the Colorado Project would be hard hit. And with all the association's prestige, it could not only nullify the project report but discredit the entire AF investigation.

Dr. Condon, in an attempt to stop the public discussion, appealed to AAAS heads. When this failed he urged Vice-President Agnew to use his influence to cancel the symposium. The Vice-President refused to interfere.

By then the AF had realized it not only would have to thwart the AAAS but forestall other such attacks. It would take powerful action, tougher than any they had tried before. Up to then, the AF Office of Scientific Research had not officially accepted the CU Report because of recognized flaws. But under the growing pressure this was swiftly changed.

On December 17, just nine days before the scheduled AAAS meeting, the AF threw a devastating blow at its critics and all the thousands of UFO witnesses. The networks and wire services, taking the AF claims without question, repeated the main points in nationwide stories:

—The Colorado Project investigations were highly approved and its conclusions were fully accepted.

—The AF had never found the slightest evidence that UFOs were unknown craft or machines.

—Not one witness had ever sighted an alien spacecraft. Every person who reported a UFO had had an optical illusion, a mental delusion, or had been misled by ordinary objects, or had perpetrated a hoax.

—Project Blue Book was closed and the AF UFO investigation was ended.

As the AF intended, the December 17 action almost ruined the AAAS symposium. Because of the AF hard-boiled statements the discussions got little publicity.

As HQ strategists also had planned, the harsh ridicule silenced most UFO witnesses. This outrageous treatment of responsible observers was a new low in character assassination. Though the AF avoided using names, thousands of witnesses had been publicized in their communities, some of them nationally. Besides those in the armed forces and other government agencies there were men and women in most professions and trades who had made sincere reports, many of them fully verified. (See witness list in the Appendix.) Among them were lawyers, doctors, educators, state and city officials, and citizens in many types of work. Because of the AF deliberate attempt to discredit all UFO witnesses, many suffered ridicule and some were actually harmed in their business and social life.

But the secrecy-fighters, in and outside the Pentagon, doggedly hung on—even some in the Air Force, who knew the risk they were taking. Slowly their efforts took effect. Here and there, witnesses began to make their sightings public, though most big cases were hidden.

In the last part of 1970 the AF big cover-up scheme began

to backfire more rapidly, when the AF Academy UFO analysis became public. This serious evaluation had been prepared in 1968, as a means of giving senior AF cadets an appraisal of the problem. Combined evidence and discussions of the main angles were used for a special chapter in an Academy Space Science study. NICAP's documented report *The UFO Evidence*, and two of my books with verified cases and censorship proof, were among the references.

If this explosive material had been submitted to headquarters there would have been fireworks. But the UFO chapter was never sent to the Pentagon. By the time HQ found out, cadets had seen the damaging admissions, such as "we too have fired on UFOs" and the Fort Itaipu injuries case. Dismayed AF censors ordered the chapter replaced with an all-out debunking job, deleting all the case evidence and all the serious disclosures.

Meantime, hurried attempts were made to keep the original evaluation from leaking out. But a photocopy had been privately given to a NICAP Affiliate president, and another copy reached me at Washington. This was only one of the many times secrecy-fighters risked HQ anger, even a court-martial, to help end the dangerous cover-up.

When a newspaper ran part of the original analysis, HQ hastily tried to offset it with the "updated version." But a series of new developments caused it to lose effect.

The first was a sharp attack on the CU Report by the AIAA. The Institute urged the government to carry out new, unbiased, scientific investigations. It stated 30 per cent of the CU Project cases were unexplained and stressed the importance of the many earlier reports. Condon's personal conclusions, said the AIAA, differed from a number of his analysts' opinions. The Institute also rejected Condon's far-out prediction: There would not be any extraterrestrial visitations to Earth in 10,000 years. Like other critics, the AIAA indicated it was impossible to predict the actions of unknown space races. Some of the press and newscasters picked this up and compared Dr. Condon with previous experts who declared certain advances were impossible. Among them were Lord Kelvin, eminent British physicist, who called X-rays a hoax, insisted aircraft flight was impossible and that radio had no future. . . . Dr. Vannevar Bush, World War II scientific adviser to the President, who stated that long-range ICBM missiles were not possible for a very long period. . . . Rear Adm. William Leahy, who declared, as an expert on explosives, that the A-bomb would never go off, and the British Astronomer Royal who in 1957 said that talk of space travel was "utter bilge."

Shortly after this, two discoveries were spotlighted on the air. One was the AF retaliation against Dr. Hynek. Because of his courageous criticism of the CU Project he was dropped after twenty years as the AF consultant on UFOs. About the same time, it was discovered that the AF had written a blistering letter to RAND, attacking the scientists who prepared the UFO Document. In an attempt to get him fired, the AF called him a disgrace to other scientists. But RAND refused to be intimidated, and the scientist continued to stimulate interest among his associates and help build opposition to the official secrecy.

On the heels of this, the National Academy of Sciences came under attack by former Secretary of the Interior Stewart Udall. At a meeting of the AAAS, Udall labeled the NAS "a virtual puppet of the government," and he urged that it be challenged for its reluctance to oppose official policies. Though he did not mention the CU Report, some commentators linked his charges with the NAS approval of Condon's conclusions.

In 1971, more criticism appeared in the press. One of the toughest attacks was made by a *Christian Science Monitor* staff writer, Peter Henniker Heaton.

Read as a whole, the report could not conceal the considerable body of evidence which pointed to an important and inexplicable phenomenon. But the introductory summary of the report performed a hatchet job on flying saucers that has rarely been equaled in the field of scientific scholarship. And as everyone knows, when a scholar and a scientist picks up a hatchet, he does a job with it of unparalleled effectiveness and ferocity.

In April of '71 the AF and the CU Project were hit by a respected engineering magazine, *Industrial Research*. A poll of its members showed that 80 per cent rejected the CU Report; about 76 per cent believed the government was concealing some of the UFO facts, and 32 per cent believed UFOs came from other worlds.

On through 1971 public criticism and sighting reports steadily increased. Then in 1972 the pace was stepped up by an important disclosure at a meeting of the Retired Military Officers Association in Baltimore. The audience included retired officers of high rank in the Army, Navy, Marine Corps and Air Force. The revelation was made by a former Army Intelligence officer, Lt. Col. Lou Corbin, now chief commentator at WFBR, Baltimore. For over fifteen years, he had made public strong UFO evidence and censorship proof, some of it secured through high connections in the Pentagon.

"Although the Air Force will deny it," Corbin told the assembled officers, "they are still investigating UFOs. This is being done through two projects—'Old New Moon' and 'Blue Paper.' . . . The UFOs are no figment of imagination."

Afterward, as Corbin later told me, several officers, among them AF men, confirmed the continued investigations, which the AF was determined to keep hidden.

Although AF HQ learned immediately that Corbin had identified the two projects, fear of causing him to announce them on the air kept the censors silent. Growing UFO publicity was already a serious worry, with the NEA syndicate, the Detroit *Free Press* and other newspapers giving the subject new respectability.

Shortly after this Dr. J. Allen Hynek added to the serious acceptance of the UFO evidence with a book entitled *The UFO Experience: A Scientific Inquiry.*[1] Although he avoided harsh criticism of the Air Force, he clearly revealed the official mishandling of the UFO investigation and the deliberate AF deception of the public and the press. Concentrating on the Colorado Project's evasion of massive evidence and its failure to use truly scientific methods, he made plain his opinion that the CU's so-called investigation was a sorry waste of the taxpayers' money.

Between mid-June and September, several UFO reports added to the AF problems. On the night of June 17–18, two AF security policemen sighted a "bright, orange-colored object" estimated at 375 feet in diameter, near George AFB. Somehow, the press learned of the incident and it was quickly tied with other sightings at the same time, including a "scare" report.

Near the end of June, a report with frightening aspects came out of Beaufort, South Africa. According to the press, Beaufort police and a farmer named Bennie Smit opened fire on a UFO with rifles. Then on July 8 two explosions occurred just after Smit saw a UFO over his farm. When he checked, he found that a large brick reservoir had been destroyed. One press account said attempts had been made to silence Smit and his wife.

Even though this was a foreign report its publication in the U.S. added to AF uneasiness. Then on August 23 a UFO chase hidden for three years unexpectedly broke into print. The story was published by the Santa Ana, California, *Register*, after a checkup by David Branch, president of a NICAP Affiliate, and an associate investigator, Robert B. Klinn.

On May 11, a glowing object had been seen north of Yucca Valley, California. The witnesses were a scientific researcher and four other residents. At one time the UFO shot a powerful beam downward, illuminating a wide area. After the beam

[1] Regnery, 1972.

was cut off the witnesses heard the sound of jets and then saw three jet interceptors racing toward the UFO. Before the jets could get near it the object accelerated to high speed and disappeared.

Before this hidden case was published, editor Bob Kirkpatrick asked the AF if interceptors were still chasing UFOs. The reply came from Lt. Col. George L. Salem, Chief of the AF Information Office in Los Angeles.

"The Aerospace Defense Command takes whatever actions are necessary to identify objects appearing on defense radarscopes," stated Colonel Salem. And this, he said, included launching interceptors. But he avoided any details of intercepts "since Project Blue Book was terminated." It would be impossible, he explained, to justify the work of compiling a report on intercepts.

"The U. S. Air Force," said Colonel Salem, "is not pursuing the investigation of UFOs today." He added that there was no requirement for an AF investigation, and that no new regulations had been implemented. He did not mention the emergency reporting system CIRVIS—Communications Instructions for Reporting Vital Intelligence Sightings—set up by the Joint Chiefs of Staff, nor the JANAP-146 warning of stiff penalties for anyone revealing a CIRVIS report— both of which are still in effect. (Photocopy of the AF letter in author's files, relayed by the Los Angeles NICAP Subcommittee.)

Two days after the 1969 hidden jet chase was revealed, the UPI released a serious account of a UFO encounter in Wisconsin.

In the early hours of August 25, a motorist sighted a flying disc hovering at treetop level. It was about thirty feet in diameter. The driver slammed on his brakes, to watch the object, but it took off in a few seconds. Then he discovered that his lights, horn and radio would not work. A police investigation showed skid marks where he had suddenly braked.

It was also found that all the car fuses had been blown, and the engine was overheated from some unknown cause.

As UFOs came back into the news, some of the press belatedly began checking the CU Report. One I knew was a Washington TV commentator. Halfway through, he told me he was amazed by the positive evidence ignored in the main conclusions.

"I see now why the AF rushed it through without giving us time to read it. I think the whole AF investigation is phoney, and I'm going to put it up to the network to bust it wide open."

But two weeks later he told me higher-ups had vetoed it.

"They said we'd look like fools for backing the report without knowing what was in it. Also we'd set off a big row. Not just with the AF—there are millions of people who don't want to believe that we're being watched by some race that's way ahead of us."

This was true, as I already knew. Many people sincerely believed space visitors were not possible. One who had denounced the idea was Sir John Eccles, noted British brain physiologist who was then in the United States.

"Extraterrestrial spaceships are an impossibility," he said. "Earth is the only place where intelligent life exists. This puts us on top of everything in the universe."

Many non-believers had also been reassured by self-appointed debunkers like Dr. Donald Menzel, who compared the idea of manned spaceships with "concepts of witches, fairies, elves, hobgoblins, or the devil" (statement in the congressional record of UFO Hearings in 1968).

Back of all the debunking is an increasingly serious situation. By now, the AF and the CIA know that the big scheme of December 1969 has failed. Some high AF and CIA officials cling to the hope that there is a block—physical or mental—to aliens meeting with humans, and that they will soon give up and return to their own world. Even if they do not leave, there could be a longer delay, and officials evidently believe we may have time to improve present space weapons or build new ones, in case the aliens prove aggressive.

But meantime the continued chases and capture attempts increase the possibility of alien retaliation. In spite of this and other hazards, communication attempts are still blocked.

Fear of contact with an advanced race is still a factor, as some highly respected scientists have recently admitted. One was Harvard's Nobel Prize-winning biologist Dr. George Wald, who took part in a Boston University symposium on "Life Beyond Earth and the Mind of Man." Discussing the communication possibility, Dr. Wald said the prospect of contact with a technically superior race was "a little terrifying" to him. Like Professor Z. Kopal and certain other leading scientists, he warned that such contact could prove to be a nightmare, resulting in the destruction of our civilization.

During all the years of the UFO reconnaissance there has been only one official step taken toward possible communication with another world—a feeble step with odds of a trillion to one against success.

In March of 1972 a 570-pound space device called Pioneer 10 was launched from Cape Kennedy, equipped with scientific apparatus to probe for the secrets of the universe and report back to Earth by radio until the distance becomes so fantastically great that communication ends. Before that time, listening Earth scientists may through the years find clues to the present mysteries of our galaxy and the infinite space beyond.

Attached to the antenna struts of Pioneer 10 was a gold-anodized plaque showing a naked man and a naked woman, our planetary system, and several technical symbols. The purpose: To show where this unmanned spacecraft came from, when it was launched and the type of beings on our planet.

This space-probe was not aimed at any particular target except to pass Mars at a distance, later to circle Jupiter and then go on past Pluto into the heart of the Milky Way galaxy. It is expected that, barring accident, Pioneer 10 will travel millions of years on this tremendous voyage, unless it should be intercepted by spacecraft from some advanced world or if by some chance it might land on a far-distant planet.

If this happened, the advanced race might be so different it could not interpret the symbols. Even if it did, there might be no interest in attempting an answer—which could take thousands of centuries to reach Earth, assuming our planet still existed.

Considering the remote chance of any benefit, even to our descendants trillions of years from now, there was not the slightest need for the symbolic plaque carried by Pioneer 10.

But there *is* an urgent need today—a need to end the long deception about UFOs and start preparing the public for whatever may develop.

The scientific groups like AIAA are trying to help. In Dr. Hynek's "Invisible College" group there are many top scientists who are only waiting, as Hynek has said, for the stigma to end so they can come out in the open with their valuable aid.

But the need for action is *now*. A sudden new wave of sightings, as in 1965 and 1966, could bring a new crisis. There are a dozen ways in which the secrecy might break down. One proven danger is the risk of UFO-airliner collisions, or serious injuries caused by hasty evasions. This hazard is greater with today's huge fast jets.

"It was bad enough," a veteran airline captain told me recently, "when only prop planes were involved. Remember that TWA case when Captain Schemel dived under a UFO? He was cruising around 300 or less when he dived, and it wasn't a steep dive, either—but a dozen people got hurt.

"Ever think what it would be like with a 747? You've usually got about 350 passengers and also twenty stewardesses moving around. Most passengers don't keep their belts fastened, either. Just imagine what would happen if a UFO came in on a collision course. With a jet cruising over 500 miles an hour, the captain would have maybe two seconds. No matter what he did—dive or zoom—he'd throw two or three hundred people around. A lot of them would be hurt, some might even be killed. And the panic—you couldn't tell what would happen in the cabin. Even if the captain got control and managed to get down okay nobody could possibly hide a thing like that. An hour after he landed it would be all over the country. You can take it from there."

Such a catastrophe may never happen. But no matter how the secrecy broke down, hysteria would probably follow, because of the long deception.

There is one sane, practical way to reduce the present hazards:

End the jet chases, then begin a program to learn the crucial answers and start preparing the public.

It can be done. The plan is ready. The key—Operation Lure.

16

Operation
Lure

The first *planned* meeting of aliens and humans could be the start of mutual adjustments, leading to great advances for our world. But adjustments might prove too difficult, leaving us with serious problems for all mankind.

For this first crucial meeting to have a fair chance of success, the humans involved should already know two vital facts:

1) The aliens' physical appearance. 2) The beings' general reactions to humans.

To learn this much before ever meeting an alien may seem impossible. But it can be done. It is the first goal of Operation Lure, a unique but practical plan which avoids the strongly opposed radio and television communications.

The basic idea was first suggested by a NICAP Special Adviser, Robert Spencer Carr, former Director of Educational Research, Walt Disney Studios, a specialist in visual-aid education who has served with the Army Orientation Service and has produced educational films for the State Department. Since the original suggestion, I have privately expanded the plan with aid from Carr, linguists, psychologists and experts in other fields.

There is nothing mysterious in this operation, though some of the steps may be surprising.

The Lure will be an isolated base with unusual structures

and novel displays, designed to attract the UFO aliens' attention. The space beings' curiosity has been demonstrated hundreds of times in their close approaches to cars, trains, ships and aircraft, also in their repeated hovering over outdoor theaters, power stations and unusual buildings.

The first attempt to attract aliens was made by Canada's Defence Research Board, when it established a top secret "UFO Landing Field" in 1958. The project failed because there was nothing unusual to catch the aliens' attention.

The Lure will have three or more dummy UFOs, disc types with domes, built of aluminum. Each one will have glass panels to show that no one is hiding inside. There will be no attempts to capture aliens or UFOs. The base will be unmanned, and the nearest humans will be stationed at hidden observation posts over a mile distant. No aircraft or ground traffic will be allowed near the Lure, and all interceptor chases will be ended.

Near the dummy UFOs will be several one-story "education buildings" containing a variety of exhibits intended to interest the UFO crews. To emphasize that no humans are concealed, the roofs will be made of shatter-proof glass, so the interiors can be seen from the air. Each building will have one glass wall to permit inspection on the ground. Behind the other walls, however, there will be hidden TV cameras and microphones, connected by buried wires with Lure Control—the main observation post.

All the observer posts are to be below ground level, except for their camouflaged roofs, below which will be high-power movie cameras with telephoto lenses and concealed high-power telescopes. Each post will be connected with Control by telephone.

At Control, teletype machines and telephones will be linked with "Relay," a communications station twenty-five miles away. In an emergency, Relay can connect Control with the White House, the Defense Department or other government agencies. It also will be connected with several radar stations which will constantly monitor the Lure approach areas for UFOs.

The fabricated dummy UFOs will not be erected until the very last, so the aliens will not start investigating while the base is still under construction. When the base is finished the observer posts will be manned and Operation Lure will begin, with the decoy UFOs and the education buildings floodlighted from dusk to dawn.

It may be several days before there is any reaction, but there are solid reasons to believe the Lure will work. If the aliens had intended to attack or invade our world, they could have done so long ago. During the long surveillance there have been well over 3,000 UFO chases, including the capture attempts. Yet the space beings have shown surprising restraint. From all the evidence, it seems clear their main purpose requires peaceful contacts and co-operation with humans.

One indication is the aliens' answering signals by humans, as frequently reported. In 1967, a typical case was reported by a former AF radar operator, Gary M. Storey. On the night of July 26, a low-flying UFO was sighted over Newton, New Hampshire, by Storey and his brother-in-law and sister, Mr. and Mrs. Francis Frappier. The device made several passes over the group, and each time they could see five lights which flashed on and off in a definite sequence.

Pointing a flashlight at the UFO, Storey tried three one-second flashes as a signal. The object quickly retraced its path, then blinked its lights three times. Before Storey could signal again two AF jets came roaring in and the UFO swiftly climbed out of sight.

Besides many signal reports, some by pilots, verified landings also indicate a desire to make contact with humans, if it can be done safely. Stopping all UFO chases should greatly increase the probability of landings at the Lure base.

Probably the first action will follow a call from Relay—a radar report of a UFO circling high above the Lure. Then the hidden observers see it slowly descend. At a low altitude it stops and hovers; apparently the aliens are scanning the dummy UFOs and the glass-roofed buildings. After an interval the craft leaves without landing.

It may take a few days of cautious inspections, but sooner or later a UFO undoubtedly will land. For the concealed watchers it will be a tense moment. But on this first landing probably no one will emerge. The craft may be remote-controlled—a test to see if this is a trap.

During another test landing the Lure observers may catch a brief glimpse of moving figures inside the craft, before it takes off. Even though the watchers get no definite picture, the tension increases. Almost certainly, the space beings intend to land and examine the Lure equipment, once they believe it is safe. The prospect of actually seeing creatures from another world brings a sobering, if not frightening thought.

What will these aliens be like?

Many analysts of the UFO evidence have tried to answer that question. By human logic, the odds indicate humanoid beings similar to us, if not identical. If the aliens' purpose requires peaceable meetings and adjustments with beings on another planet, it would seem vitally important to seek out their own kind—at least beings not unlike them. Any frightening difference would make adjustments extremely difficult, if not impossible. The UFO aliens would have realized this in a fairly short time—that neither they nor the humans could meet without fear and revulsion. They would have two choices—a forcible invasion to attain their ends, or giving up their plans for Earth as hopeless. The long worldwide surveillance, without attacks, seems proof that humans and the UFO aliens are not too unlike in appearance.

But this is not proof. Human logic could be wrong, a result of wishful thinking. The men at the Lure will know this as they wait, uneasily, for the answer.

The aliens may continue landings without appearing. If so, then Control may try to convince them there is no danger.

On a platform near one decoy UFO there will be a large, horizontal movie screen, with a remote-controlled projector beneath it. At Control, an operator will switch on the projector and a specially prepared animated picture will be visible to any aliens above the base. The film will show a flying disc with interceptors not far away. Suddenly the jets will reverse course, leaving the UFO alone. After repeating this sequence several times, the last scene will show the jets' landing lights flashing on and off as they depart—an intended "good-by" signal.

Whether or not this is decisive, the aliens are almost bound to appear at the Lure for a more thorough inspection of the dummy UFOs and the education rooms' exhibits.

It will be a dramatic and tense moment when the hidden Lure observers see the first space being emerge from a UFO. In that second they may see a creature who resembles Man— or one so different it will be a shock.

If the "human logic" analysis proves right, the watchers will see, with sudden relief, a humanoid figure. Undoubtedly there will be minor differences. He may be taller or shorter than the average man. His arms, legs and torso may have somewhat different dimensions. His eyes, mouth and ears could vary noticeably from those of most humans, but not to a frightening extent. Essentially, however, he may resemble *Homo sapiens* enough to reduce the observers' fears.

Probably the aliens will first examine the decoy UFOs, as the fascinated observers watch every step. After a careful check of an education room, through the glass wall, presumably they would enter—or perhaps only one or two, the others remaining outside to warn of any sudden appearance of humans, or approaching interceptors.

At Control, operators switch on the concealed TV-type cameras for close-ups of the aliens, as they view the first exhibits. In one building, they would see a visual display of our country's development, from the early settler days on through the nineteenth century to the first aircraft flight, early cars, to the Space Age beginning. In scores of other exhibits a general picture of our civilization is built up by animations and other visual aids.

Back at Control, medical men, psychologists and anthropologists will watch every movement, assessing the beings' strength, quickness of reaction and any unusual features.

The next important step will be to determine whether the aliens use speech to communicate with each other. If they do not use speech sounds then linguists and visual-aid experts will have to devise methods to converse by sign language, drawing and animation. But there is evidence that the UFO beings can hear and understand us.

During the excitement at Washington National Airport, in 1952, several UFOs were tracked over the area. One was sighted by Capt. Casey Pierman, a Capital Airlines pilot, as he approached the field. When he radioed the airport, Chief Traffic Controller Harry Barnes asked him to head toward the object for a closer look. Instantly, the UFO shot straight up, accelerating at tremendous speed. From other incidents that night, Barnes was convinced that the aliens heard and understood his radio transmissions. Scores of similar incidents have been reported by airline and military pilots, here and abroad.

If speech sounds are heard at Lure Control, linguists and cipher experts will immediately set to work on the recordings, aided by automatic translating machines.

In addition to the numerous exhibits, the education rooms will contain television sets linked by closed circuits with Control. Selecting sections of movie films, newscasts and TV programs for display to the aliens, the concealed observers will try to tell whether the space beings understand English— and also French, Spanish and other most common languages.

If they do seem to understand English, the watchers at Control will test their reactions to our Westerns, space fiction, comedies, crime programs and news reports.

Probably the aliens will quickly realize the purpose of the TV programs and the exhibits. They may suspect that armed men will suddenly arrive, or that AF jets will try to keep them from taking off. Possibly they will end this first visit abruptly. But with Lure Control carefully avoiding any disturbing actions, their curiosity and evident desire to contact humans can be expected to bring them back.

After one or two other visits, Control will take the first step toward a meeting. Using the pictures taken by hidden cameras, visual-aid men will prepare an animation showing two or three aliens slowly approaching the same number of humans. It will be in an open area, away from the Lure structures.

The two groups will stop fifty feet or more apart. Besides the need for caution, there is another problem to be settled —the danger of contamination from strange disease germs. Some time ago, this hazard was analyzed by a group of biologists. Afterward, Dr. Colin S. Pittendrigh of the Space Science Board drew up this grave warning:

The introduction into Earth's atmosphere of destructive alien organisms could be a disaster of enormous significance to mankind. We can conceive of no more tragically ironic consequence of our search for extraterrestrial life.

But this could also be a two-way danger, as the aliens would undoubtedly know. If our linguists managed to understand the space beings' speech, and they understood ours, it would speed the solution of this problem. It might take weeks, or longer, for the aliens to agree to a quarantine such as our astronauts went through when they returned from the moon. In return, the humans would have to submit to whatever steps could be taken to protect the alien visitors. However, this would not necessarily delay the exchange of vital information. Discussions could be held by avoiding close approaches, or by the two-way closed circuit television.

If the aliens agree after the contamination problem has been controlled, the first face-to-face meeting should finally take place.

For the humans involved there will be tense moments, no matter how carefully they have prepared. For the space beings, too, it probably will be the same. How long it will take for the first actual adjustment we cannot even guess. But if no unfortunate development occurs, continued meetings should bring the answers to our most important questions:

What were the reasons for the UFO-caused injuries, the fatal crashes of AF interceptors and airliners, the burning of the Ft. Itaipu sentries? What happened to the F-89 which disappeared during the UFO chase over Lake Superior? If aliens caused the great Northeast blackout, why was this done? Why the close, dangerous passes at airliners which led to passenger injuries? And most important of all—why are they here? Why the long surveillance of our world?

The aliens may claim all these incidents were accidental. They may blame the AF chases and firing at UFOs, and admit retaliating a few times to discourage such attacks. They might even admit that the blackouts and other EM interference cases were displays of their technical advances, intended to impress humans and lead to an end of our hostile reactions. They might have other reasons we have never considered.

Over the years, serious analysts have suggested a number of possible motives for the long observation of our world.

1) Migration, as suggested by Col. W. C. Odell, AF Intelligence. In Colonel Odell's opinion, space beings from a dying planet are probably looking for a "second home," where they could perpetuate their race, and Earth might be similar enough to their world to be their choice. If so, said Odell, planet Earth might become—willingly or not— "a host to extra-terrestrial life." In this case, the aliens could be weighing several problems—the hazard of a worldwide nuclear war, increasing pollution, hostility between nations and the threat of overpopulation. The extensive surveillance might not seem long to the space beings; as Dr. Hynek has suggested, they may have a much longer life-span.

2) The UFO aliens are maintaining a watch on our space operations, in fear that we might become a threat to other inhabited worlds. If this is the answer, then they may intend to warn us or take action before we can begin aggressive, large-scale space explorations.

3) If the aliens originate on Mars, or have established a large base there, they may fear a nuclear war on Earth could start a chain reaction that could affect the planet's orbit. In turn, this might change conditions on Mars or another solar system planet. This suggestion is usually based on Dr. George Gamow's theory that some unexplained change on Saturn caused our ice ages.

4) The aliens may wish to establish a large space base on our planet; since Earth is on the outer edge of our galaxy, it might be considered a suitable takeoff point for travel to a different galaxy—the one nearest our own. The decision might involve an improvement in conditions on Earth, which could explain the continued surveillance without any action.

There have been other suggested answers, of course, including outright attack and invasion. But most of the analysts who have studied the possibilities of extraterrestrial life and who know the UFO evidence do not believe we are in great danger.

If we make contact with space beings, says Dr. Allen Hynek, it may be a great adventure leading to tremendous benefits. Dr. Hermann Oberth, who believes the UFOs come from a planet of Tau Ceti or Epsilon Eridani, is convinced the aliens are scientific observers with no hostile intentions. Space authority Arthur C. Clarke, who once feared we might encounter malevolent beings in space, now holds a different belief: "With superhuman knowledge there must go equally great compassion and tolerance." Dr. Frank Drake, the Project Ozma director who has continued working toward eventual communication with aliens, expects that we shall learn many valuable lessons on ending disease, prolonging life and attaining knowledge beyond our grasp today. Among the great advances might be our acquiring the technical secrets of the UFOs, for peaceful purposes and as a deterrent against any hostility by another nation.

But even if the aliens are humanoid this will not guarantee they are altruistic. One space authority who has stated this warning is Dr. Donald N. Michael, a top NASA consultant.

"Space beings may be ethical, moral, immoral, aesthetic or something different from us. Such beings may have ideas on proper relationships among creatures inhabiting planets which may or may not support our most cherished beliefs."

If the aliens' purpose should be migration to Earth, it would set off a wave of fear and hysteria. They might offer their superior technical knowledge in exchange for a limited small-scale migration, but there would always be the risk of eventually being taken over.

The aliens might threaten force to carry out migration; the present relatively small number of UFOs possibly would be increased, with the aid of huge spacecraft. But attacks could easily wreck their hopes of migrating to Earth. Even if U.S. and Russian missiles failed to stop them, our nuclear weapons would cause fallouts over a great area. Deadly radiation in many parts of the planet would prevent occupation. Even if killing humans meant nothing to them, the chance of migration would be ended for many years.

If the aliens' purpose is not migration, the chance of adjustments would be much greater. There still would be potential dangers; such an advanced race could try to impose their ideas on us, in order to improve our civilization. At best our world and our lives would be changed in many ways. It is not impossible, however, that we might keep control and that we might benefit, as some scientists believe, in many ways leading to a better world.

But if the alien beings should prove unlike humans, then adjustments would be almost impossible. Such beings might be peaceable, they might intend no harm to our world. A small, carefully trained group of humans at the Lure might possibly have a cautious meeting with a few aliens similarly prepared to face frighteningly different members of our race. In spite of the strain and tension, the two groups might be able to exchange information. But any contact with the public would be hopeless. Even a glimpse of such a being, on television, could set off a wave of panic.

When all the factors are weighed it is possible to understand the reported CIA belief that the public can never be prepared. But accepting such a hopeless attitude is a grave mistake.

As already explained, the odds are against terrifying space beings, and the massive evidence so far does not indicate any definite menace. At first, it may seem too difficult for our world to accept alien beings—even if they are similar to us. But continuing to mislead the public will only increase the problems, leaving our people unprepared for any landings and contacts.

If Operation Lure had been tried earlier, by now we probably would have at least some of the answers to help in preparing the public. During the sixties the plan was discussed privately with several Washington officials who believe the secrecy is dangerous. I was told there was then no chance —the CIA and the AF would be sure to block it. In 1965, NICAP member John Kelly sent me a layout sketch similar to the Lure, though without the exhibits and special plans. At the same time he submitted a copy to NASA, but no action was ever taken.

One reason for the official fight against communicating with aliens has been stated by NASA's Dr. Michael. Referring to the probable effect of messages proving the existence of an intelligent space race, Dr. Michael said: "I would imagine this discovery would present very real threats to the Pentagon. . . . One threat, becoming obsoleted by the advance of society . . ." A message from other-world beings, Michael said, would be a threat for most public figures and spokesmen.

"They would try to bolster present beliefs rather than try to cope with the situation by new approaches."

But there is one way to get around this determined opposition. It would be a crash program created by the President under his emergency powers.

Such a program, similar to the famous Manhattan Project which produced the A-bomb, could be carried out by unbiased scientists, engineers and education specialists directly under the President. The administrator would be under strict orders to allow no interference by any government agency. There would be no chance for the Lure to be turned into a trap, to capture aliens and UFOs.

The cost would be far less than an Apollo moon shot or other major space operation. In 1972, NASA attempted to put a powerful new telescope into orbit to study distant stars and galaxies. The venture failed, costing taxpayers $98 million. The Lure, even with a high-speed crash program, should not cost much more, and the results could be of tremendous importance.

When the Lure construction started, or even before, the first public preparation program would begin. It might take a presidential order, but it would have to be done as a vital part of the plan. Gradually presenting proof of UFO reality and emphasizing the high percentage of harmless encounters, it would get the public ready for the final disclosures.

If the UFO aliens proved to be humanoids with no alarming intentions toward Earth this would be carefully revealed over a period of time. The shock impact would be reduced if the White House or Lure Control could also disclose the chances of valuable aids and benefits from this advanced race.

If the beings unexpectedly proved to be unlike us, to a startling degree, it would create an appalling problem. Undoubtedly this would be kept secret if possible, to prevent panic. If the aliens did not already know it, they might soon realize that successful meetings with humans were utterly impossible.

Even revealing contact with human-like aliens will be a frightening problem for those who have to make this momentous disclosure.

"It will be a terrifying responsibility," says space authority Arthur Clarke, "merely to inform the public of messages from an unknown space race. But waiting, hoping communication and meetings will never happen, could be a losing gamble."

For too many it has already been a losing gamble—the passengers and crews of airliners who died in UFO-caused crashes; the family that perished in a blazing car at Walesville; Captain Thomas Mantell and other AF pilots who lost their lives in pursuing UFOs, and other Air Force pilots ordered to chase the strange machines who were never seen again.

The time has come to stop the long deception, the deliberate discrediting of thousands of honest witnesses.

At any time, there could be a sudden development for which we are totally unprepared. The secrecy, the censorship must be stopped.

We must end the dangerous gamble which could involve us all.

Epilogue

In 1973, as UFO reports rapidly increased, censors redoubled their efforts to discredit witnesses and silence critics of the cover-up.

For some time there had been a rumor of official pressure on NICAP, long known as the most powerful and determined foe of the secrecy. The rumor suddenly grew when NICAP's executive director was interviewed on KFI, Los Angeles. Asked about the evidence of UFO reality, he startled thousands of his audience.

"NICAP doesn't have actual proof," he said. "As a matter of fact, we don't really feel we've ever come up with solid proof that something extraordinary occurred."

Veteran NICAP investigators and other listeners who knew the facts were amazed at this statement. It was practically a complete reversal of NICAP's published evaluations and the opinions of most Board members, based on a mass of verified reports by top-rated observers. The broadcast, quoted in the press, had a bad reaction on dedicated, long-time investigators and technical advisers who took it to mean an end to NICAP's original goals, carried out during my 13 years as director.

Concerned over this development, and acting as a member of the Board, I wrote NICAP's president, John L. Acuff, who is also chairman of the Board. In reply, he told me NICAP disagreed with the executive director's statement on KFI.

"We do have solid proof that something extraordinary has occurred. I do not know why he made the statement."

By this time a number of Subcommittee investigators and technical advisers had resigned, dissatisfied with what they considered policy mistakes. Hoping the situation could be corrected, I put some key questions to Acuff.

Regarding secrecy, Acuff stated: "We all know that the Government classified many documents in the UFO field which were withheld from NICAP and the general public, and (they) probably are still doing so."

On the Colorado Project, Acuff expressed a negative view. At my request he promised NICAP would make a policy statement rejecting the Condon Report conclusions.

After a special meeting with NICAP's executive director, the chairman and members of the Los Angeles Subcommittee told me he had made this disturbing admission—NICAP would not criticize the Air Force any more. When I queried Acuff he denied this statement was true.

Some of NICAP's trouble, it appears, has resulted from serious differences of opinion at the administrative level. I have advised President Acuff to make a public correction of the KFI statement and to take steps to avoid other such errors.

In addition, I have urged that NICAP try to regain the competent Subcommittee investigators and technical advisers it has lost and that it return to our original operating program and goals: To put the verified evidence on record, to expose the secrecy dangers and to end the cover-up. To secure public attention I also have urged an up-to-date public review of the most powerful evidence and proof of UFO reality accepted by NICAP Board members.

If NICAP agrees, as I sincerely hope, and follows through with determination, it will play an important role in speeding the end of the long deception. Such an all-out fight should also remove any suspicion that it was under official pressure or control.

Regardless, the forces now building up will make the final break inevitable. As the ridicule lessens, responsible witnesses have reported their sightings in the U.S., England, Austria, Argentina and a dozen other countries. More and more, members of Congress, the press and the public have come to realize the serious situation of which the late Dr. Carl Jung, the famous Swiss analyst, warned some years ago. A member of NICAP, he wrote me from Zurich.

Dear Major Keyhoe:

I am grateful for all the courageous things you have done in elucidating the thorny problem of UFO-reality . . .

If it is true that the AAF (American Air Force) or the government withholds tell-telling facts, then one can only say that this is the most unpsychological and stupid policy one could invent. Nothing helps rumors and panics more than ignorance. It is self-evident that the public ought to be told the truth . . .

I remain, dear Major,

Yours,
C. G. Jung

If the documented evidence in this book has convinced you that the UFO problem is serious you can help by writing your senators and congressman. You can ask them to aid in ending the secrecy and revealing the truth. You have a right to know—whatever the answers may prove to be.

Appendix A

The growing number of scientists who take the UFO problem seriously is indicative of a new, factual approach and the release of important information withheld from Congress and the public. The following list shows only a small percent of the scientists who have urged a new, intensive and unbiased investigation—and an end to secrecy.

Dr. Charles P. Olivier, President, American Meteor Society.

Dr. William S. Bickel, physicist, Univ. of Arizona.

Dr. Darrell B. Harmon, Jr., Deputy Program Manager, McDonnell Douglas Corporation.

Dr. Frederick F. Cranston, physicist, former member of the Nuclear Physics Staff, Los Alamos Laboratory (ten years). Now professor of physics, Humboldt State College.

Dr. Charles Gaston, space and atmospheric sciences, IBM.

Dr. Roger W. Westcott, Chairman, Dept. of Anthropology, Drew Univ., N.J.

Dr. H. E. E. Greenleaf, Head, Dept. of Mathematics and Astronomy, DePauw University.

Dr. Robert H. Williams, radiation chemistry, research and development, Mobil Corporation.

Dr. Garry C. Henderson, Senior Research Scientist, Space Sciences, General Dynamics.

Dr. Fulton Koehler, Institute of Technology, Univ. of Minnesota.

Dr. Magoruh Maruyama, Dept. of Psychology, Univ. of California.

Dr. Robert Hall, professor of sociology, Univ. of Illinois.

Dr. Stanton Friedman, Westinghouse Astronuclear Laboratory.

Dr. H. H. Damm, former German rocket engineer, now a U.S. citizen.

Dr. Robert Baker, Dept. of Astronomy, UCLA.

Col. R. B. Emerson, U. S. Army Reserve, nuclear physicist and head of Emerson Testing Laboratories.

Research Associate Frank J. Sgro, Research Center, Rutgers University.

Dr. James A. Harder, associate professor of engineering, Univ. of California.

Dr. Roger N. Shepard, Dept. of Psychology, Stanford Univ.

Astronomy Specialist Robert Bulkley, Jet Propulsion Laboratory, Caltech.

NASA upper-atmosphere physicist Leon B. Katchen, Goddard Space Flight Center.

NASA experimental specialist Alan C. Holt, Manned Spacecraft Center.

Dr. Norman S. Wolf, radiation biologist, Univ. of Washington.

Dr. Frank Salisbury, ecologist, Utah State Univ.

NASA physicist Frank Rawlinson.

Dr. D. H. Bragg, Head of Dept. of Education, Drake Univ.

Several scientists, after extensive studies and experiments, have endorsed the "saucer" or disc shape as suitable and desirable for space travel.

One of the earliest to experiment with the disc shape was Dr. W. F. Hilton, Chief Aerodynamicist for Armstrong-Whitworth Aircraft Company in England. Dr. Robert A. Cornog, physicist for Space Technology Laboratories in Los Angeles, is another scientist who has shown similarities between UFOs and high-speed craft proposed for the future. In a report to the American Rocket Society, Dr. Cornog said that a rocket liner of the future would look like a "flying saucer." As it traveled through the sky, at 3,000 mph or more, it would glow red-hot. But the passengers and crew, he stated, would feel no discomfort.

Further backing for circular-shaped craft has been put on record by Dr. Martin Gerloff, aerodynamic expert with General Electric. The disc shape, he said, can operate efficiently in dense air, rarefied areas and in empty space. It is far superior to ordinary aircraft in takeoff, climb and cruising. For power it could use a closed water turbine heated by solar energy, which would give it a large reserve of power for high-speed maneuvers.

All this is only a hint of what can be in store for us when our leading scientists use their influence to lift the "ridicule lid" and bring the UFOs and their advanced technology into the open.

Appendix B

STATEMENTS BY ARMED FORCES MEMBERS
INDICATING UFO CENSORSHIP

Many members of the armed forces believe UFO secrecy is a grave mistake. Because of official policies most of those on active duty have avoided public criticism, and in the Air Force the restrictions are supposed to apply also to those in a reserve or retired status. In spite of this, some retired or reserve members have had the courage to speak out. Here are a few of the group who have gone on record:

Lt. Gen. Curtis LeMay, USAF, Ret., former head of the Strategic Air Command, and later the AF Chief of Staff. In 1965, General LeMay discussed UFOs with Pulitzer Prize writer MacKinlay Kantor, with whom he co-authored *Mission With LeMay. My Story*. In contradiction to the AF claims, the general stated there were unsolved sightings by scientists, pilots and other responsible observers.

"There were some cases we could not explain," LeMay emphasized. "Repeat again. Never could."

Col. Howard Strand, Detachment Commander, Air National Guard Base, Battle Creek, Michigan. During flights in F-94 all-weather interceptors Colonel Strand had three encounters with UFOs.

"They were no figments of imagination. Too many intelligent, competent observers have reported UFOs. My conclusion is that this is a reconnaissance by an advanced civilization. I urge a congressional investigation of UFOs and the military secrecy surrounding them."

Col. Joseph Bryan, USAF, Ret., Special Assistant to the Secretary of the Air Force during early UFO operations and later assigned to the staff of Gen. Lauris Norstad. After stating that he was aware of many cases of UFO sightings and radar trackings by competent observers, Colonel Bryan added: "The UFOs are interplanetary devices systematically observing the Earth, either manned or remote-controlled or both. Information on UFOs has been officially withheld. This policy is wrong and dangerous."

Lt. Col. James McAshan, USAFR: "In concealing the evidence of

UFO operations the Air Force is making a serious mistake. The public should be informed as to the facts."

Lt. Col. Richard T. Headrick, Senior Pilot, USAFR, indicated his opposition to the secrecy in releasing his sighting of two UFOs to NICAP.

Maj. Paul Duich, SAC Navigator, USAF, Ret. In a statement to NICAP's director, Major Duich agreed UFOs are interplanetary and the AF secrecy is hazardous.

Maj. Dewey Fournet, former AF HQ monitor of the UFO Project: "The AF withholds UFO information, including sighting reports."

Former AF Maj. William D. Leet, with three sightings while a bomber pilot, accepts the evidence that UFOs are interplanetary and agrees that the secrecy is dangerous.

Maj. John F. McLeod, USAFR: "I do not believe in censorship, especially when it gets to be so dogmatic and ruthless as that imposed on dissemination of information about UFOs."

Maj. Edwin A. Jerome, retired USAF Command Pilot, fully backs the struggle against "this inane veil of security classification. I suggest we are several centuries behind the intellects of other planets. . . . The national policy should be to educate the public."

Former AF Maj. F. Thomas Lowrey, a graduate of Carnegie Institute of Technology, with World War II service as an engineer at the Aircraft Laboratory, Wright-Patterson AFB. "I am thoroughly convinced that the 'flying saucers' come from some extraterrestrial source. I cannot understand the AF policy of pretending they do not exist."

Besides these and other AF members, highly responsible officers in the Navy, Marine Corps and Army have also publicly opposed the censorship.

NAVY: Vice-Adm. R. H. Hillenkoetter, former CIA Director; Rear Adm. D. S. Fahrney, formerly head of the Navy guided missile project; Rear Adm. H. B. Knowles, an investigator of UFO evidence for several years, Capts. K. C. McIntosh and H. C. Dudley, and Lt. Comdr. John C. Williams, a witness during a mass sighting.

U. S. MARINE CORPS: Lt. Gen. P. A. del Valle, leader of the World War II attack on Okinawa and other major actions: "There should be a serious investigation of authentic reports, and all factual evidence and possible conclusions should be given to the public."

ARMY: Col. Robert B. Emerson, USAR, a physicist in private life, whose long and detailed evaluations at his testing laboratories convinced him the UFOs were real and under intelligent control. Lt. Col. Samuel Freeman, Army liaison pilot in World War II, later operator of an air service in New Jersey.

The group listed here comprises only a very small part of the military members opposing UFO secrecy. In addition to those in the Reserve or retired, there are many on active duty who share the same concern about the censorship hazards. Some are privately supporting efforts to create a practical program for preparing the public and ending the cover-up, and these efforts are steadily increasing.

Appendix C

In December of 1969, when the AF claimed its UFO investigations were ended, it had over 15,000 reports in its files—at least 3,000 unsolved, as confirmed by the former AF scientific consultant Dr. J. Allen Hynek. At that same time, NICAP had more than 12,000 reports, hundreds of them duplicating AF cases.

The witnesses named in the following list are only a small fraction of those whose factual evidence of UFO reality has been submitted to the Air Force and to NICAP. But even this small cross section demonstrates the observers' competence and reliability, completely disproving official claims that all UFO witnesses had delusions, or were unable to recognize familiar objects, or were guilty of perpetrating hoaxes.

AIR FORCE OBSERVERS

AF Wing Commander Donald J. M. Blakeslee, the leading AF ace in World War II, who vainly tried to intercept a high-speed UFO.

Col. Howard Strand, Detachment Commander of the Air National Guard Base, Battle Creek, Michigan, with three logged encounters with UFOs.

Col. Henry Carlock, in private life head of the Physics Department, Univ. of Mississippi, who sighted a UFO with lighted windows.

Lt. Col. Richard Headrick, who observed AF jets vainly trying to intercept two UFOs.

Former Lt. Col. E. Garrison Woods, Executive Officer at Godman AFB when Capt. Thomas Mantell was killed in a UFO chase. Along with most of the base staff, Colonel Woods clearly observed the UFO and watched it through binoculars.

Maj. Paul Duich, Master Navigator, Strategic Air Command, who sighted a large UFO with small devices circling around it—a sighting witnessed by a score of other SAC officers at Offutt AFB.

Maj. William D. Leet, bomber commander, who with his crew sighted a huge flying disc over Japan, faster than any known aircraft.

Maj. James B. Smith, one of two pilots ordered to intercept a UFO near Wright-Patterson AFB. The unknown machine quickly outdistanced the pilots.

Capt. William Patterson, whose jet fighter was suddenly surrounded by UFOs during an attempted intercept over Washington National Airport.

Capt. Edward Ballard and Lt. W. S. Rogers, who reported that a UFO eluded them at over 900 mph when they tried to close in.

Lt. George Kinnan, who reported that a disc-shaped UFO made repeated head-on passes at his fighter plane, zooming over the canopy with only a few feet to spare.

Navy Observers

Capt. R. B. McLaughlin, Navy missile officer at White Sands.

Cmdr. M. B. Taylor, guided missile expert, who with hundreds of other witnesses watched a maneuvering UFO above an air show.

Lt. Cmdr. John D. Williams, a Navy pilot for ten years, who with twelve other witnesses sighted a flying disc at least 300 feet in diameter.

Cmdr. L. H. Witherspoon, another Navy witness in a multiple sighting.

Lt. Cmdr. Thomas M. Lasseter, USNR, who reported a glowing disc hovering at treetop height, about 150 feet from his location. As the UFO rotated, a row of ports or lights was visible around the rim.

Lt. J. W. Martin and Chief Petty Officer R. E. Moore, pilots, saw a domed disc make a swift pass in front of their planes.

Marine Corps Witnesses

Maj. Charles Scarborough, Maj. E. C. White and Capt. Charles Stanton, daylight observation of sixteen discs in precise formation. When the Marine jet pilots tried to box them in, the UFOs, Scarborough reported, evaded them at almost unbelievable speed.

Capt. Don Holland, an encounter with a high-speed UFO; report verified by Maj. Gen. William Manly, USMC.

Lt. E. J. Ambrose; a report of a futile UFO chase.

Lt. Edward Balocco; another vain pursuit of a rocketlike craft, over Virginia.

Army Observers

Lt. Col. Robert R. Staver, rocket expert; report of UFOs maneuvering at more than 1,000 mph over Los Altos, Calif.

Lt. Col. Samuel E. Craig, circular object flying at great speed below observer's Army plane.

Maj. Herbert W. Taylor, Signal Corps; a disc observed to descend, hover briefly, then speed out of sight.

Capt. Clayton J. Boddy and other Army Engineers; gleaming, "saucerlike" devices seen operating over New Mexico.

Capt. J. B. Douglas, 489th Field Artillery; World War II observation of a UFO over Holland.

SCIENTISTS AND ENGINEERS

Dr. Clyde Tombaugh, discoverer of the planet Pluto and head of the armed forces search for unknown orbiting objects. In his report Dr. Tombaugh described a swiftly moving unknown object with rectangular ports or windows.

Dr. Seymour Hess, head of the Dept. of Meteorology, Florida State Univ.; a report of a powered disc seen in daylight.

Aerospace engineer and aircraft builder William Lear, who with his co-pilot sighted a flying disc from his executive plane.

Dr. Charles H. Otis, biologist, who sighted a formation of rocketlike UFOs.

Geologist John Zimmerman and civil engineer Charles Fisher, who observed two flying discs dive in front of an aircraft, then make tight loops around it.

Many other verified reports by engineers, including: Nathan Wagner, White Sands missile safety chief; C. T. Zohm, specialist on a Navy missile project; aeronautical engineer Paul R. Hill; Harold Lamb and three other Rocketdyne engineers; Victor G. Didelot, aviation research engineer; Charles B. Moore, aerologist at White Sands, and J. J. Kaliszewski, researcher on a Navy cosmic-ray project.

AIRLINE PILOTS

American Airlines. Capt. Willis Sperry, whose plane was circled closely by a UFO, near Washington, D.C. Capt. Raymond Ryan, who pursued a UFO by AF instructions. Capt. Peter W. Killian, who was silenced by the AF after reporting a UFO encounter. Capt. Paul Carpenter and Capt. W. R. Hunt, verified reports on record.

Eastern Airlines. Confirmed reports by Capt. C. S. Chiles, Capts. William Call, Truman Gile, Robert E. Reilman and other EAL pilots.

Pan American Airways. Capt. Matthew Van Winkle, who had to zoom to avoid a possible collision with a UFO. First Officer (now Senior Captain) W. B. Nash, who saw a formation of 100-foot discs fly under the airliner he was piloting. Other PAA pilots on record:

Capts. Jack Adriance, Ned Mullens, Joseph L. Flynn, H. Dunker, Kenneth Brosdal, Charles Zammett, Robert Harris, James King and William Hutchins.

Trans World Airlines. Capts. Robert Adickes and Robert Manning, whose TWA flight was closely paced by a glowing UFO, near South Bend, Ind. Capt. Charles Kratovil, who reported a similar pacing near Boston. Others with confirmed reports: Capts. W. H. Kerr, D. W. Miller, M. H. Rabeneck, Arthur Shutts, Irving Kravitz and G. W. Schemel, whose near-collision encounter is detailed in Chapter 1.

Since 1947, UFOs have been reported by pilots of all major airlines and most of the others. Because of limited space, relatively few have been named, but there are hundreds of other equally capable airline pilots who have encountered UFOs, such as Capt. Emil J. Smith of United, Capt. William Bruen of National, Capt. Max Jacoby of Pioneer Airlines and Capt. B. C. Carlson of Northwest. The hundreds of verified reports by these highly trained observers constitute a powerful segment of the UFO evidence, factual proof of the strange objects' reality.

Index